Educating European Lawyers

Editors:
Aalt Willem
Heringa
Bram Akkermans

Educating European Lawyers

intersentia

METRO

Ius Commune Europaeum

Editors:
Aalt Willem Heringa
Bram Akkermans

Educating European Lawyers

Intersentia Ltd
Trinity House | Cambridge Business Park | Cowley Road
Cambridge | CB4 0WZ | United Kingdom
mail@intersentia.co.uk

ISBN 978-1-78068-018-7
NUR **823**/845

British Library Cataloguing in Publication Data. A catalogue record for this book is available from the British Library.

CONTENTS

LIST OF AUTHORS

Bram Akkermans
Assistant Professor of European Private Law, Maastricht University, the Netherlands

Sjoerd Claessens
Lecturer in European Law, Maastricht University, the Netherlands

Mariolina Eliantonio
Assistant Professor of European Administrative Law, Maastricht University, the Netherlands

Sjef van Erp
Professor of Civil Law and European Private Law, Maastricht University, the Netherlands. Deputy Justice Court of Appeal 's-Hertogenbosch, the Netherlands

Jaap Hage
Professor of Contract Law and Law of Obligations in General, Maastricht University, the Netherlands

Aalt Willem Heringa
Dean, Faculty of Law, Maastricht University; Professor of Comparative Constitutional and Administrative Law; <www.maastrichtuniversity.nl/law>

Philipp Kiiver
Associate Professor of European and Comparative Constitutional Law, Maastricht University, the Netherlands

André Klip
Professor of Criminal Law, Criminal Procedure and Transnational Criminal Law, Maastricht University, the Netherlands

Nicole Kornet
Dr. Nicole Kornet BA LL.B.(Hons) LL.M. is Assistant Professor of Commercial Law, Maastricht University, the Netherlands

Tanja van der Meer
Lecturer in Legal History, Maastricht University, the Netherlands

Mieke Olaerts
Assistant Professor Company Law, Maastricht University, the Netherlands

Jan M. Smits
Professor of European Private Law, Maastricht University, the Netherlands and Research professor of Comparative Legal Studies in the University of Helsinki (Finland).

C.H. (Remco) van Rhee
Professor of European Legal History, Maastricht University, the Netherlands

Hildegard Schneider
Professor of European Union Law, Maastricht University, the Netherlands

Remme R. Verkerk
Assistant Professor at Maastricht University until September 2010. He currently practices law at Houthoff Buruma

Ellen Vos
Professor of European Union Law, Maastricht University, the Netherlands

Bruno De Witte
Professor of European Union Law, Maastricht University, the Netherlands

LIST OF ABBREVIATIONS

AD	Anno Domini
ADR	Alternative Dispute Resolution
A.G.	Advocate General
ALI	American Law Institute
Art.	Article
BC	Before Christ
BCL	Bachelor of Civil Law
BGBl.	Bundesgesetzblatt
BGH	Bundesgerichtshof
BSE	Boviene spongiforme encefalopathie
CCBE	Conseil des barreaux européens (Council of Bars and Law Societies of Europe)
CDE	Cahiers de Droit Européen
CELE	Coaltion for European Legal Eduction
CETS	Classroom Educational Technology Services
CFR	Common Frame of Reference
CFSP	Common Foreign and Security Policy
CJEU	Court of Justice of the European Union
CMLR	Common Market Law Review
CoPECL	Common Principles of European Contract Law
CPE	Common Professional Education
DCFR	Draft Common Frame of Reference
DRiG	Deutsches Richtergesetz
DUE	Diritto dell'Unione Europea
EC	European Commission
ECHR	European Court of Human Rights
ECJ	European Court of Justice
ECR	European Court Reports
ECtHR	European Court of Human Rights

ECTS	European Credit Transfer System
ELI	European Law Institute
ELR	European Law Review
ELS	European Law School
ELS-ET	European Law School - English Track
ELS-ELT	European Law School - English Language Track
EPC	European Private Company
EPR	Europarecht
EU	European Union
EUI	European University Institute
FEMM	Droits de la Femme et Égalité des Genres (Women's Rights and Gender Equality) Committee European Parliament
HRG	Hochschulrahmengesetz
Id.	Idem
IGC	Intergovernmental Conference
JOR	Jurisprudentie Onderneming & Recht
JORF	Journal Officiel de la République Française
JURI	Legal Affairs Committee European Parliament
LIBE	Civil Liberties, Justice and Home Affairs Committee European Parliament
LL.B	*Legum Baccalaureus*, Bachelor of Laws, Bachelor of Common Law
LL.D.	Doctor of Laws
LL.M.	*Legum Magister*, Master of Laws
MIC	Magister Iuris Communis
MJ	Maastricht Journal of European and Comparative Law
NGO	Non-Governmental Organisation
OJ	Official Journal
OLG	Oberlandesgericht
PBL	Problem-Based Learning
PECL	Principles of European Contract Law
PhD	Philosophiæ Doctor
RDUE	Revue du Droit de l'Union Européenne
REDE	Revista Española de Derecho Europeo
ROA	Research Centre for Education and the Labour Market
RTDE	Revue Trimestrielle de Droit Européen

SE	Societas Europaea
SE	Statute for a European Company
SPE	Societas Privata Europaea
SPE	Statute for a European Private Company
TEU	Treaty on European Union
TFEU	Treaty on the Functioning of the European Union
UK	United Kingdom
UNESCO	United Nations Educational, Scientific and Cultural Organization
UNIDROIT	International Institute for the Unification of Private Law
US/U.S.	United States

Aalt Willem
Heringa
Bram Akkermans

INTRODUCTION

The reasons to make this book were manifold. Legal education, although constantly evolving remains a predominantly national domain. Witnessing the growth of Europeanization, multi-level governance, rule making, the increasing internationalisation of the legal domain and the workplace of lawyers, we feel the need to start a discussion about a proper European legal education. Are we right in thinking that it is time to reflect upon a model of truly European legal education? How to cope with questions about the proper curriculum, the links with the labour market, the existence of teaching materials and academic output?

A primary reason was found in our own (maybe preliminary) answers to the a foregoing questions. In 1995 we set up a European Law School programme, in 2006 we set up a bachelor program taught in English, the European Law School English Track, as well as a master program with the same name. Four years of law studies in English, not so much (and sometimes not at all) focused on a domestic legal system, but about European law, comparative law and the common law of Europe (*Ius Commune*), with evidently also a substantial doses of international law and globalization trends. This program is, we humbly submit an academic challenge as well as a pioneering endeavour to work towards a truly European legal education and perhaps can serve as the basis for the development of other programmes.

Evidently we have stumbled upon many issues, some major ones to be analysed and described in this book. Some relate to the language of instruction; the existence of teaching materials; the relationship with legal professions; and didactical aspects, to name but a few.

So, basically we aim at achieving two things with this book. Starting and bringing forward the discussion about European legal education, and secondly bring into that debate our internal discussion, attempts, achievements and obstacles as well as our belief, founded upon the qualities we believe our European Law School programme possesses, that the proper way forward is to construct a truly European legal education for a selected group of future European lawyers. This project is not finished with this book and will be ongoing and we seek advice and comments as well as also solicit support from other schools and professors who have a similar vision of a future European legal education model. We seek support from politics on the domestic and European level to enable a European legal education model to come into being and be recognized by national legislatures, bar organizations and European decision makers.

This book's title Educating European Lawyers is inspired by the US Carnegie Foundation for the Advancement of Teaching publication 'Educating Lawyers: Preparation for the Profession of Law', that proposes reform of US law schools.[1] In this book the authors propose to rethink the methodology underlying the curriculum in American Law Schools, adapting the methods to the needs of our current time.

The book before you is divided into two parts. The first part deals with general aspects of European Legal Education and offers general insights into European legal education. The second part deals with subject specific aspects. In this part challenges in a specific field of law will be dealt with. The book concludes with an outlook and a proposal where to go next.

Maastricht, May 2011

Bram Akkermans & Aalt Willem Heringa

1 See <http://www.carnegiefoundation.org/publications/educating-lawyers-preparation-profession-law>.

PART I

LEGAL EDUCATION

Aalt Willem
Heringa

TOWARDS A TRULY EUROPEAN LEGAL EDUCATON. AN AGENDA FOR THE FUTURE

1. Introduction

Though the title of this chapter suggests otherwise, there is no such thing as a uniform European Legal Education. Not within the context of the European Union (27 Member States), let alone in the context of the Council of Europe (47 Member States). In this chapter, I will briefly describe the state of affairs of legal education in Europe after and with the Bologna declaration.[1] I will focus upon the impact of European law on legal education and the connection with present-day legal research focusing upon comparative law, European law, international law, Europeanization and globalization. Subsequently I will focus upon the Maastricht initiative to establish the European Law School, as a new and innovative law school focused upon training the lawyers and academics of the future. And finally I will indicate a way forward in setting up legal education for European lawyers.

Between the 27 EU Member States great disparities exist in the length of the curriculum, the intake of students, the labour market for the students (access to the bar e.g.), who sets the curricula and whether there are any bar (or state exams) after graduation, the access to professional legal training afterwards, the content of the curricula and the courses, the languages of instruction, the requirements for teachers and professors, the teacher-staff ratios, the qualities of the buildings and facilities, etc. And also, there is (apart from the European University Institute in Florence (only offering PhD training) and the European Colleges in Belgium (Bruges) and Poland (Natalin) (only offering LL.M programmes)) no European legal education or no general discussion or let alone a common understanding of a European Law Curriculum, as there is no common European labour market for lawyers.

1 See Joint Declaration of the European Ministers of Education: The Bologna Declaration of 19 June 1999, available at <http://www.bologna-bergen2005.no/Docs/00->.

I submit here that legal education is through this lack in a common training is legging behind the legal and political developments of the EU and of EU Law.

Evidently a major problem is that the EU has no competence over (legal) education nor that there is no joint understanding of a European labour market; also European law and domestic law are interrelated. However, the issue I do raise here, whether it is not time to seek such a common European legal education in parallel to the many developments in European law that have taken place. I would suggest to work towards a number of schools in Europe providing European legal training which will train the students for European wide careers and which will be recognized by the different competent bodies in de Member States as lawyers in their own right, possibly after having done a very basic bar exam as to domestic law. Or going even further and setting up a European Bar Exam or mutual recognition of national bar exams? Very basic indeed, since they are already lawyers, a basic exam (comparable to the bar exams in the US) might suffice.

Before I develop this argument further, let me first briefly do some stock taking and describe in a basic manner the main developments upon which my proposals rest.

2. The Bologna Declaration

The idea that the Bologna Declaration and the ensuing process of harmonizing higher legal education has led to a uniform model of higher education is a myth; one of the reasons is that the Bologna document is based upon a voluntary approach; and another is that the several participating states have seen fit to implement Bologna according to their own higher education history and finances. Famously, Bologna introduced the three-tier system: bachelor, master, Ph.D. That concept sounded simple enough; however, some states started with a four-year bachelor's degree;[2] most with a three-year model;[3] many set up a two-year master,[4] others only a one-year master,[5] or a mixed model: both two-year and one-year masters.[6] Some states were quick in reforming higher legal education in the Bologna format,[7] others (most notably e.g. Germany) have been very slow so that only incidentally German universities (or law schools) have set up a Bologna-model of bachelors and masters.[8]

The fact that this is so, and that even within the European Union (EU) no uniformity or complete equivalence has been created, is caused, or explained, by the fact that the EU has not been given the rule-making power in this domain. There is simply no authority (competence) for the EU to regulate education. The best way to have a European impact upon higher legal education is by making funds available

2 E.g. France and Austria.
3 E.g. Belgium.
4 E.g. Belgium.
5 E.g. the Netherlands.
6 E.g. France and the Netherlands.
7 E.g. the Netherlands and Belgium.
8 E.g. Bucerius Law School in Hamburg.

for desirable projects, such as research, student and staff mobility, and student exchanges (Erasmus/Socrates,[9] Marie Curie, Erasmus Mundus,[10] Jean Monnet).[11] But since the Member States carefully guard and protect their sovereignty in the domain of education, the Bologna process, while a joint process, is still a voluntary.

In law, the situation is even further complicated by the fact that the domestic regulation of the legal profession is very much a domestic issue, partially regulated by the domestic bars and, at least, very much linked to national aspects, traditions, and (legal) culture. The process to become a practicing lawyer, or judge, or prosecutor, is very much in the hand and discretion of legislatures and/or the legal profession. The role of legal education varies; so does the labour market, the intake of students, the length of studies, the content of the studies, the accreditation processes etc.

Without doubt these developments, setting up a coherent model, facilitating exchanges of staff and students, developing a common credit system known as ECTS, all helped in preparing the scene for more changes and common developments. Evidently in transnational sciences such as engineering, medicine, and chemistry it is a lot easier to develop joint curricula and allow for the simple recognition of degrees. But law has for the last centuries been linked with national sovereignty and domestic legal systems. In the nineteenth century Codes have been adopted and the development of the law in many European countries has been nationalized and became an increasingly domestic matter. Domestic legal culture mattered; the domestic bars and judiciaries developed their own admission criteria; lawmakers created their own educational systems and models, and the study of law had to fit in the requirements of the bars and the legislatures. Therefore, what we have witnessed in the nineteenth and the most part of the twentieth century was an increasing nationalization of the study law. It has been a recent development, under the influence of the EU, that European law has increasingly impacted upon national sovereignty and (therefore) also on the domestic law. Increasingly law became European and also global. Parts of the sovereign law making powers became European; not only in the domains of the internal market in Europe and all its related aspects, but also in areas such as torts, contracts, property, administrative law, criminal law: areas of the law long considered to be purely and exclusively national!

What also happened was that scholars (and I will come back to that in more detail later) started to work on the Europeanization of the law, and evidently they needed a common language, since law and language are inherently interrelated, and gradually it seems to me that the English language has occupied this role. This trend was unmistakably furthered by the growth of the EU and the increasing trend

9 See generally European Commission, Education and Training, <http://ec.europa.eu/education/lifelong-learning-programme/doc80_en.htm>.

10 See generally Erasmus Mundus – Scholarships and Academic Cooperation, <http://ec.europa.eu/education/external-relation-programmes/doc72_en.htm>.

11 See generally The Jean Monnet Programme: understanding European Integration, <http://ec.europa.eu/education/lifelong-learning-programme/doc88_en.htm> (hereinafter Jean Monnet Programme).

there towards the English as a most prominent language: English as the *lingua franca*.

And, related, larger law firms opened shop in Brussels, seeking international alliances, and increasingly operated in English and also wanted to hire new lawyers with international (European) backgrounds: students who had studied abroad, were fluent in English (next to their native language) and had knowledge of European law but also of more than one (their own) legal system. This means educating students who could work in a European setting and could work in European law *strictu sensu* but also within and between different legal systems and with lawyers from different legal backgrounds.

And this was not only the case in commercial legal practice, but also within governments: the increase in EU policies and law making made it necessary to have civil servants who spoke their languages, had foreign experiences and could work with different legal cultures and legal systems.

But whatever these trends were and have been taking place, I am under the impression that legal education as a whole did not catch up quickly, and when it did, that domestic bar associations, were and are very reluctant in adapting and making the necessary changes. The feeling being that what has been the proper way for raising lawyers in a one size fits all model, must still be good in these times of Europeanization.

Although there is much more to be said, for the purposes of this paper, this brief description must do.

3. Development of 'European' Law

Luckily the situation that the study of law is predominantly a domestic issue and is therefore governed by domestic rules and traditions only, is very much in flux. Although the above seems to indicate a deadlock in the sense that legal education seems to be fixed and domestically oriented, there is still a lot of movement below the surface. Bologna and Socrates have triggered a lot of gradual changes and all kinds of reforms, having an impact upon both European legal education and European law faculties.[12] Also, other EU rules and principles have been leading toward progress in this area.[13]

In the first place, the EU has set certain rules regarding the freedom of services and free movement of workers within the EU relating to qualifications and recognition of diplomas that also affect the profession of lawyers ('attorneys-at-

12 Developments such as student and staff exchanges have led to the development of joint programs; courses that could be followed by exchange students; and collaboration between law faculties. Courses for exchange students often related to courses in the domain of European, international and comparative law, thereby adding new courses to existing curricula.

13 An example is the increasing impact of EU rules and principles in areas like consumer law, social law, freedom of movement, migration, establishment, freedom of services, contract law, tort law, and proportionality, as it relates to institutional and constitutional law.

law').[14] Basically, the EU rules allow a person who is qualified to practice as a lawyer in one state to also practice in another state.[15] Lawyers can also acquire the lawyer title of their host Member State, either after practicing the law of that state for three years or by passing an aptitude test.[16] Much still needs to become clearer in this respect, through decisions by the ECJ and possibly through new EU directives, but the trend is clear towards an increasing movement of lawyers and their services.

Secondly, many areas and domains of domestic law are increasingly influenced or determined by EU regulations or directives.[17] This means e.g. that important aspects of company law appear to be domestic law and being part of domestic legislation and codes, but that they are basically translations and implementations of EU directives. Many aspects of what used to be purely domestic law are now, in effect, European law, as such and in disguise. Primary examples are company law, competition law, public procurement law, consumer law. This harmonization implies that students, when properly educated, all over Europe will be taught the same substantive law. And this evidently also applies to European law proper. This is not to say that all European legal curricula properly cover European law and its broad implications. In fact, many universities still mainly focus upon domestic law while in my view neglecting European law and its impact. But, here the situation is gradually and steadily improving (one of the stimuli in this respect has been the Jean Monnet program, funding chairs and courses in European subjects).[18] Another nice illustration of what is going on here is the (quality of the) participation in the annual European Law Moot Court Competition, showing the growth in European law in curricula all over Europe as well as its depth. However, I still have the impression that much can and should be improved. A glance over many law curricula in Europe still make me doubt whether enough is being done. This impression is underlined by noting the knowledge of European law among new master students in my own faculty of law in Maastricht. We teach an advanced course in European law and note that many students, who came from all over Europe, have significant difficulties in catching up because of limited knowledge of European institutional law and substantive law.

As a consequence of the previous aspect of increasing importance and impact upon domestic law of EU law, and also as a separate independent development,

14 See generally European Commission - The Single EU Market: Professional qualifications, <http://ec.europa.eu/internal_market/qualifications/index_en.htm>. Judges' professional qualification are not regulated therein, because most member states still require that the judge be a national of their country, before acceding to the vocation.

15 See Council Directive 98/5, Facilitate Practice of the Profession of Lawyer on a Permanent Basis in a Member State Other Than that in Which the Qualification was Obtained, 1998 *OJ* (L 77/36 (EC).

16 See *idem* Art. 14.

17 One only has to consult the Official Journal and the case law of the Court of Justice and the new EU treaties as amended by the Lisbon Treaty to see the expansion of the policy areas of the EU and how EU rules and regulations impact criminal law, environmental law, immigration, contracts, non-discrimination, social security, state aid, competition, public procurement etc.

18 See Jean Monnet Programme, *supra* note 11.

legal academics started to research (also for the benefit of drafting new European legislation) common rules and principles and their transformation in domestic legal concepts. As part of its endeavour to promote trade and business within the EU and between the Member States, the European Commission has even mapped out a course of seeking to codify these principles into European principles.[19] Many academics now work in different projects and collaborative initiatives drafting common principles of tort law, contract law and property law. In Maastricht, we have translated these efforts in making grand case books on common European principles of tort, contract, property, civil procedure, judicial review, non-discrimination, each underpinning as a research project the codification exercises and enhancing our knowledge for teaching purposes.[20] These developments do not take place as purely autonomous efforts, irrelevant for legal practice. They are merely the consequences of European legal developments; the expansion of a concept such as freedom of movement for workers, goods and services - implying that it is easier to contract across borders when one knows that there are similarities (e.g. in the domain of consumer law which has been very much regulated by the EU[21]); or the development of an own EU concept of tort (the Francovich case law and its aftermath[22]), developed by the ECJ; or the relationship between the notion of freedom of (financial) services and cross-border mortgages which might have an impact upon property law. In general, the EU has seen tremendous political and legal development: its powers have been expanded with a series of treaties (Single European Act 1986;[23] Treaty of Maastricht, 1992;[24] and subsequent treaties of Amsterdam;[25] Nice;[26] and now, on December 1st, 2009, the entry into force of the Lisbon Treaty[27]). In less than a quarter of a century, the EU has emerged as a strong polity, with, for many members, a common currency, and a whole new list of powers for the EU's institutions.[28]

And powers, explicit or implicit which have seriously impacted upon domestic law; and have also led to reflecting upon domestic law and to a larger attention for comparative law. Harmonization of laws of Member States also means that one has to know how they are and what can be done; what are common traditions and principles which could be relied upon in European law making or in

19 See European Private Law (CoPECL), <http://www.copecl.org/>.

20 See METRO - Ius Commune Casebooks, <http://www.unimaas.nl/default.asp?template=werkveld.htm&id=OO11IA6XU2XFTA11S02P&taal=en> (last visited 4 September 2010).

21 See Treaty Establishing the European Community, 10 November 1997, 1997 *OJ* C 340/169 [hereinafter EC Treaty].

22 See Francovich and Others, Joined Cases C-6/90 and C-9/90, [1991] ECR I-5357.

23 See Single European Act, 28 February 1986, 1987 *OJ* L 169/1.

24 See Treaty on European Union (Treaty on Maastricht), 7 February 1992, 1992 *OJ* C 191.

25 See Treaty of Amsterdam Amending the Treaty on European Union, the Treaties Establishing the European Communities and Certain Related Acts, 2 October 1997, 1997 *OJ* C 340/1.

26 See Treaty of Nice Amending the Treaty on European Union, the Treaties Establishing the European Communities and Certain Related Acts, 26 February 2001, 2001 *OJ* C 80/1.

27 See Treaty of Lisbon Amending The Treaty On European Union and the Treaty Establishing The European Community, 13 December 2007, 2007 *OJ* C 306/1.

28 See EC Treaty, *supra* note 21, Arts. 4-6.

the case law of the European Court of Justice. Studying European law proper is therefore benefited by the knowledge of domestic legal systems; and working in a domestic legal system for instance in preparing a domestic law implementing an EU directive, or for negotiations in Brussels it might be necessary to be immersed in comparative law and the search for communalities and differences.

My point here is that unmistakably European law has advanced to such an extent that it certainly warrants its legal education proper: training in European law, comparative law, the interaction between domestic law and European law, lead to a new European wide legal education.

The question could be asked whether there is sufficient 'substantive' European law (in the broadest sense) to be able to construct a law curriculum with enough system and doctrine to warrant and fill a legal curriculum. It is my conviction that there is: as well as with European law proper as with comparative law courses; the latter lend themselves for academic training in law. Even better so than with purely domestic law courses. Let me briefly explain why, though the response relates to the reason of being of academic university teaching of law as distinguished from professional training for the bar and the judiciary. For the latter, it is indeed important to know and understand the law as it stands with the pertinent case law. For the former it is indispensable to train legal minds: students who can reflect and ponder solutions for social and legal problems; to understand the basics of contract law and the variations, and also for other domains of the law; students who can reflect on the quality of the law and look and find creative new solutions. For these purposes, comparative law courses lend themselves excellently; they teach truly academic training and make it subsequently easier to study one specific system for legal practice.

A major method to do so in comparative law is to start from general legal questions and doctrines, such as the making of a contract, the termination, requirements for tort, separation of powers etc, and subsequently construct on the basis of abstract analysis as well as through comparative analysis which abstract solutions might exist and which ones do exist in practice. And well in the laboratory of a (comparative) lawyer, *id est* comparing legal systems. These approaches give a student infinite insight and academic training in legal thinking and analysis. It might therefore lead to a truly academic legal training.

4. Law School Curricula

All the above developments have found their places in many curricula in European law schools; however, I submit that still, in too many law schools and European universities, developments have been too slow in fully making room for the EU's expansion. For this very, very slow integration, there are, in my perception and based on conversations with law professors in a variety of institutions many factors, including:

1. the interests (and in some countries, powers) of incumbent professors: many do not like to create room for EU-related subjects;
2. the sometimes overwhelming influence of the domestic bar associations;
3. the conservative nature of lawyers;

4. the scarcity of good people with knowledge of EU law and the competition with law firms (who generally pay higher salaries than universities);
5. the political climate;
6. the absence of power for law school deans or university presidents to make reforms;[29] and
7. the difficulty (yet necessity) to integrate EU law in existing curricula (to integrate aspects of EU law in e.g. a course on contracts) due to the absence of good materials and a lack of knowledge on the part of professors.

Finally, I would like to draw attention here to the immense impact upon the future generation of lawyers and upon the development of new courses, of the new lingua franca (English, or maybe better Euro-English); of collaboration between European law schools and the emergence of new European law journals, through not only the previous developments but also by the Erasmus/Socrates exchanges, facilitated by the European Commission, as well as a pan-European credit system (ECTS: 60 ECTS per academic year).[30]

European law schools have developed new courses in English, developed courses adapted to exchange students, or designed courses based upon the development of EU law and research findings. However, as I argued before,[31] these developments have been more advanced in some places than in others. Some countries have been slow in adopting English-taught courses for reasons of domestic language policy or because foreign students came also for a study in their domestic language (Germany, Spain, Italy, France). Others quickly adapted to the need to have English-taught courses in order to cater to foreign exchange students (Sweden, the Netherlands). Belgium also moved along these lines but was hindered by domestic legislation prohibiting law schools to offer more than a few English-taught courses. Obviously the United Kingdom (UK) did not have to change, as all courses offered were already taught in English; Moreover, even the courses offered basically remained unchanged, addressing domestic law.

In the beginning, the courses that were taught in English in Dutch law schools were the obvious courses: international law, various courses on European law, and comparative law.[32] Gradually, under the influence of the increasing impact of European law within and upon domestic legal orders, we started to design courses that focused upon areas of law, integrating comparative law and European law.[33] These courses build upon academic research with respect to common principles of

29 Due to the *modus operandi* of universities in some states and the relative lack of power of deans.

30 See European Commission – Education and Training, European Credit Transfer and Accumulation System (ECTS), <http://ec.europa.eu/education/lifelong-learning-policy/doc48_en.htm> (last visited 4 September 2010).

31 See *supra* paragraph 3.

32 See generally Maastricht University, European Law School English Track, <http://www.maastrichtuniversity.nl/web/Faculties/FL/TargetGroup/ProspectiveStudents/BachelorsProgrammes/Programmes/EuropeanLawSchoolEnglishLanguageTrack1.htm> [hereinafter European Law School English Track].

33 See *idem*.

European law, in combination with comparative law, seeking for the 'common law' of Europe.

Law school curricula in Europe are characteristically primarily focused upon domestic law and, necessarily and consequently, taught in the domestic language(s) of the country with electives that might have been developed in English for exchange students on comparative law or international and European law. In only a few countries apart from the evidently English-speaking countries such as the UK and Ireland, English-taught LL.M programs have been developed (Scandinavia, the Netherlands, and Belgium). Toulouse University in France is now also in the process of setting up an English-taught, one-year masters program on international, European, and comparative law; in Germany, a private Hamburg-based law school runs an English-taught program; and Mannheim University is also constructing an English-taught LL.M program. In Switzerland, the new Luzern University Law School also offers a great variety of English-taught courses. However, despite these and possibly some more initiatives, the predominant feature is that law is taught in the domestic language, with some added courses on European law and occasionally a number of courses in English for exchange students.

5. Labour Market and Intake; Tuition and Funding

Before moving on to describing and discussing further law school curricula and efforts to change and adapt them to modern-day European needs and the needs of a partly globalizing labour market for lawyers, a few words need to be said about student intake and output. The intake of students into universities and law faculties is very different from country to country. In Scandinavia, access to university is very selective: only the best students will be admitted. In the UK, there seems to be a shortage of places and the top schools have the first pick. In Belgium, France, Italy and Germany there is open access: all students who qualify (successfully graduate from secondary school) must be admitted. This is also the case in the Netherlands, but legislation allows law faculties to expel students (after one year) who do not meet the standards set by the school.

Funding is most commonly provided by the state: public funding seems to be the rule, with most countries allowing for no fees or only very low fees (a few hundred Euros). In the Netherlands, the fee is around 1,650 euros per year and in the UK, fees are even higher.[34] Public funding means that there is less and limited access for private funding (of education); for research the situation is different and more competitive.

[34] State of affairs 2007/8: Austria: (prices in euro): 363 per semester; Belgium 500-800 per annum; Bulgaria 50-200 per annum; Cyprus: 0; Czech Republic: 0; Denmark: 0; Estonia: 420-1.200 per semester; Finland: 0; Germany: 0 in some states; between 100 and 500 per semester in others; Greece: university fees; Hungary: 16-48 per month; Ireland: 0; Italy: minimum 750 per annum; Latvia: 700-5,811 per annum; Lithuania: 0-3,475 per annum; Luxemburg: 100 per semester; Malta: 0; the Netherlands: 1,600 per annum; Norway: 0; Poland: 0; Portugal: 500 per annum; Romania: 350-650 per annum; Slovak Republic: 0; Slovenia: 0; Spain: 550-900 per annum; Sweden: 0; UK: up to 3,070 per annum. See *idem*.

Law faculties in most European countries train lawyers, but not necessarily solely or predominantly for law firms or the judiciary. Many graduated lawyers do not take the bar but use their legal education as an academic training and pursue other labour market avenues: legal departments in companies; civil servants in governments and the European Commission; policy advisors and policymakers; legal experts in agencies; consultancy firms; NGOs; lobby organizations, etc.

6. Research and Journals

As I have mentioned before, research in Europe among legal academics started to develop in the areas of comparative law, common European principles, Europeanization of domestic law, and related aspects. Many projects flourished, one of them in the Maastricht law faculty which set up a major collaborative research school, with Leuven, Utrecht and Amsterdam: the Research School 'Ius Commune'.[35] Journals were set up on European constitutional law, European private law, and European and comparative law (such as the Maastricht Journal on European and Comparative Law: MJ).[36] Maastricht started the mentioned case books project, under the supervision of Prof. Walter van Gerven.[37] Maastricht also started a Ius Commune book series.[38]

7. Maastricht European Law School: Its Start in 1992

In the context of European developments, we perceived in Maastricht that it was necessary to reflect upon the future of legal education in Europe and upon European legal education. Our perspective was the gradual growth of European law and of European common law, leading up to the future need to educate European trained lawyers. Lawyers with a good training in European institutional law and substantive law; who have a good command of Legal English (as a second legal language); and who were trained in the common principles of European legal systems so that they could operate across boundaries and were able to communicate with foreign colleagues about drafting new European rules and decisions and contracts. For that purpose, we started in 1992 a commercial post-graduate LL.M. program, entitled Magister Iuris Communis (Master of European and Comparative Law).[39] In this program we offered, for domestically trained lawyers, a curriculum

35 See Ius Commune Research School Homepage, <http://www.iuscommune.eu/startpagina.aspx?language=English>.

36 See Maastricht University, Maastricht Journal of European and Comparative Law, <http://www.unimaas.nl/default.asp?template=werkveld.htm&id=IHA3VONPFP25175R1IJP&taal=en>.

37 See Maastricht University, Ius Commune Casebooks for the Common Law of Europe, <http://www.unimaas.nl/default.asp?template=werkveld.htm&id=OO11IA6XU2XFTA11S02P&taal=en>.

38 See Maastricht University, Ius Commune Europaeum Book Series, <http://www.unimaas.nl/default.asp?template=werkveld.htm&id=M772225M74X20LMX367H&taal=en>.

39 See University, Master's Programmes, <http://www.maastrichtuniversity.nl/web/Main/ProspectiveStudents/MastersProgrammes.htm>. This MIC programme has been reformed →

with courses on European law proper as well as on European and comparative tort, contracts, property law; administrative law, company and business law etc.[40]

In 1995, we used the knowledge and experiences gained with this master program to offer a European Law School program (at that time, pre-Bologna), a four-year program with courses on Dutch law in the first two years and English-taught courses in the latter two years, focusing on the subjects mentioned and expanded with courses on criminal law, trade law etc.[41] This program has been a great success but suffered from two great disadvantages:

1. it was difficult to attract foreign students (because of the first two years in Dutch); and our idea was to seek a way to have an international class room in which comparative law can flourish and which is truly European;
2. the need to train lawyers under Dutch law in order to educate them for a European labour market; i.e. the absence of a Europe-wide system of legal education and of Europe-wide standards of access to the legal profession, or at least the absence of some commonality in this respect.

8. The Modern-Day European Law School LL.B. and LL.M.

In 2006, Maastricht University dared to take the next step: offering a full fledged program on law, taught in English, from day one, with a focus on European law, comparative law and international law. This step was obvious: considering the many developments in the domain of European Union law and the growing expertise in European and comparative law, we decided to reform the European Law School curriculum once more and to add a track (taught in English from day one) which basically is a three-year bachelor in International, European and comparative law. For those who opt for access to the legal profession we offer them a third year in Dutch in which we train them in Dutch law (which gives them two years to learn Dutch by the way).[42] If a student does not have the desire to enter the bar, (s)he will simply finish the LL.B with English-taught courses.[43]

The full curriculum is relatively simple and straightforward, and not very revolutionary if not for the focus upon international, European and comparative law; teaching courses such as: Introduction to Law, Legal English, Skills, Moot court training, comparative contract, comparative tort, comparative property, comparative government, European legal history, International and European law,

now into a master on International and European Economic Law, since the Maastricht European Law School LL.M includes the courses previously taught in MIC. See *idem*.

40 These are casebooks analyzing case law in different EU member states seeking for common principles and solutions.

41 See Maastricht University, Bachelor's Programmes, <http://www.maastrichtuniversity.nl/web/Faculties/FL/TargetGroup/ProspectiveStudents/BachelorsProgrammes/Programmes.htm>.

42 See European Law School English Track, *supra* note 41.

43 See Maastricht University, Bachelor's Degree – Programme Structure, <http://www.maastrichtuniversity.nl/web/Faculties/FL/TargetGroup/ProspectiveStudents/Bachelors/Programmes/DutchLaw/ProgrammeInformation/ProgrammeStructure.htm>.

European Law Foundations, European Substantive Law, comparative criminal law and criminal procedure, European company law. In the subsequent master program, students take further courses on these areas in addition to courses on competition law, civil procedure, European criminal law, etc.

Evidently, we still feel hindered by the second disadvantage mentioned before; we still have to offer possibilities for students to take the bar if this is what they want. They can still opt for Dutch law courses (but must learn Dutch), or they can go for the one-year English CPE (Common Professional Education, training students with a non-English law bachelor and preparing them for the Bar Vocational Course).

However, despite these bar access problems, we see many benefits in our program and we also believe that, with the assistance of large law firms who operate at a truly European level, gradually the barriers will dwindle and disappear. II certainly see the benefits of our program, and that is why our graduates are very much wanted, for a variety of reasons:

1. the students attracted are very motivated students;
2. they have been trained in different languages (native language and (legal) English);
3. their international and European legal training meets a real need in the market for lawyers; and
4. their comparative approach and knowledge have trained them better than others for European labour market demands.

The exercise of setting up this curriculum very much went hand in hand with research and the development of novel, tailor-made teaching materials. I already referred to the case book project; also Philipp Kiiver and Nicole Kornet published a book with comparative, international and European legal provisions needed in our courses.[44]

9. Labour Market for these New Lawyers

It is premature to provide solid data with respect to the labour market perspectives of our European Law School graduates. The students in the classic European Law School were very much welcomed on the labour market and, compared to other law programs in the Netherlands; they entered international jobs on a large scale. Also, we found that a large proportion (larger than in other Dutch law school programs) found jobs in large law firms (25 per cent).[45] Recent figures relating to access to the bar even showed higher percentages for Maastricht graduates: in 2009, 154 of Maastricht law graduates entered the bar (out of the 309 Maastricht master degrees awarded in the same year; and out of the 999 total number of applicants to the

44 See generally Kiiver & Kornet 2008.

45 ROA (Research Centre for Education and the Labour Market) research done for the Faculty of Law in 2004.

Dutch bar in 2009).[46] For them, as well as for other law school graduates, the labour market was positive.[47]

The perspectives for the European Law School students cannot be predicted; law firms still hire new graduates, but certain areas (mergers and acquisitions) seem to suffer. On the other hand, qualitatively good students still find jobs and are still very much in demand, especially if they have done something different or extra such as internships, study abroad, language courses and the like. On domestic levels, there is also an increasing demand for these new lawyers; governments seek lawyers and other civil servants with excellent knowledge of European law, the interface between European law and domestic law, and legal English. The interaction between Brussels and domestic governments are so intensive that governments are desperate for expertise.[48] Recently, the European Council of the EU also called upon the national governments to improve legal training and expertise. One of the reasons for this was a general consensus that domestic lawyers and domestic judiciaries lack the necessary expertise and knowledge in the relevant domains of European law and its intricacies and entanglement with domestic law.[49]

10. Conclusion and Agenda

Many interesting developments take place in Europe and in European legal education. I have not even touched upon benchmarks or features of what might constitute a good law curriculum.[50] Nor have I discussed how to teach (Socratic method, case method, problem based learning and others), or how to install an academic attitude in students, or how to distinguish between academic training and professional training, or how to teach and integrate skills, or how to peer review curricula within countries and transboundary, nor have I touched upon what constitutes good teaching materials, case books and other materials and whether and how to include other sciences,(economics, psychology, forensics, philosophy, criminology etc.) in a legal curriculum. Some of these issues are discussed by other contributors to this book and all are items that I will certainly commit myself to in

46 Since Maastricht is the smallest law school in the Netherlands with in total 9 law schools, this means that a large share of Maastricht graduates enter the bar (*Jaarverslag Orde van Advocaten 2009 – Annual Report of the Dutch Bar*, p. 52); in 2009 almost 50 per cent of the Maastricht graduates entered the bar: 154 out of 309: which is an exceptionally high number (*Annual Report/Jaarverslag 2009 Maastricht University*, p. 10).

47 Loopbanen na Maastricht University: metingen 2008, Research Centre for Education and the Labour market/ROA, 2010, ISBN 978-90-5321-485-5.

48 I have no specific data on this but conclude from interaction with recruiters and government officials that they specifically seek students with knowledge of both English and European law.

49 See Council Resolution 2008/C 299/01, Resolution of the Council and of the Representatives of the Governments of the Member States meeting within the Council on the training of judges, prosecutors and judicial staff in the European Union, 2008 *OJ* C 299/1.

50 See Centre for Higher Education Development, Ranking, <http://www.che-ranking.de/cms/?getObject=613&getLang=en>. There is not yet a European-wide benchmark for European higher education; the best (and increasingly covering more universities) is CHE; it is not yet available for non-German speaking law schools.

other writings. The present article purports to briefly describe legal developments in Europe, heir consequences as I see them for legal education and how we can prepare the stage for tackling these issues and build a European legal education and do so European wide.

At this stage, I submit that in Europe there is certainly room to move forward with regard to discussing European legal training. Europe needs lawyers who are fully trained in academia in languages, European law, comparative law and the interaction between domestic legal systems and European law. A challenging new approach in this respect is the Maastricht European Law School project. Still, we have to find a solution to ensure that these new lawyers will be accepted as full fledged lawyers and be recognized for what they are: European lawyers.

Let's therefore turn our attention to what might be the road ahead and the actions to be undertaken. I submit the following model for European legal education.

1. The first conclusion is to recognize a two tier approach: in some selected schools focus is to be had on 'European' legal training (which I will explain shortly); in most schools the law is taught as it is now for the domestic bar and legal professions with a curriculum which is primarily nationally oriented with the proper attention to (the impact of) European and international law.
2. For the 'European Law Schools' the mission will be different;

2.1 Access for students will be selective and limited;

2.2 These schools will need an internationally diverse student body;

2.3 They will need an internationally diverse faculty;

2.4 They will teach European (and international) law and comparative law for two to three years as a general basic legal academic training, in English;

2.5 They will join efforts and resources in a joint consortium aimed at discussing and improving courses and curricula; engage in staff and student exchange; this consortium will also develop into an accreditation and quality assurance organization;

2.6 The consortium will be the partner for the European Commission and will have to be sponsored and funded, as an important means and tool to improve legal education and work towards the goal of increasing the knowledge of European law and its effective application and implementation.

3. The legislatures of the Member States and its bar associations will work towards a recognition of the degrees obtained in the European law schools by setting up bar exams allowing the students to have access to legal professions.
4. On the European level the consortium will work with the Commission and a representation of the bar associations and other stakeholders to allow for a common European Bar exam for European Law School graduates, to allow them access to European legal jobs as well as the bar in domestic jurisdictions, and recognition of the European bar exam.
5. The European Law Schools will strive to establish professional trainings for domestic judges and lawyers and assist in training them in the domain of European law in the broad meaning of the term (including comparative law).

6. The consortium will make available a platform for discussions about European legal education and the setting of the agenda for a future oriented European legal education of high quality, combining academic training and professional skills.

Bibliography

Kiiver & Kornet 2008
Kiiver, Ph. & Kornet, N. (eds.), *Selected National, European and International Provisions from Public and Private Law; The Maastricht Collection,* Groningen: Europa Law Publishing, 2008.

Bruno De Witte

EUROPEAN UNION LAW: A COMMON CORE OR A FRAGMENTED ACADEMIC DISCIPLINE?

1. Introduction

The study of European Union law is a common element of legal education everywhere in Europe. This chapter revisits the discipline of EU law as it is taught and thought about today, with one particular question in mind, namely: how common is that common element of European legal education? To what extent can one say that European Union law is a unified academic discipline, and that the shapers of that discipline, those who professionally write about EU law, constitute a true community? Are they a unified group or are they deeply fragmented along national or other lines? This chapter does not aim at dealing with other, related, questions, such as that of the substantive characteristics of EU law legal scholarship (what are its main themes? which are the ideological currents?) or that of the influence of legal academics on the actual development of EU law.[1]

The first thing one can note is that legal scholars display a surprising lack of interest in legal scholarship, or at least they tend not to make it an object of their writing. There is no apparent interest in 'mapping the field' of the kind which one finds in political or sociological scholarship.[2] This general characteristic of legal academia is also true in the field of European Union law. The scholars specializing in this field rarely, if ever, indulge in self-reflective inquiries. They write frequently about the nature of their object ('what is European Union law?') but not about the nature and state of their own trade ('what is European Union legal scholarship?'). The few writings by EU law scholars that deal with the state of the academic discipline mainly deal with the content of scholarship,[3] and only very few deal also

1 For a comparative law essay about the influence of legal academics on the development of the law (but without specific reference to European law), see Twining, Farnsworth, Vogenauer & Tesón 2003. Specifically on the UK, see Duxbury 2001. And on Germany, see Vogenauer 2006.

2 But see the intriguing essay by Twining 2000, Chapter 6.

3 See for example: Shaw 1996; von Bogdandy 2000; Walker 2005; Curtin 2006.

with the structure and organisation of EU law scholarship,[4] which is my concern in this chapter.

Treating the individuals who freely indulge in legal writing (in the case of judges or practitioners), or who are contractually obliged to produce legal writing (in the case of university-based academics), as potentially forming a community is itself an idea which makes more sense in some countries than in others. In a recent study of German legal academia, the author stated that 'German lawyers take it for granted that there is a body of persons, writings and opinions that, in its entirety, constitutes "the doctrine" (*die Lehre*), "the legal doctrine" (*die Rechtslehre*), "legal science" (*die Rechtswissenschaft*) or "the literature" (*das Schrifttum*)'.[5] Similarly, in France and in Italy, *la doctrine* and *la dottrina* have traditionally been conceived as an abstract entity beyond the collection of individuals that compose it.[6] This is not the case in other countries, such as the United Kingdom. So, already at the meta-level of whether it makes sense to conceive of legal academics as a body with collective views and opinions, there is a cultural fragmentation along national lines.

In the following pages, I will first (in section 2) present the 'unity hypothesis', that is, the factors that might lead us to conceive of EU legal scholarship as a relatively unified academic discipline, and then move to consider (in sections 3 and 4) the main elements that have caused, and continue to cause, fragmentation, with an emphasis on the existence of geographical and disciplinary boundaries.

2. The Unity Hypothesis

There are several reasons why one would expect EU legal scholarship to form a relatively close-knit and homogenous community. First of all, the academic 'branch' of European Community law was created quite some time ago and quickly assembled all the paraphernalia of a true legal sub-discipline. More precisely, one can date the emergence of the academic discipline of Community law to the early and mid-60s, and localize it, obviously, in the original six Member States of the European Communities.[7] A number of Institutes of European Law were created in those years, in places such as Brussels, Leiden, Utrecht, Cologne, Paris, Liège and Padova, offering an infrastructure for teaching and research in the brand-new discipline. In some countries, particularly the Netherlands, special chairs for European Community law were established, whereas in other countries new courses in EC law were offered by academics belonging to an established discipline (this is an issue which we will address later in this paper). A number of specialized journals were started one after the other, including *Common Market Law Review*,[8]

4 But see: Schepel & Wesseling 1997; Shaw 2003; Arnull 2008.

5 Vogenauer, *supra* note 1, p. 631.

6 See in particular Jestaz & Jamin 2004 and Jestaz & Jamin 1998. For Italy, see Braun 2006, at p. 680.

7 On this period of emergence of EC law, see Vauchez 2008, at p. 21-22, and also Vauchez 2007.

8 The *Common Market Law Review* was founded in 1963 at the University of Leiden in the Netherlands. The mission of the Review was defined, in its first editorial, as that of building a bridge between the continent and the UK, and providing interested readers in the UK with a →

Cahiers de droit européen, Revue trimestrielle de droit européen, Europarecht, Rivista di Diritto Europeo, all still alive and thriving except for the last named. In each Member State, associations of European Community lawyers were set up and together they formed a *Fédération Internationale de Droit Européen,* which still exists today and manifests its existence essentially by the organisation of large two-yearly conferences.

This early group of Community law scholars had a clear common purpose. Apart from commenting the concrete legal developments in EC legislation and case-law (which were very modest compared to what they are today), they devoted much of their intellectual energy to highlight the novel characteristics of the Community legal order. Based on an analysis of the judgments of the European Court of Justice in *Van Gend en Loos* (1963) and *Costa* v. *ENEL* (1964), they propagated the need for the uniform application of EC law and its integration in the legal orders of the Member States. Thus, from the start, EC law aspired to become truly uniform law, in contrast with traditional public international law whose domestic application was (and still is) very uneven depending on the different constitutional rules and practices of each country. In fact, the uniform application of EC law has become a *leitmotiv* in the case law of the ECJ. Whereas most norms of Community law, whether contained in directives or in regulations, are implemented and applied by national authorities and courts, the European Court has insisted that this domestic transposition and application of European norms should not distort the content of the norm. It has often held that 'the need for uniform application of Community law and the principle of equality require that the terms of a provision of Community law which makes no express reference to the law of the Member States for the purpose of determining its meaning and scope must normally be given an autonomous and uniform interpretation throughout the Community',[9] and that this requires, among other things, a consideration of all the language versions of a given Community law measure.[10] It is clearly utopian to think that national courts or authorities will be able to consult and compare all the (more than 20) language versions of an EU law norm,[11] but stating this as a rule of interpretation certainly expresses a strong invitation to look 'across the border' when interpreting and applying EU law. This aspiration to uniformity, a true hallmark of the EC legal order as it was developed from the 1960s, is thus a reason to expect the emergence of an academic community which is fairly homogeneous across national lines. Since EU law applied in Germany must be the same as EU law

view of legal developments in the Community of the Six. Its initial board of editors had 4 British and 4 Dutch members, and one each from Belgium, France, Germany and Italy. The vast majority of the contributors, in the years prior to UK accession, were based on the continent.

9 ECJ, Case C-188/03, *Irmtraud Junk v. Wolfgang Kühnel,* judgment of 27 January 2005, para. 29. Similar language can be found in many judgments of the Court.

10 *Ibidem,* para. 33.

11 Indeed, it is difficult enough for the European Court of Justice to deal with discrepancies between the language versions of a given text in its own interpretation of EU law; see, for example, Van Calster 1997, p. 374.

applied in Poland, one would expect EU legal writing to adopt a cross-national outlook in its comments and analysis.

Another factor of unity, which was duly noted by Schepel and Wesseling in their pioneering empirical study of 1997,[12] is the active participation of lawyers working for the European institutions, and members of the Court of Justice and their legal secretaries, in scholarly writing, including the writing of textbooks[13] and the editing of legal journals. They showed, in their study, that since the early years of the Communities a close connection was established between academics and practitioners, including frequent circulation of individual scholars from one sub-field to the other, with university professors becoming judges or members of the Commission or the Council legal service and vice-versa, and many persons exercising both functions simultaneously. One typical figure of EU law is, in fact, that of the member of the Court of Justice who writes abundantly in scholarly journals, is an editor of a few of them, and teaches EU law in places such as the College of Europe. This close-knit interaction caused *la doctrine* to be, at least in the early decades, very supportive of the work of the EU institutions, and in particular of the Court.[14]

In a more recent publication dealing with another subject, one of the authors summed up and confirmed the views outlined in the 1997 article in the following terms:

> 'Les communautaristes forment un groupe très uni, qui circule tout naturellement entre l'université, les institutions politiques et le monde économique. Leur ethos est profondément pragmatique, ouvertement hostile aux idées grandioses, et sous-tendu par une conception clairement instrumentale du droit. Leur engagement collectif en faveur de l'intégration estompe leurs divergences politiques et leurs controverses techniques.'[15]

We find, in this passage, a nutshell definition of an academic discipline which is institutionally well-integrated and which possesses a common sense of purpose.

However, each of the three sentences contains highly disputable statements which may have been true at some earlier epoch, but may no longer be true today. The last sentence assumes that EU law scholars, taken as a whole, support the deepening of European integration. Yet, one increasingly finds legal writing that criticizes the general direction taken by the integration process (for example, at the time of the drafting and adoption of the Constitutional Treaty), and of particular pieces of legislation and judgments of the European Court of Justice. Today, legal writing in the leading journals is as critical of EU law-making and judicial interpretation as comparable national legal scholarship, and *la doctrine*, taken as a whole, is no longer throwing its weight behind plans for 'more Europe'. The second

12 Schepel & Wesseling, *supra* note 4.

13 For example, one prominent English-language textbook of EU law is co-authored by a current judge at the ECJ and by one of his *référendaires*: Lenaerts & Van Nuffel 2005.

14 On this phenomenon, see Schepel & Wesseling, *supra* note 4, and also Shaw, *supra* note 4, at p. 336 *et seq*.

15 Schepel 2005, at p. 152.

sentence, referring to an ingrained pragmatism and instrumental view of the law, is probably less true than it used to be. As the number of academics specializing in EU law increases, there is more room for theoretically inclined and normative assessments of the evolution of EU law and its different branches. But the remainder of this paper will deal, in particular, with the plausibility of the statement in the first sentence: do EU legal writers really constitute *un groupe très uni*?

3. Fragmentation through Legal Education

A theoretical basis for scepticism about the existence of a single Europe-wide scholarly community is provided by the 'law-as-culture' school in comparative law.[16] Writers of this persuasion have expressed deep scepticism about the feasibility of comparative legal analysis and about transplants of norms and institutions between legal orders. They posit the 'incapacity on the part of those immersed in one legal system to appreciate the deep context and meaning of other systems.'[17] Their emphasis on the incommensurability of legal cultures and legal systems has become influential (though controversial) in the field of comparative law, but the views of these writers are clearly relevant also for the field of European Union law. In part, this is because EU law is only partly uniform and partly absorbed into 27 different national legal systems. But also where EU norms are formally speaking uniformly applicable throughout the territory of the Union (as in the case of the rare EU regulations that do not require national implementing measures), they will be understood and handled in a different way by lawyers depending on the legal culture to which they belong. The domestic interpretation and application of EU law does not involve the interpretation and application of a norm belonging to a *foreign* legal system (as is the case in comparative law scholarship and in the practice of legal transplants), but it still concerns a norm from *another* legal system than one's own - and this otherness is faced by academics as well as by judges and practitioners, since EU law is another legal system than the one in which they were trained and whose culture they have absorbed during that training process. The EU law that is studied in each country is therefore a 'legal hybrid', a European law which is contextualized and transformed by the national legal order in which it is articulated.[18] Professor Jolowicz put it in the following metaphorical terms, some 30 years ago:

> 'It is not to be expected that the insertion into different legal systems of a single text will produce identical or even similar results in all those systems any more than it is to be expected that the addition of a litre of green paint to four litres of yellow will give

16 Characteristic writings from this school include: Legrand 1999; Legrand 2003. For discussion of this approach to comparative law, see Cotterell 2006.

17 Walker 2002, at p. 258 (the author of this description is not himself part of the school).

18 Walker, *supra* note 3, at p. 583.

> us the same colour as the addition of the same quantity of the same paint to four litres of red.'[19]

In fact, the validity of the 'law-as-culture' thesis appears to be crucially linked to the conditions of legal education. A child born in Birmingham is not a natural common lawyer, nor does the young Tuscan acquire a *'civiliste'* frame of mind already in secondary school. It is, rather, university and professional legal training that instil the deep understanding of law as expression of a particular legal culture. Now, to what extent can it be said that the understanding which legal academics have of EU law is determined by the particular legal system in which they received their early training?

The training of many EU law academics took indeed place within the confines of a national university system, in which the emphasis is clearly on learning about the national legal system first, and learning about European Union law (if at all) in the light of the categories and ways of argument of the national system. Thus, their perspective on European law was formed on the basis of a university *curriculum* which situated the national legal system at the centre of the legal universe. The fragmentation effect which this causes is visible both in terms of academic content and academic style.

As to academic content, the themes of EU law which scholars explore are often determined by the importance given to them in the university canon of their own country. This question has never been properly studied, at least not for EU law,[20] but, to give just one example, it is surely no coincidence that much of the legal writing on the system of sources of EU law has been produced by French scholars, and that UK scholars fail to even to register this as a distinct topic of EU law scholarship.

The same is true for academic style. For example, the French rigid writing structure (with the *plan en deux parties*) applies to EU law as much as to any other legal discipline. Similarly, scholars of EU law who have been educated in a German law school will typically display a style of EU law scholarship which corresponds to the dominant style used by domestic law scholars. It is characterised, according to a description proposed by a German academic working in the UK, by a 'struggle for rationality, systematic coherence, logical consistency, building on first principles, obsession with taxonomy, abstractness, precision and clarity of concepts.' It is, to put it in a nutshell, 'still very much under the spell of nineteenth century 'legal science''.[21]

This form of fragmentation is of course self-perpetuating: to the extent that university teachers are themselves steeped in their national legal traditions, and use the EU law literature written in their own language, the legal education system will

19 Jolowicz 1978, at p. 244.

20 But see the attempt to map the distinctiveness of German legal scholarship in the neighbouring field of public international law, in 'Typisch deutsch...: Is there a German Approach to International Law?', special issue of the *German Yearbook of International Law*, 2007, p. 15-456.

21 Vogenauer, *supra* note 1, at p. 657.

tend to perpetuate this nationally-coloured outlook on EU law for the next generation of students. On this point, one would need to have a closer look at textbooks, which are the privileged means through which EU law scholarship is passed on to students, but it is probably safe to assume that these textbooks, because of their synthetic approach, will be even more clearly focused on scholarship produced within the country or within the language community than other more specialized legal writings. If one takes, for example, the most widely used English language textbook of EU law, Craig and de Búrca's *EU Law – Text Cases and Materials* (4th ed., 2008), each of the 28 chapters is followed by a list of further references comprising from a minimum of 5 to a maximum of about 30 items of legal writings; none of those is written in another language than English. The same is true, by and large, for the other English-language textbooks. This instils in young EU law scholars the feeling that it is possible and normal to write intelligently about EU law as if it were exclusively produced and commented upon in English. Textbooks in other main European languages similarly refer predominantly to writing in their own language, although this may be changing gradually. Examples of a new, more plurilingual approach, are a recently published *Introduction au droit européen*, written by two scholars of the younger generation, who refer extensively also to writing on EU law in English,[22] and Ulrich Haltern's *Europarecht*, which uses as much, if not more, English as German literature.[23]

It would seem, therefore, that national systems of legal education have a massive fragmenting effect on EU law scholarship. However, a number of factors weaken the 'nationalizing' impact of legal education on the formation of future EU law academics.

The *first of these factors* is that a large number of students (especially among the bright students who might become academics) actually study EU law in other countries than the one in which they receive their basic legal training. From the start, training in European law was not an exclusively national affair. In the early decades of European integration, when EC law was integrated in the national law *curriculum* to a very limited extent, knowledge of EC law was typically acquired in a specialized post-graduate programme, such as those of Nancy, Strasbourg and Saarbrücken. The most important of those programmes was the College of Europe in Bruges, a true breeding ground of EU law specialists who, for many of them, went on to work for the EU institutions.[24] At the more specific level of training future legal academics, the European University Institute in Florence has played a similar role of denationalization of legal scholarship, although the emphasis of its Law doctoral programme (unlike in Bruges) was never exclusively on EU law, and its unifying role is probably more implicit than deliberate.[25] More recently, this de-nationalization of the study of European law started to occur at undergraduate level as well. We can observe, today, that many Erasmus exchange students study EU

22 Bergé & Robin-Olivier 2008.

23 Haltern 2007.

24 For a sociological study of the role played by the College of Europe in general (that is, also in other fields than the law), see Schnabel 1998.

25 See Snyder 2000; see also the Autumn 2005 issue of the *EUI Review* (available online).

law also, or even mainly, during their exchange period abroad rather than in their home university. This happens for a number of reasons, which include the perception that EU law is a more easily accessible subject in a foreign university context than courses in the law of the host university's country! As a result of these developments, a sizeable number of EU academics[26] have obtained their first or advanced training in EU law in another country than their own, so that their understanding of EU law becomes 'transnationalized' and partly divorced from their understanding of the domestic law of their country of origin.

A *second factor* is also linked to the operation of the Erasmus programme. The programme has, contrary to its stated ambition of strengthening cultural diversity in Europe, promoted the diffusion of English as EU law's *lingua franca*. Indeed, many universities in the smaller countries of Northern Europe have decided to offer English language courses in order to be sufficiently attractive to foreign students; in the case of law studies, the parts of the *curriculum* that were most easily anglicized were EU law and international law, rather than the courses dealing with the various branches of national law. The Erasmus-induced student mobility has thus led to the large-scale use of English and English-language literature for teaching EU law outside the UK and Ireland. Examine, for example, the webpage of the University of Edinburgh's School of Law dedicated to its Erasmus exchanges.[27] It lists the participating institutions and mentions the languages they use: there are five French universities where courses are taught in French, three German universities where courses are taught in German, three Spanish universities where they are taught in Spanish, whereas for all other European destinations, namely Belgium, Denmark, the Netherlands, Norway and Sweden, the webpage reassuringly indicates that the courses will be taught in English (which presupposes that the Edinburgh students will not venture to take courses in Belgian, Dutch etc. law, but will stay with the selected English language offering of their host institutions, which invariably includes one or more courses of EU law). Obviously, the switch to English and to English language literature also applies to the 'home' students of those law schools, since the schools often cannot afford the luxury of offering parallel courses of EU law in the national language and in English. Thus, a Dutch student who studied European law at Maastricht University based on the *EU Law* textbook by Craig and de Búrca has imbibed a vision of EU law that does *not* reflect Dutch legal culture.

This 'blurring' of legal cultures also happens at later stages of the academic career. Indeed, the *third factor* that counteracts national fragmentation in university education is the fact that, in a number of countries, university positions in the field of EU law are wide open to foreign nationals. In theory, all university positions are now open to all EU citizens, on the basis of the rules on the free movement of persons of the EU Treaty. In practice, though, the mobility of university professors

26 Although it is true that less than 4 per cent of university students take part in an Erasmus exchange during their studies, the percentage is probably much higher (although once again, I have no figures...) among EU law academics – that is, of course, among those who obtained their law degree during the last 20 years.

27 <www.law.ed.ac.uk/erasmus/institutions>.

and lecturers is rather limited,[28] and this is particularly so in the field of legal studies. The rules on academic recognition and the recruitment practices of universities, particularly in the large continental countries France, German, Italy and Spain, are organized in such a way that it is very difficult for foreign-trained scholars to be appointed.[29] In contrast with them, countries such as the United Kingdom and the Netherlands are easily accessible to foreign-trained scholars and both these countries might, today, have a majority of EU law academics who obtained their initial legal training in other countries than the UK or the Netherlands. For academics who are based, and teach, in another European state than the one in which they received their basic legal education, the national legal system of reference may become, with time, that of the country in which they live or else (and perhaps more frequently) they may form islands of truly trans-national research on EU law.

The *fourth factor* is the recent phenomenon whereby a small, but increasing, number of students opt for complete *undergraduate* legal studies at a foreign institution, which may involve either student mobility or the cross-border provision of legal education. Both these modalities of transnational education are permitted by the application of EU Treaty rules on freedom of establishment, freedom to provide services and Union citizenship. It is not uncommon, now, for a Greek student to obtain her legal education in France (or from an English university through distance learning), or for a German student to obtain a Dutch law degree. Luxemburgers necessarily had to study law abroad in the absence, until very recently, of a university at home, and this allowed for the emergence of some typically 'cosmopolitan' jurists such as former ECJ judge Pierre Pescatore, who had both studied and worked in several European countries other than his own.

The *fifth factor* relates to the non-academic segment of EU law scholarship. Many of the legal specialists working for the EU institutions have made most or all of their career inside these institutions, and have become thoroughly socialized into the frame of mind of the 'supranational' EU lawyer. This is reflected in their writings which, after some years, feel more like 'Brussels' than like Dublin, Heidelberg or Salamanca.

To conclude on this point, we find that the legal culture of many European law academics is a disaggregated and recomposed legal culture. The field is composed of two rather different groups of scholars: those who have been trained inside the traditions of a national legal system, and have encountered EU law within that context; and those (a growing number) who have a transnational perspective of the discipline, either because they lack a specifically national vantage point altogether or because they have become thoroughly socialized in a transnational professional context.

28 See the recent discussion of this lack of openness and mobility in European academic systems by Grigolo, Lietaert & Marimon 2010.

29 On the legal academic recruitment patterns in a selected group of countries, see the symposium papers edited by Mattei & Monateri 1993, p. 351 *et seq*. Little has changed since 1993…

4. Fragmentation in the Production of Legal Scholarship

After our summary examination, in the previous section, of the degree to which legal education structures promote fragmentation in EU law scholarship, we will now turn to another (not unrelated) dimension of the unity v fragmentation debate, namely the way in which the diffusion of EU law scholarship is organized. Here as well, the first impression is not that of a closely-knit community of scholars continuously speaking to each other (as the Schepel/Wesseling study of 1997 suggested), but rather that of a deeply segmented field with groups of scholars organised along national/linguistic and disciplinary lines.

4.1. *National/Linguistic Fragmentation*

We will start with the most obvious source of fragmentation in the diffusion of EU law scholarship: the fact that it takes place in different languages and through separate publication channels without much interaction between them. As one indicator of this degree of territorial fragmentation, I propose some data (presented in Tables at the end of this paper)[30] relating to the geographical origin of the contributors to some of the leading European law journals. With geographical origin, we mean here the country of the author's principal professional affiliation rather than her nationality. We made separate categories for each of the 15 'old' Member States, and lumped the twelve Member States that joined after 2004 together in one category 'New Member States'. In addition, we added a category 'EU' for the authors who work for one of the European Union institutions (or for the European University Institute in Florence), and therefore cannot be assigned, professionally speaking, to one particular country. The data relate to the years 2005 and 2006, and also to the years 1995 and 1996 in order to signal any major changes that may have occurred over the last decade. They indicate a very clear divide between on the one hand the German, Italian and Spanish journals which are overwhelmingly written by authors from the country in which the journal is based and on the other hand the English language journals which present a very diverse picture in this respect. The French language journals are situated in between. This pattern has not changed much during the last decade.

More specifically, we found for the Italian journal *Il Diritto dell'Unione Europea* that 33 of the 38 authors for the year 2005, and 31 out of 36 authors for 2006 were based in Italy, and the remainder (with one exception) was affiliated with the EU institutions. In *Europarecht,* 38 out of 39 authors in the year 2005 were based in Germany, and 40 out of 41 in 2006. Among the French-language journals of our sample, there is a clear difference between the *Revue trimestrielle de droit européen,* based in France, whose contributors are predominantly located in France (though with a large number of EU-based contributors in the year 2005) and the Belgium-based *Cahiers de droit européen,* which has a more varied pattern, but with Belgian

[30] The data were collected by Gracia Marín Durán, research assistant of the Academy of European Law at the European University Institute in Florence.

authors forming the largest group in most years. One finds a similar distinction between the two English-language journals included in the sample. Whereas the *European Law Review*, based in the UK, recruits about half of its contributors from the UK, the *Common Market Law Review*, based in the Netherlands, has a much wider spread. In fact, this journal has traditionally had a very diverse range of authors including, along those based in Britain, also an important number of Dutch, Belgian, German and EU-based authors.[31] The *Revue du Droit de l'Union Européenne* is different from all others. This journal was founded by jurists working for the European Commission, and its contributors are still overwhelmingly affiliated with one of the EU institutions; although their articles are all published in French, the nationalities of the authors are quite diverse.

This compartmentalization of the non-English journals is largely due to language barriers. For example, very few non-Italian scholars are able to write in Italian and Italian journals do not have the means to make more than the occasional translation of a foreign text. This language-induced fragmentation may be compared with the neighbouring field of public international law. There, one can observe that in Germany, Spain and Italy, alongside journals in the national languages, there are also periodical publications that have adopted English: the *German Yearbook of International Law*, the *Italian Yearbook of International Law* and the *Spanish Yearbook of International Law*. The former of these switched to English long ago (in 1976) and publishes the work of numerous authors who are not based in Germany, as well as contributing to the diffusion of German scholarship abroad. This cosmopolitan character contrasts quite sharply with the Germany-centred composition of the journal *Europarecht*, whose valuable articles are rarely perceived abroad, due to the language factor.

This summary view, based on the examination of a limited number of mainstream EU law journals over a limited number of years, provides only a rough indication of the degree of 'output' fragmentation of EU law scholarship. It would need to be complemented and qualified by consideration of other, less mainstream journals, which offer a very different perspective. For example, the *Revista de Derecho Constitucional Europeo*, an online-journal edited by the University of Granada,[32] contains very many (often translated) contributions by authors from outside Spain. One should also mention here the *European Law Journal* which has moved its editorial seat from Italy to France and then to the UK and has a cosmopolitan authorship to an even greater extent than the other two English-language journals mentioned above. It also has a special feature, namely the annual publication of a set of papers written by young European law authors based in institutions spread all over Europe and beyond, selected from among those presented at an annual International Workshop of Young Scholars.

31 Three other English-language journals based in the Netherlands that deal, to a large extent, with EU law, namely the *Legal Issues of Economic Integration*, the *European Constitutional Law Review* and the *Maastricht Journal of European and Comparative Law*, show the same pattern of multinational authorship.

32 <www.ugr.es/~redce>.

A more refined indicator of geographical closure (or, conversely, cross-national fertilisation of ideas) would be the practice of referring to publications in other languages than the one in which one writes. There, the picture is quite different from the one sketched above. Although I cannot offer concrete data here, there are some noticeable differences between countries on this point. Generally speaking, scholars writing in Italian and Spanish, despite the existence of a rich literature in their own language, tend to make frequent reference to the foreign-language literature, and not only in English. The same is true, of course, for those writing in the smaller European languages. In contrast, most authors writing in German and French hardly use any literature in other languages than their own, although there is a growing minority of mainly young authors who examine also the scholarly production in other languages (in fact, mostly English in both cases).[33] Among those writing in English, there is also a majority/minority cleavage, but of a different nature: here the smaller group of those who make frequent use of foreign language literature is mainly composed of those authors who are not based in Britain or Ireland. For example, a Dutch academic writing for an English-language law journal will quite naturally include Dutch, German and perhaps French writers among her references to the literature. Interestingly, though, the many EU law scholars of foreign origin who are employed by British universities tend to adopt the habit of their British-born colleagues of using exclusively English-language sources. It is a sure sign of the growing hegemony of English that these authors, who have easy mother-tongue access to other European languages, do not bother using the legal literature produced in those other languages.

So, it may be tempting to divide EU law scholarship in two groups: English-language scholarship and the rest. The former group is multinational in its composition, and is rather widely read and cited by their colleagues operating through other languages; the latter group operate *en vase clos*, in the sense that they may form a thriving and lively scholarly community within their language area, but are largely ignored by the rest of the world unless they make the effort to occasionally publish in English. There is, thus, a tendency for the English-language cluster, composed of many British and Irish scholars, a smaller group of Americans, and a growing group of scholars from Northern and Central Europe, to dominate the field, but this dominance is not absolute and uncontested.

More particularly, it is difficult to argue that English-language scholarship is more influential than the rest when it comes to the actual evolution of EU law. It is, of course, difficult to measure influence, but one small indicator is the extent to which legal writing is transmitted to the European Court of Justice through the opinions of the Advocates-General. Indeed, it is rather common for such opinions to refer to the scholarly literature dealing with the legal issue that is at stake in the case at hand.[34] A.G. Poiares Maduro, for example, cited ten pieces of legal literature in his opinion of 21 May 2008 in the case *Arcelor* (dealing with the interpretation of the

[33] A good example of the new trend is the sample of EU law scholarship from Germany and Italy published in English in the series of *Jean Monnet Working Papers* of New York University: von Bogdandy & Weiler 2003; Toniatti & Weiler 2007, 06-07 to 12-07.

[34] See Lasser 2004, at p. 122 *et seq*.

principle of equality and the relationship between the European Court and national courts),[35] A.G. Bot cited thirteen pieces of legal writing in an opinion of 8 July 2008 in a dispute between the Commission and Italy dealing with the regulation of motorcycle trailers,[36] and A.G. Trstenjak, in her opinion of 3 July 2008 in *SELEX Sistemi Integrati* (a competition case) cited fifteen different academic writings.[37] It would seem that the national origin of the Advocate-General is an important factor in the choice of the literature: whereas all A.G.s tend to use French and English literature, the use of writings in other languages is more sporadic and depends on the language skills of the A.G. and his/her collaborators. Some Advocates-Generals tend not to mention the *doctrine* at all; for example, in an opinion of A.G. Mazak of 10 July 2008 in the *Förster* case, which dealt with a controversial problem of Union citizenship on which there is abundant legal writing, one finds references to literally dozens of earlier ECJ judgments but not a single reference to the literature. It seems that the influence of legal scholarship on lawmaking and judicial decisions is limited by its fragmentation. The existence of national sub-communities means that it is much more difficult for something like a 'European prevailing opinion' to emerge, which could play a similar role as the *herrschende Lehre* in the German legal culture. In Germany, the *herrschende Lehre* (the 'prevailing doctrine') is a well-known concept which plays a practical role, in the sense that even judges and lawmakers feel under an obligation to give good arguments when they wish to depart from the prevailing doctrine.[38] There is no such thing in EU law.

4.2. *Disciplinary Fragmentation*

In 1989, the European Commission started its Jean Monnet Action Programme, a funding scheme which sought to promote university teaching on questions of European integration. Much of the funding since then went to the creation of new chairs or course modules of EU law. The Commission considered, indeed, that such a financial incentive was needed in order to convince the conservatively minded national education authorities and universities to give EU law its rightful place within the *curriculum*. It is true that prior to the Jean Monnet Programme only a few countries, such as Belgium and the Netherlands, had created specialized chairs in EU law. In most countries, EU law was incorporated into existing legal disciplines. In the early decades, this was often public international law, a logical choice since the European Communities had been created as advanced international organizations. In France, the main cleavage in legal studies between private law and public law ran right through EC law, so that EC law scholarship was fragmented, from the early days, between the *publicistes* and the *privatistes*, with separate courses and textbooks that deal either with the *droit institutionnel de l'Union européenne* or with the *droit communautaire des affaires*. When Spain joined the EC, it was decided

35 Of which 5 in French, 4 in English and 1 in Italian.

36 Of which 9 in English and 4 in French.

37 Of which 9 in German, 5 in French and 2 in English.

38 Vogenauer, *supra* note 1, at p. 631 and p. 652. And, more generally, on the role of 'prevailing opinion': Drosdeck 1989.

not to create separate chairs or departments, but rather to allow the new field to be 'carved up' between the existing departments of international law, administrative law or constitutional law, according to the dynamics and *rapport de force* in each university. Each Member State thus offers its own micro-story of the way in which the new legal reality of EU law was absorbed into generally very conservative university structures and academic circles.

More generally, with the expansion of EU law into ever-new areas such as environmental law, contract law, administrative law, health law or criminal law, the legal doctrinal analysis of EU law has also to a growing extent been 'redomiciled'[39] in the various substantive disciplines of national law. EU legal scholarship is now incomparably more voluminous, richer and interesting than twenty years ago, but it is, unavoidably, also more fragmented. If a French EU law scholar wants to follow the periodical literature in his field, he can no longer limit himself to read the specialized European law journals (the three journals mentioned above and the monthly *Jurisclasseur Europe)*; he now also needs to browse through the *Revue trimestrielle de droit civil*, the *Revue française de droit administratif*, *Droit social*, the *Revue critique de droit international privé*, the *Revue du droit public*, and several others, because all of them may contain important pieces of scholarship dealing with one corner of EU law. Faced with this abundance of domestic legal scholarship, he may well decide that there is no time left to read also the English-language or Italian journals of EU law. In this way, disciplinary fragmentation strengthens national/linguistic fragmentation.

Apart from this fragmentation which follows the lines of the traditional legal disciplines, one can see the appearance of another cleavage line in EU law scholarship which is based on different general understandings of 'how to study law'. In particular English-language EU law scholarship has been subject, in the last two decades, to a radical transformation which is much less visible in the scholarship in other languages. This transformation thesis was recently expounded by Tony Arnull.[40] According to this author, the Community law literature was marked until the end of the 1980s by 'two essential characteristics: first, it was essentially sympathetic to the integration project; second, it was traditional in character, 'based on the exposition of legal doctrine and the analysis of judicial decisions.'[41] After that, there occurred a 'theoretical turn' whereby a number of younger EU law scholars started to follow the model of American legal academia, where traditional doctrinal studies are neglected in favour of theoretically inspired and interdisciplinary research. However, as Arnull continues to argue, the American influence has had only a limited impact on English-language EU law scholarship: 'to the established tradition of sophisticated doctrinal analysis have been added the insights afforded by theoretical, contextual and interdisciplinary work,'[42] but this is an addition rather than a displacement. In fact, English-language EU scholarship seems to be marked by the coexistence of several approaches,

39 Walker, *supra* note 3, at p. 582.
40 Arnull, *supra* note 4.
41 Arnull, *supra* note 4, at p. 416. The internal quotation is from Snyder 1990.
42 Arnull, *supra* note 4, at p. 431.

ranging from the very doctrinal to the very theoretical, but without any animosity between different schools.[43] This 'rude health'[44] is probably due, in part, to the variety in national origin and academic background of the scholars. One could say that the capacity of English-language scholarship to overcome traditional national fragmentation, and its relative insensitivity to the well-established pattern of legal disciplines, allows it to be more open to new ways of studying the law.

43 For a similar view by a German scholar, see Haltern 2005, at p. 33.

44 Arnull, *supra* note 4, at p. 431.

ANNEX:

Country of professional affiliation of the authors of some leading European law journals

Journals included in the sample: *Cahiers de droit européen* (CDE), *Common Market Law Review* (CMLR), *Diritto dell'Unione Europea* (DUE), *European Law Review* (ELR), *Europarecht* (EPR), *Revue du Droit de l'Union Européenne* (RDUE), *Revista Española de Derecho Europeo* (REDE), *Revue trimestrielle de droit européen* (RTDE)

TABLE 1: 2005

Journal	**Place of Authors' Professional Affiliation (principal)**																		**Total Nr of Authors**
	Old EU Member States															**New EU MS**	**EU**	**Non-EU**	
	AT	**BE**	**DE**	**EL**	**FI**	**FR**	**GE**	**IR**	**IT**	**LX**	**NL**	**PT**	**SP**	**SW**	**UK**				
CDE (BE-based)		**8**	**1**	**3**		**4**							**1**				**4**		**21**
CMLR (NL-based)	**1**	**9**		**1**	**1**		**10**	**1**	**8**		**8**			**1**	**10**		**7**	**2**	**59**
DUE (IT-based)									**33**								**5**		**38**
ELR (UK-based)		**4**	**1**	**3**		**2**	**4**	**1**			**2**		**1**	**1**	**21**	**1**	**5**	**4**	**50**
EPR (DE-based)							**38**										**1**		**39**
RDEU (FR-based)				**1**		**4**			**1**		**1**		**2**				**27**	**1**	**37**
REDE (SP-based)							**1**						**15**			**1**	**5**		**22**
RTDE (FR-based)		**3**				**22**									**1**		**7**		**33**

TABLE 2: 2006

Journal	Place of Authors' Professional Affiliation (principal)																		Total Nr of Authors
	Old EU Member States															New EU MS	EU	Non-EU	
	AT	BE	DE	EL	FI	FR	GE	IR	IT	LX	NL	PT	SP	SW	UK				
CDE (BE-based)		4		3		6			1								4		18
CMLR (NL-based)	1	8	2	1	2	1	8		1	1	9		1		19		9	3	66
DUE (IT-based)									31						1		4		36
ELR (UK-based)		2		1		1	2	2		2	6				25	3	8	2	54
EPR (DE-based)							40				1								41
RDEU (FR-based)	1	2				3			3								30	2	41
REDE (SP-based)	1								1				19				2	2	25
RTDE (FR-based)		2				20			2		1				1		1		27

TABLE 3: 1995

Journal	Place of Authors' Professional Affiliation (principal)																		Total Nr of Authors
	Old EU Member States															New EU MS	EU	Non-EU	
	AT	BE	DE	EL	FI	FR	GE	IR	IT	LX	NL	PT	SP	SW	UK				
CDE (BE-based)		11		1		4	1		2		1		1		1		3		25
CMLR (NL-based)	2	8	1				3		1		11		2		13		16	4	61
DUE (IT-based)																			0
ELR (UK-based)		2	2		1		1	2			4				19	1	7	2	41
EPR (DE-based)	2						17										4		23
RDEU (FR-based)		4		1		3			4		2						26		40
REDE (SP-based)																			0
RTDE (FR-based)		1		1		18	1						1				3	1	26

TABLE 4: 1996

Journal	Place of Authors' Professional Affiliation (principal)																		Total Nr of Authors
	Old EU Member States															New EU MS	EU	Non-EU	
	AT	BE	DE	EL	FI	FR	GE	IR	IT	LX	NL	PT	SP	SW	UK				
CDE (BE-based)		10				2											6	1	19
CMLR (NL-based)	1	8				1	6	1	1		7				17		11	2	55
DUE (IT-based)									31								7		38
ELR (UK-based)		2					1	1			7			1	25		1	1	39
EPR (DE-based)	1						18			1							3		23
RDEU (FR-based)		13				2							3		2		20	2	42
REDE (SP-based)																			0
RTDE (FR-based)		2				16					1				1		2		22

Bibliography

Arnull 2008
Arnull, A., 'The Americanization of EU Law Scholarship', in Arnull, A., Eeckhout, P. & Tridimas, T. (eds.), *Continuity and Change in EU Law – Essays in Honour of Sir Francis Jacobs*, Oxford: Oxford University Press, 2008, p. 415-431.

Bergé & Robin-Olivier 2008
Bergé, J.-S. & Robin-Olivier, S., *Introduction au droit européen*, Paris: Presses Universitaires France, 2008.

Braun 2006
Braun, A., 'Professors and Judges in Italy: It Takes Two to Tango', *Oxford Journal of Legal Studies*, 2006, p. 665-681.

Cotterell 2006
Cotterell, R., 'Comparative Law and Legal Culture', in Reimann, M. & Zimmermann, R. (eds.), *The Oxford Handbook of Comparative Law*, Oxford: Oxford University Press, 2006, p. 709-737.

Curtin 2006
Curtin, D., 'European Legal Integration: Paradise Lost?', in Curtin, D., Klip, A., Smits, J. & Mccahery, J.A. (eds.), *European Integration and Law*, Antwerp: Intersentia, 2006, p. 1-54.

Drosdeck 1989
Drosdeck, T., *Die herrschende Meinung: Autorität als Rechtsquelle*, Berlin: Duncker & Humblot, 1989.

Duxbury 2001
Duxbury, N., *Jurists and Judges: An Essay on Influence*, Oxford: Hart Publishing, 2001.

German Yearbook of International Law 2007
'Typisch deutsch...: Is there a German Approach to International Law?', special issue of the *German Yearbook of International Law*, 2007, p. 15-456.

Grigolo, Lietaert & Marimon 2010
Grigolo, M., Lietaert, M. & Marimon, R., 'Shifting from Academic "Brain Drain" to "Brain Gain" in Europe', *European Political Science*, 2010, p. 118-130.

Haltern 2005
Haltern, U., *Europarecht und das Politische*, Tübingen: Mohr Siebeck, 2005.

Haltern 2007
Haltern, U., *Europarecht – Dogmatik im Kontext*, Tübingen: Mohr Siebeck, 2nd ed., 2007.

Jestaz & Jamin 1998
Jestaz, P. & Jamin, C., 'The Entity of French Doctrine: Some Thoughts on the Community of French Legal Writers', *Legal Studies*, 1998, p. 415-437.

Jestaz & Jamin 2004
Jestaz, P. & Jamin, C., *La doctrine*, Paris: Dalloz Sirey, 2004.

Jolowicz 1978
Jolowicz, J.A., 'New Perspectives of a Common Law of Europe: Some Practical Aspects and the Case for Applied Comparative Law', in Cappelletti, M. (ed.), *New Perspectives for a Common Law of Europe*, Berlin: de Gruyter *et al.*, 1978, p. 237-265.

Lasser 2004
Lasser, M., *Judicial Deliberations – A Comparative Analysis of Judicial Transparency and Legitimacy*, Oxford: Oxford University Press, 2004.

Legrand 1999
Legrand, P., *Fragments on Law-as-Culture*, Deventer: W.E.J. Tjeenk Willink, 1999.

Legrand 2003
Legrand, P., 'The Same and the Different', in Legrand, P. & Munday, R. (eds.), *Comparative Legal Studies: Traditions and Transitions*, Cambridge: Cambridge University Press, 2003, p. 240-311.

Lenaerts & Van Nuffel 2005
Lenaerts, K. & Van Nuffel, P., *Constitutional Law of the European Union*, London: Sweet & Maxwell, 2nd ed., 2005.

Mattei & Monateri 1993
Mattei, U. & Monateri, P.G., 'Selecting Minds', *American Journal of Comparative Law*, 1993, p. 351-500.

Schepel 2005
Schepel, H., '*Professorenrecht?* Le champ du droit privé européen', *Critique internationale*, 2005, No. 26, p. 147-158.

Schepel & Wesseling 1997
Schepel, H. & Wesseling, R., 'The Legal Community: Judges, Lawyers, Officials and Clerks in the Writing of Europe', *European Law Journal*, 1997, p. 165-188.

Schnabel 1998
Schnabel, V., 'Elites européennes en formation. Les étudiants du «Collège d'Europe» et leurs études', *Politix*, 1998, p. 33-52.

Shaw 1996
Shaw, J., 'European Union Legal Studies in Crisis? Towards a New Dynamic', *Oxford Journal of Legal Studies*, 1996, p. 231-253.

Shaw 2003
Shaw, J., 'The European Union: Discipline Building Meets Polity Building', in Cane, P. & Tushnet, M. (eds.), *The Oxford Handbook of Legal Studies,* Oxford: Oxford University Press, 2003, p. 325-352.

Snyder 1990
Snyder, F., *New Directions of European Community Law,* Cambridge: Cambridge University Press, 2nd ed., 1990.

Snyder 2000
Snyder, F., 'The EUI Law Department and the Europeanisation of Law: An Introduction', in Snyder, F. (ed.), *The Europeanisation of Law – the Legal Effects of European Integration,* Oxford: Hart Publishing, 2000, p. 1-11.

Toniatti & Weiler 2007
Toniatti, R. & Weiler, J.H.H. (eds.), 'Symposium: European Legal Integration - The New Italian Scholarship', *Jean Monnet Working Papers,* 2007, 06-07 to 12-07.

Twining 1999
Twining, W., 'Mapping Law', *Northern Ireland Legal Quarterly,* 1999, Vol. 50, No. 1, p. 12-49.

Twining 2000
Twining, W., *Globalisation and Legal Theory,* Cambridge: Cambridge University Press, 2000.

Twining, Farnsworth, Vogenauer & Tesón 2003
Twining, W., Farnsworth, W., Vogenauer, S. & Tesón, F., 'The Role of Academics in the Legal System', in Cane, P. & Tushnet, M. (eds.), *The Oxford Handbook of Legal Studies,* Oxford: Oxford University Press, 2003, p. 920-949.

Van Calster 1997
Van Calster, G., 'The EU's Tower of Babel - The Interpretation by the European Court of Justice of Equally Authentic Texts Drafted in More than One Official Language', *Yearbook of European Law,* 1997, p. 363-393.

Vauchez 2007
Vauchez, A., 'Une élite d'intermédiaires - Genèse d'un capital juridique européen (1950-1970)', *Actes de la recherche en sciences sociales,* 2007, No. 166-167, p. 54-65.

Vauchez 2008
Vauchez, A., 'Integration-through-Law - Contribution to a Socio-History of EU Political Common Sense', *EUI Working Papers RSCAS,* 2008/10.

Vogenauer 2006
Vogenauer, S., 'An Empire of Light? II: Learning and Lawmaking in Germany Today', *Oxford Journal of Legal Studies,* 2006, p. 627-663.

von Bogdandy 2000
von Bogdandy, A., 'A Bird's Eye View on the Science of European Law: Structures, Debates and Development Prospects of Basic Research on the Law of the European Union in a German Perspective', *European Law Journal,* 2000, p. 208-238.

von Bogdandy & Weiler 2003
von Bogdandy, A. & Weiler, J.H.H. (eds.), 'Symposium: European Integration - The New German Scholarship', *Jean Monnet Working Papers,* 9/2003.

Walker 2002
Walker, N., 'Culture, Democracy and the Convergence of Public Law: Some Skepticism about Skepticism', in Beaumont, P., Lyons, C. & Walker, N. (eds.), *Convergence and Divergence in European Public Law,* Oxford: Hart Publishing, 2002, p. 257-271.

Walker 2005
Walker, N., 'Legal Theory and the European Union: A 25th Anniversary Essay', *Oxford Journal of Legal Studies,* 2005, p. 581-601.

Jan Smits

EUROPEAN LEGAL EDUCATION, OR: HOW TO PREPARE STUDENTS FOR GLOBAL CITIZENSHIP?*

1. Introduction

It is well known that legal education is gradually moving away from the teaching of national law towards a more European, transnational, or even 'global' way of teaching. Such international legal education has now firm roots in Europe, the United States, and in many other countries throughout the world. The form this international legal education takes, however, differs enormously from one institution to another. While some law schools only recently started to offer mandatory courses on some international aspect of the law - Harvard Law School being one example[1] - others offer full bachelor programmes that no longer aim at teaching one national law. The two best-known examples of such programmes are the combined bachelor degree of civil law (B.C.L.) and common law (LL.B.) at McGill University[2] and the European Law School bachelor at Maastricht University.[3] Although both programmes differ in scope, content, and the type of graduates they aspire to produce (at McGill, these are lawyers who will work mostly - though not exclusively[4] - within the domestic Canadian legal system, while the Maastricht graduates are more likely to work in an international setting),

* This article was previously published in *The Law Teacher* 45 (2011), p. 163-180. Thanks are due to Mark Kawakami for invaluable research assistance.

1 In 2007 Harvard Law School followed other American law schools in adding an internationally oriented course to the first year as part of the first substantive change of the 1L curriculum in 130 years. First year students now have to take one of three courses devoted to Public International Law, International Economic Law, or Comparative Law.

2 There is abundant literature on the 'transsystematic' programme at McGill (taught since 1999). See the special issue of *McGill Law Journal*, 50, 2005, p. 701-1006 and most recently Dedek & de Mestral 2009, p. 889-911 and Strauss 2006, p. 161-171.

3 Apart from the contributions to this volume, the Maastricht ELS programme (taught since 1995) is discussed by Heringa 2002, p. 3-13 and Heringa 2010, p. 81-94.

4 McGill graduates are increasingly hired by the big international law firms (including those in New York) because of their ability to work in both civil law and common law jurisdictions.

they are both characterised by the same ambition: to educate lawyers in a non-national way by creating a 'transnational' or 'European' law graduate.

The aim of this contribution is to ask why we should teach law in a more international way and to explain what the *denationalisation* of legal education means in terms of *what* is taught and *how* it is taught. It will also attempt to answer the question of what this implies for the organisation of the traditional law school. Although these questions are of paramount importance, they have not been sufficiently addressed in the flourishing literature on international legal education.[5] I believe that teaching law in an international curriculum is fundamentally different from teaching (one or more) national laws: it assumes not only a different conception of law, but also a different attitude of both lecturer and student. For programmes that offer a complete transnational curriculum (such as McGill and Maastricht), it is therefore necessary to identify what makes them unique (even though some of the answers I will provide can also be valuable for programmes devoted to the study of two or more different national jurisdictions[6]).

Before discussing what is ideally taught in an international curriculum (section 3), how it should be taught (section 4) and what this means for law schools (section 5), it is appropriate to ask why - if at all - we should pursue an international legal education (section 2). Although I believe my arguments to be valid for international legal education in general, they apply in particular to the European situation.

2. Why A European Legal Education? Towards A Dialogue With Otherness

Until around 1990, legal education in Europe was primarily national: the law of one jurisdiction was taught to students of usually one nationality by lecturers of that same nationality, aiming at the production of graduates that would mostly work within their country of study. This situation had persisted for almost 200 years and, in hindsight, it is surprising that almost[7] everyone considered this to be the normal state of affairs. In the last two decades, however, this changed dramatically: apart from courses on international law and European law[8] (that were already part of the traditional law curriculum), almost everyone now accepts that it is no longer possible to teach the classical areas of law (such as private law, constitutional law,

5 See most recently the special issues of the *Penn State International Law Review*, 26, 2008, p. 811-912 and of the *German Law Journal*, 10, 2009, p. 629-1168.

6 Prime examples of such programmes are the Hanse Law School (a cooperation between the universities of Bremen, Oldenburg and Groningen, focusing on German and Dutch law) and the joint LLB programme of Paris I and King's College London (focusing on French and English law). In addition, numerous transnational programmes exist at the master and 'post-master' level.

7 Of course, there have always been dissident voices. One of the earliest is Rudolf Von Jhering's famous lament that legal science had deteriorated into a provincial field of study (Von Jhering 1852, p. 15). More recently the turn towards a European legal education received theoretical and programmatic underpinning in Cappelletti 1978 and in De Witte & Forder 1992.

8 On which De Witte 2011.

criminal law and tax law) without taking into account European and international influences. This led to whole new fields of academic study: many European law faculties now have professorial chairs for, e.g., European private law, European criminal law and European tax law to name just a few. It is also widely accepted that it is beneficial to have students and lecturers from abroad at one's own law school, and perhaps even better to have one's own students and lecturers spend some time at a foreign university.[9]

As indicated above, this phenomenal change in attitude led to different degrees of internationalisation in individual law schools. The aim of this section is to make the case for a far-going type of international legal education (such as the one offered in the Maastricht European Law School[10]). I believe three arguments can be put forward in favour of such a European bachelor programme in law. The first is based on the changing character of the law itself, the second on the requirements an academic study should meet and the third on the importance of attracting highly motivated students.

The first argument in favour of a truly European education is that the law itself is no longer a national phenomenon, but increasingly flows from other than national sources.[11] In private law (as well as in all other traditional sub-disciplines), we accept law of European and supranational origin, as well as a variety of rules originating from private initiative (ranging from the Common Frame of Reference for European Private Law[12] to standard form contracts and codes of conduct on corporate, social and environmental responsibility). Most of these authoritative rules and norms from 'sites of governance beyond the nation-state'[13] would not be recognized as binding in a traditional conception of law because they do not meet the formal criterion of being enacted by the relevant authorities. But they do set the norms for specific groups of people and are important in predicting their behaviour. Any modern legal education should take these norms into account, not only because they are indispensable in understanding the *existing* law (and consequently play a big role in practice), but also because it makes the students realise that law is not necessarily tied to the nation-state.[14] Patrick Glenn rightly observes that if law is no longer considered exclusively in terms of national sources, the discipline of law 'must assume the cognitive burden of providing information on law beyond

9 The exchange of students and staff in Europe is facilitated by the highly successful Erasmus Programme (established by the European Commission in 1987, later part of the Socrates Programme and now part of the Commission's Lifelong Learning Programme) and by the creation of the European Higher Education Area (as a result of the Bologna Declaration of 1999).

10 More in particular in the so-called 'English track' of this programme ('ELS-ET'): see on this programme, Kornet 2011.

11 See, with many references, Smits 2010a, p. 113-130.

12 The importance of which for teaching is emphasised by Akkermans 2009, p. 803-814.

13 De Búrca 2009, p. 101-158, at p. 104.

14 For an elaboration of the idea of private law beyond the nation-state: Michaels & Jansen 2006, p. 843-890; Jansen & Michaels 2007, p. 345-397 and the special issue of the *American Journal of Comparative Law*, 56, 2008, p. 527-843.

national borders.'[15] This does not mean that the law is taught 'without the State',[16] but it does imply that a legal education exclusively based on the intricacies of national legislation and court decisions is a poor one.

At this point, it is important to address a likely counterargument. It is sometimes argued that a European legal education is impossible because a European private law, criminal law or constitutional law do not really exist: such fields would (at least to a large extent) not be based on the authoritative statements of legislatures and courts, but at best be 'a brooding omnipresence in the sky'.[17] The flaw with this argument is that it gravely misunderstands the nature of legal authority. Apart from the fact that there is a rapidly increasing number of European treaties, regulations, directives and court decisions in these fields, it denies that the authority of legal sources is not necessarily dependent on the political institutions. Thus, when the University of Bologna started teaching the *Corpus Iuris Civilis* in the eleventh century, it taught a law that was not in force anywhere. Roman law gradually derived its authority from how it was taught and from its acceptance by the legal profession - how could it have been different in the absence of State structures in medieval Italy? In fact, it is often the legal profession and not the legislature that determines the authority of a text.[18] This makes it important not to limit legal education to those elements that are laid down in legislation and court decisions: law schools should not only *react* to legislatures and courts, but they also play an important role in *shaping* the future law.[19]

It would be possible to argue that this plurality of sources does not prompt us to adopt a far-going type of international legal education: one could still teach the national law and add some international and comparative elements here and there. I do not deny this as a possibility (it is even common practice at most law schools), but I do not think that this is the best way to teach students in today's globalising world. Even if one would assert that the only goal of legal education is to offer a professional training for future practitioners (which I would deny[20]), these practitioners should be able to work in the different legal systems of various countries to meet their clients' needs.[21] Even when the graduates stay in their home country, they are increasingly advising multinational and foreign clients who want to know about different solutions.[22] This calls for a much more rigorous international curriculum in which alternative approaches are sketched from the first day onward. Teaching one national law does not adequately prepare students for the world they have to work in.

15 Glenn 2006, p. 57-65, at p. 59.

16 Arthurs 2009, p. 629-639, at p. 637.

17 *Southern Pacific Company* v. *Jensen*, 244 *U.S.* 205, at 222 (1917), opinion of O.W. Holmes.

18 See the recent book by Jansen 2010, at p. 28; cf. p. 43: the 'abstract authority of a text giving expression to a legal norm consists in the legal profession accepting it as an ultimate source of the law'.

19 Cf. Kennedy 1990, p. 58.

20 See below, text surrounding footnote 24.

21 Strauss 2006: today's lawyers should be 'resourceful in imagining alternative approaches to clients' needs, drawing on the full range of the law's possibilities'.

22 See on the increasing importance of 'legal tourism' (in Dutch) Smits 2010b.

The second argument in favour of an international legal education is that it better meets the requirements of an academic study. This is not the place to summarize the extensive literature on what requirements an academic study has to meet,[23] but in my view a legal education should do at least two things: it should offer a specialized professional training in becoming a lawyer *and* it should shape students to become academics. In brief, students should learn to use the law not only as an instrument, but also to think about law in an intellectual way.[24] Martha Nussbaum aptly argues that in today's world, this academic aspect means that students have to be prepared for 'global citizenship':[25] they should learn how to become a citizen, not only of their country or local community, but also of the increasingly interlocking and interdependent world they live in.

This means that an academic legal education, in my view, should educate students about the contingency of the law. In other words, students have to be exposed to legal diversity, not only through grasping common law and civil law (and the varieties within these legal families), but also by extending their understanding to Nordic, Asian and Islamic laws. They should learn about the fact that different societies give different weight to issues such as social justice, efficiency, equality of man and woman and the value of life. They should learn to think through the consequences of choices made in different societies, to understand why these choices were made, and to argue why they think one choice is better than the other. If this 'dialogue with otherness'[26] is at the core of legal education – as I think it is – to focus on only one or two jurisdictions would be a poor and rather limited curriculum. A true legal education is only worth its salt if it shows to a full extent alternative outcomes to common problems and teaches students to think through the arguments and their alternatives.[27]

It must be emphasized that this argument is not just to advocate teaching students about multiple legal systems, but it is about promoting students to learn *the legal way of thinking* (to 'think like a lawyer'). In a similar way as economists do not focus on the study of one particular economy but adopt a method of analysis ('the economic approach'[28]), law is ideally not regarded as a subject but as a method. Students then no longer study Dutch law or German law, but learn to apply a legal approach towards the questions they are confronted with. They then learn that views on what ought to be necessarily differ from one jurisdiction to another and that legal scholarship deals with exploring and contrasting the implications of these

23 See, instead of many, the overview by Bell 2003, p. 901-919 and the recent book by Kronman 2007.

24 Cf. Strauss 2006, at p. 165: the goal must be to 'catch students in a University enterprise'.

25 Nussbaum 2003, p. 265-279, at p. 265 and for a more general account Nussbaum 1997.

26 See Morisette 2002, p. 12-28, at p. 22. Cf. Rakoff & Minow 2007, p. 597-607, at p. 606: 'The focus will be more on alternatives, choices, and living with the sequential consequences of earlier choices'.

27 This view fits in with what I think is at the core of normative legal scholarship, namely a concern with the *ought*, on which opinions will always differ: see (in Dutch) Smits 2009.

28 Becker 1992. Cf. Levitt & Dubner 2009, at p. 13: economics is not a subject matter, but 'a decision to examine the world a bit differently'.

conflicting normative positions.[29] Legal scholars do not search for what is *the* just society, but discuss alternatives.[30] Although after 200 years of teaching only one law, many law schools may find it difficult to adjust to this ambition, this does not mean that it is impossible.[31] One should realise that of the almost 1000 years in which law is taught at universities, the last 200 years have been exceptional: before 1800, students learnt about more than one law, be it Roman law and Canon law, common law and mercantile law or Roman law and local law. It was self-evident that all these laws had a rationality of their own and could not be brought under one heading. The names of the academic degrees and titles law graduates receive still remind us of this practice.[32]

The final argument for why an international legal education is preferable over a national one is that it will attract better motivated students. In this respect, the success story of the curriculum reform made by Langdell at Harvard is telling: before Langdell became the dean of Harvard Law School in 1870, law was taught by way of lectures, textbooks and moot courts. This was good enough for the great majority of the students, but it did not give any real intellectual stimulation for the best among them. This changed when Langdell introduced the case method (and combined it with the Socratic method): it attracted ambitious students because of the academic rigour of the programme. After graduation, these students were hired by the top law firms in New York because of their ability to deal with more than one State jurisdiction.[33] At present, to study law is in most European countries not particularly the most ambitious thing to do. This is at least partly caused by the way in which law is usually taught: as given by an authority and as inalterable. First year law students often learn to give up their inquiring state of mind and trade it in for learning their national system.[34] I believe this is wrong. A European or cosmopolitan legal education can be a real intellectual challenge, attracting more capable students and producing better graduates.[35] If it in fact *does* so, is of course dependent on what is taught and how it is taught. These are the topics of the next two sections.

29 Cf. Rubin 1988, p. 1835-1905, at p. 1893: 'The conflict of norms is the essence of normatively-based scholarship (…)' and Smits 2009.

30 Also see Sen 2009, at p. 106: we should 'have something to say about the choices that are actually on offer'.

31 On the strong tradition of having (and teaching) only one law (the *ius unum*): Glenn 2003, p. 839-862.

32 Apparent in the use of the terms LL.B (*legum baccalaureus* or Bachelor of Laws), LL.M (*legum magister* or Master of Laws) and LL.D (Doctor of Laws).

33 See Strauss 2006.

34 Cf. Posner 1990, at p. 431-432: (national) doctrinal work is now '*work for followers rather than leaders*', if not '*old-fashioned, passé, tired*'.

35 There is more than just anecdotal evidence that the graduates of McGill and the Maastricht European Law School get better job opportunities than traditional graduates.

3. What Should We Teach? On Doctrines, Arguments and Principles

The mandatory curriculum of traditional law schools in Europe is well known.[36] In the bachelor stage, students are usually introduced to the main fields of study (not only private law, criminal law, constitutional law, procedural law and European and international law, but in many countries also company law, administrative law, labour law, tax law, legal history and philosophy of law). This bachelor is almost invariably followed by a master, in which students specialise in a specific field. In both stages of study, these substantive mandatory courses are supplemented by skills training and optional courses on a wide variety of topics.

This section raises the question of what is covered by the ideal curriculum in a European legal education. One aspect of this question can be easily answered: the very same subjects that are part of a bachelor of national law should also be part of a European curriculum.[37] Instead of Dutch, English or Polish law, the curriculum then consists of courses on European Private Law (possibly split into European Contract Law, European Tort Law and European Property Law), European Criminal Law, European Constitutional Law, European Procedural Law and European and International Law *per se*. Courses on these topics are at the heart of any law study in Europe, not only because many countries require these courses in order to enter the bench and the bar, but also because of their substance: they *make* the discipline of law.

Another aspect of the question is much more difficult to answer: what do we actually teach in these 'European'[38] courses? In so far as private, criminal, constitutional and procedural law are governed by binding rules of European origin (as is increasingly the case), it is still possible to teach these topics in the same way as one teaches national law. This traditional way of teaching usually takes the form of telling students how 'the law' reads: they are informed of the law as it stands today in the particular country they study in. I do not deny that some lecturers are able to escape this authority paradigm, even when teaching the law of one national jurisdiction, but they are the exception. The textbooks predominantly used in teaching national law confirm this conclusion. What Patrick Atiyah and Robert Summers wrote almost 25 years ago is still true today:[39]

36 But important variations exist among countries and universities. A useful overview is provided at <http://www.europaeische-juristenausbildung.de> (last consulted 8 September 2010).

37 See for the same view Heringa 2002.

38 The term 'European' is not completely correct. I use it to indicate an approach that seeks to teach lawyers about alternative approaches, not necessarily restricted to those adopted in the European Union. Ideally, terms like 'contract law' and 'constitutional law' would already out of themselves imply that these topics are treated in an international way: likewise, one should not teach 'comparative law', but law. As the current understanding of these terms is different, I add the term 'European' to denote this international aspect.

39 Atiyah & Summers 1987, at p. 394.

> 'The tone of textbooks is often dogmatic, with decisions presented as if they were strict decisions from basic principles. (...) The ultimate and all-pervasive aim is to lay out the law as it stood on the day the book went to press.'

But while I think it is wrong to teach national law in this way, it is outright impossible when teaching European courses. In order to cover the whole field of, e.g., contract law or criminal law, there is simply not enough binding law produced by the European institutions. This calls for a different approach.

It was argued in section 2 that the main aim of legal education is to explore and contrast the implications of conflicting normative positions. Students should not just learn one system of law, but ought to be exposed to alternative ways of achieving justice. This provides the answer to the question of what materials we should use and what we should focus on when studying these materials. The focal point is no longer the national legislation and case laws of a particular doctrinal system. Instead, the full range of materials that informs us about how we can possibly deal with normative conflicts should be brought to the fore. These materials can come from civil law and common jurisdictions, but also from, e.g., Chinese law, ethics, conventions, religion or private documentation (such as contracts, general conditions and memorandums of understanding). When discussing these materials, the emphasis is on the *arguments* behind the choices made by the relevant authorities (and others) and not on the doctrinal intricacies. Therefore, one no longer learns the law 'through the eyes of a distinguished commentator'.[40] It also means that the starting point of the discussion is a case or a problem that is functionally defined (such as 'When is a contract binding?') and not some doctrinal term (like 'consideration'). It is out of these materials that students can construct their own understanding of the problem and its possible solutions. Paraphrasing Peter Strauss: 'such a class, organized around a conceptual problem, might hop from Germany to England to China to nineteenth century France, forward and back in time and space without apparent concern.'[41] I emphasise that to give this method its full meaning, we should not confine our materials to Western jurisdictions only, but give ample attention to the differences among North and South and West and East[42] and move beyond the State-centred paradigm by involving sub-national and private producers of law as well.

Accepting this ambitious teaching method means a turn away from teaching law as an authoritative system. Case law and legislation are no longer regarded as authoritative statements about what is law in a certain jurisdiction, but viewed as empirical material on how to deal with conflicting normative positions. It is used to unveil the arguments pro and against certain outcomes. Existing jurisdictions are thus seen as experimenting laboratories[43] and it is through the comparative method

40 Strauss 2006.

41 *Ibidem.*

42 Cf. Mattei, Ruskola & Gidi 2009, Preface.

43 After the famous expression of Louis Brandeis in *New State Ice Co.* v. *Liebmann*, 285 *U.S.* 262. Cf. Smits 2009, No. 39.

that we learn about alternative outcomes to similar questions.[44] To make this the goal of legal education may have as a consequence that graduates are less versed in the details of one particular legal system, but this is compensated by their ability to apply the legal way of thinking in various jurisdictions.

This approach is well captured by Todd Rakoff and Martha Minow. In a recent article, they put it like this:[45]

> 'Students ought to be presented with relatively dense materials that lay out a situation, experienced as a problem for a person, or group of people, for legal treatment. Students should face a choice that challenges them to identify options and that permits multiple resolutions (...). The problems ought not to be situated in one doctrinal area, but should present opportunities for mental manoeuvring around the legal universe. Teaching should emphasise generating alternative solutions as well as appropriate grounds for choosing among them. And criteria for resolution should include legal, normative, and practical considerations.'

It is important to emphasise two things. The first is that this method may invoke the criticism that students no longer learn to reason in a clean and precise way. This is wrong: analytical reasoning must be a quality every law graduate must possess and I believe that a broader European legal education is much more conducive to teaching this skill than a purely national education. Related to this is the critique that students would not learn how to think in a doctrinal way. This criticism is also flawed. As doctrinal thinking is an essential part of many civil law jurisdictions,[46] it has to be part of a European legal education, not as the only possible way towards a certain outcome, but as one of the alternative avenues of legal reasoning. Law schools thus teach students both practical ('know how') and propositional knowledge (understanding the law).[47]

The second point is admittedly a contested one. An important strand of legal scholarship claims that the ultimate goal in fields like European private law and European criminal law is to draft and implement common European principles. In particular, private lawyers have invested a lot of time and energy in such projects, leading to, *inter alia*, principles on European contract law, tort law, trust law, family law and private law in general.[48] Apart from the objections one can have against representing law through principles,[49] it cannot be denied that they are useful in teaching. Their importance should however not be overestimated. Too much focus on what jurisdictions have in common can conceal very real divergences, endangering what is at the core of the legal discipline: divergent views of what is

44 The importance of the comparative method in teaching law is also stressed by Hage 2011.
45 Rakoff & Minow 2007, p. 597-607, at p. 604.
46 On the importance of doctrinal thinking in French law, see the much discussed book by Jestaz & Jamin 2004.
47 See for this distinction in the context of teaching: Mincke 1992, p. 285-294.
48 See resp. Lando & Beale 2000 and Lando *et al.* 2003; European Group on Tort Law 2005; Hayton *et al.* 1999; Boele-Woelki 2004; Von Bar & Clive 2009.
49 Cf. Smits 2000, p. 221-223.

the right answer to a legal problem. European legal education therefore should not only seek common ground, but also expose difference.[50]

4. How Should We Teach? No Comfort of the Familiar

It became clear in the previous section that the ideal type of legal education exposes students to alternative ways of achieving justice, making the comparative method the most essential learning tool. What kind of teaching method this requires was already alluded to earlier: it is one in which a functional problem is identified and solved, thus allowing students to construct their own understanding of the possible solutions. This rather abstract statement is elaborated in this section. It looks at some, admittedly disperse, aspects of how to teach law in an international curriculum:[51] the sequence in which the various jurisdictions come to the fore, the approach to teaching, assessment of students and finally the teaching materials and language of instruction.

The first question is in what sequence the various legal systems are to be discussed. Two different approaches are possible. The first is to introduce students consecutively to different jurisdictions: one starts with one legal system and gradually confronts others. This is the model followed by many traditional law schools: they want their students to first obtain a profound knowledge of one law (e.g. Dutch law) and add some international component by requiring students to take capstone courses on foreign law or comparative law in the second or third year (or by stimulating them to study abroad). This model was also adopted in the original international programmes at McGill and Maastricht University. In McGill's 'National Programme', taught from 1968 to 1999, common law and civil law were taught sequentially. The original European Law School programme consisted of a first year in which exclusively Dutch law was taught and a second year in which courses on Dutch law were combined with European courses. Only in the third year were students fully exposed to a truly international curriculum. This was motivated by the belief that an integrative approach would confuse the students and that they need a training in one coherent legal system first before being able to engage in comparative study.[52]

The second approach is to expose students to civil law, common law and other jurisdictions right from the start. This means legal systems are examined and contrasted simultaneously: teaching never takes place on basis of one national law, but integrates alternative approaches to functionally defined problems. Interestingly, both McGill and Maastricht changed the structure of their original curriculum to adopt this integrative approach.[53] This change was prompted by the idea that it is much more natural to look at law in a comparative way if one is used

50 See for a theoretical foundation Legrand 2003, p. 240-311.

51 Also see Valcke 2004, p. 161-182 and Catá Backer 2007 (last consulted 8 September 2010).

52 Heringa 2002, at p. 7.

53 McGill did so by introducing its 'transsystematic' programme (see the text surrounding footnote 2 above) and Maastricht by adding an 'English track' to its European Law School (see footnote 10 above).

to doing so from the very beginning (in particular for students expecting to participate in an international programme).[54] In the case of Maastricht, there was also the practical aspect that requiring students to start with one year of Dutch law (naturally taught in Dutch) was not helpful in building up an international student population. The European bachelor can then be followed by a master on the law of one particular jurisdiction (e.g. Dutch or Finnish law). This makes sense because law schools specialising in international legal education will still be eager to offer a full programme, having the additional benefit that such masters can host colleagues excelling in national law.

Which of these two approaches is to be preferred? I have no doubt that the integrative model is best suited to meet the needs of an international legal education. Students addressing a specific problem by moving back and forth from one jurisdiction to another is much more conducive to the 'dialogue with otherness' than the sequential model. Starting with one jurisdiction makes it likely that students regard all the rest as irrelevant. Jaakko Husa warns for this 'mind fixing' in the following way:[55]

> 'The problem with the traditional law-teaching approach is that it constructs a primary epistemic foundation for legal understanding, which is based on one mother-system. This creates an implicit mono-epistemology, which makes lawyers regard their own system as "normal" and other systems as "non-normal" or, at least, something that is "less-normal". From this mono-epistemic platform, the law student is first immersed in the one-approach-thinking, which later makes it difficult to epistemologically adapt to transnational pluralism and to genuinely accept different approaches.'

In this approach, students are denied 'the comfort of the familiar',[56] which forces them to develop a pluralistic legal mind. Within their first year, they have to realise that legal views differ and that there is not *one* legal system or *one* solution to the problem at hand.[57] This view is motivated by the same reason why I believe it is so important to have the law school's best academics teach in the first year: it is in the first months of their university career that students are to be imprinted with what it means to study law.

A second important question concerns the approach to teaching: what model of teaching is the most effective in persuading students to consider a wide variety of sources to construct their own understanding (and not that of the learned author) of the legal problem? I am less concerned with educational theories here than with what works in practice. In my own experience, confirmed by distinguished colleagues elsewhere, the ideal teaching method is certainly not to focus on

54 Cf. Junker 2005, p. 789 *et seq.*

55 Husa 2009, p. 913-926.

56 Arthurs 2009, at p. 638.

57 Also see Rakoff & Minow 2007, at p. 607, who point at the lesson of Langdell: 'the template for legal thinking established in the first year of law school has real staying power'. The advocated approach may be difficult to apply, but 'the greater fear is that, if we do not make the effort to challenge students in this way, students will learn to think of the legal system as only so many rooms, so many pieces of furniture, that they can never reorder'.

doctrinal questions or to teach 'comparative law' as such. What works best, is to select a topic and to provide materials on how this topic is dealt with in various jurisdictions. What follows then, is aptly described by Kurt Lipstein:[58]

> 'The student must in his time examine the reading matter, possibly have recourse to further literature and practice cited there before coming to the classroom. Here accounts given by members of the class reporting on unfamiliar topics will be amplified, collected and explained by the lecturer (...). This exchange (...) requires a much greater participation by the directing lecturer and the audience (...).'

If this *exchange* is a central goal in teaching, it is clear that lecturing to a large group is not the ideal method to achieve it. This is confirmed by educational research: one person ('the sage on the stage') giving a two hour-lecture is generally rejected and dismissed as a non-effective way of teaching.[59] Small group teaching, with the lecturer as an initiator of discussion and students giving presentations and writing papers, is often seen as a much better method.[60] Working with the materials allows students to construct their own understanding of what is right or wrong, shifting the responsibility of learning away from the lecturers onto the students.

I believe this practice fits in with various 'teaching theories'. One of these theories is problem-based learning (PBL), adopted at various law schools throughout the world including Maastricht University's Faculty of Law.[61] PBL regards discussion of carefully designed problems in small groups, and not systematic overviews in big lectures, as the main stimulus for learning. PBL can indeed work well if it is sufficiently adapted to law teaching[62] and understood in a broad sense as focusing on a discussion of problems with multiple solutions. PBL, however, still leaves open the issue of how to practically organise the learning process, other than that there is a strong emphasis on individual study and skills training. In my own experience, it is of vital importance that the lecturer is a highly qualified academic and much more than a mere 'facilitator' of discussions. As Nobel Prize winner George Stigler once put it: she is 'to fan the spark of genuine intellectual curiosity and (...) to communicate the enormous adventure and the knightly conduct in the quest for knowledge.'[63] This calls for a much more active lecturer than some proponents of PBL suggest.

PBL is not the only educational theory consistent with small group teaching aimed at an exchange of ideas about alternatives for problem-solving.[64] The Socratic method, consisting of a dialogue among lecturer and students in question and

58 Lipstein 1992, p. 255-263, at p. 258.
59 Dunkin 1983, p. 63-78.
60 Cf. Nussbaum 2003, at p. 273.
61 There is a voluminous literature on PBL in law. See, instead of many, Moens 2007, p. 623-632 and Tzannes 1997, p. 180-197.
62 For an example of how to do this: Wade 1990, p. 283 *et seq.*
63 Stigler 1963, at p. 14.
64 Rakoff & Minow 2007 also see this as the core of legal education: 'the analysis of complex, rich factual descriptions of problems and (...) the generation of alternative avenues for problem-solving'.

answer format, also enables 'deep' learning.[65] In American law schools, this Socratic method is seen as a highly successful method to do the two things PBL also does: teach students to think like a lawyer and to practice their skills.[66] I do not think PBL and the Socratic method differ fundamentally, except for the fact that in PBL there seems to be a preference for groups of maximum 12 students. However, the American experience shows it is very well possible to teach larger groups of students. I therefore believe that it is worth emulating the American system of splitting the (first year) class into sections that stay together for the entire year, adding considerably to the group feeling and the perception of students that they are part of a small school. At top law schools like Yale and Chicago, these sections usually consist of no more than 30 students.[67] What Europeans may dislike about this option[68] is that not all of the sections are taught the same way or even use the same materials. Each lecturer will teach the course and assess the students as they see fit. I do not think this is wrong: differences among the different lecturers, within the parameters set for the course, will only add to the diversity of a law school.

Closely related to the method of teaching is the assessment of students. If law is taught in the non-traditional way I just described, it makes little sense to assess students in the way it is traditionally done: by way of a final examination with one 'model answer'. Student oriented teaching requires student oriented assessment. This does not rule out there is still some form of a final exam, but in my experience it is best to combine this with essays and presentations.[69] In the way we assess students, we can also learn from American law schools. One of the problems with grading systems that are too detailed is that the students focus too much on obtaining high grades, whereas their focus should be on the intellectual stimulus they get out of their study and the contribution they can make to the intellectual community they are part of. This (combined with the problem of grade inflation) is why several American law schools (including Harvard and Stanford[70]) recently decided to abandon the old grading system. Students' performance is now graded as 'honors,' 'pass,' 'low pass' or 'fail,' one third of the class to receive the top mark ('honors') and the bottom 8 per cent to receive a 'low pass' or 'fail'. I realise that this system may work better for graduate students (as law students in the United States are) than for European undergraduates, but I still think it is worth considering to adopt this system in European law schools as well.

The final point concerns teaching materials and the language of instruction. I already mentioned that most textbooks describe the law in a positivistic way and not by way of alternative answers to functionally defined questions. Already in

65 On the difference between deep and surface learning: Ramsden 2003, at p. 62 *et seq*.

66 Cf. Del Duca 2007, at p. 296.

67 Both law schools admit about 200 students per year. At Harvard, the entire first year class of about 550 is split into sections of maximum 80 students (which seems too large to pursue the type of teaching advocated in this contribution).

68 Probably (but unjustly) motivated by concerns of accountability and quality assurance.

69 On the enormous importance of students writing papers as critical examination of the materials (and oneself) see Nussbaum 2003, at p. 273.

70 Yale had already abolished letter grading in the 1960s.

1992, Hein Kötz defined this lack of truly European (or comparative) teaching materials as problematic:[71]

> 'We do not have, in Europe, a legal literature tackling the daunting task of developing in a given area a European common law. (...) True, there are books discussing legal problems from a comparative perspective. (...) What I have in mind is something else. It is a literature based on a decidedly non-national point of view, seeking to discuss its subject in a way which by no means ignores the rules national legal systems have arrived at, but treats them as merely local variations of a theme which in principle is unitary.'

Although we now have more comparative casebooks and textbooks in the traditional areas of law compared to 20 years ago,[72] we still need more. We need their authors to adopt different approaches and consider different materials. Only in that way, will we be able to create a critical mass of materials out of which students can choose what they like best. Although these materials are likely to be written in different languages, I believe they should as much as possible be written in English. One occasionally hears the argument that it is impossible to teach law in another language than the one in which the sources are available. I think this view is mistaken. The argument is certainly true for the study of one national law: it does not make any sense (and one should not try) to teach Dutch or Finnish law in English.[73] However, this is different for the type of European education propagated in this contribution: the entire point of such a programme is that it teaches students to think like a lawyer in an international setting. As it became clear in section 3, this means a necessary turn away from texts and their interpretation towards the arguments behind these texts. These arguments can very well be discussed in English for they are not dependent on one national jurisdiction.

5. Concluding Remarks. On the Law School of the Future

This contribution focused on the reasons *why* we need a European legal education, *what* we should teach and *how* we should teach it. I did not say too much about what this means for the organisation of the law school as a whole, although it is clear that the ambitious programme propagated here can form a true challenge for the law school that offers it. In this respect, it is important to emphasise that not every law school can or should offer a European or international programme. Having said this, it is also clear that the present uniformity in the European university landscape will gradually disappear. In the Netherlands alone, universities teach nine astonishingly uniform programmes on Dutch law. This will soon change with law schools opting to increasingly specialise, attracting the students they want to have. Some universities will end up attracting students from

71 Kötz 1992, at p. 39.

72 See for a brief overview in the field of European private law Akkermans 2011.

73 The suggestion is not as unworldly as it seems: it is part of the internationalisation mission of various Dutch universities to insist on all faculty (including those teaching Dutch law) teaching in English.

all over the European Union, while others will remain primarily national. This type of niche marketing is important, also to inform prospective students about the type of education they can expect when choosing for a specific university.

Meanwhile the challenges for the more internationally oriented law schools are manifold. I will mention three of them here. The first is about the relationship between teaching and research. It is no coincidence that McGill and Maastricht not only teach international programmes, but also have a strong tradition in doing internationally oriented research. The two reinforce each other considerably: students profit from the internationally acclaimed academics teaching their courses and faculty is able to try out new ideas when teaching and to attract teaching assistants from the student body. This interaction between teaching and research is essential: it would be just as unthinkable to teach an international programme without doing (comparative) research as it is to publish internationally without having the benefit of teaching students about the topics one writes about. Some law schools have been able to interlink their European teaching and research in an optimal way, but it is clear that this can be a difficult process.

The second challenge relates to the recruitment of faculty.[74] It is probably the most important factor in building up an international programme. A law school can only decide to offer European legal education if there is sufficient faculty expertise to do so, or has the resources and prestige to attract new colleagues. The alternative is to force specialists in national law to change their precincts, but this is - at least in most cases - not a very wise decision to make. Forcing talented and experienced people to re-educate and conform to a new standard often lead to mediocre results; it is better to let people do what they are best in. Attracting visiting staff and cooperating with other law schools is then a better option.[75]

The final challenge concerns the ideal organisation of the law school. It is well known that Europeanisation and internationalisation of law affect the distinction between the traditional legal fields.[76] The distinction between public and private law has set the discourse in the last 200 years,[77] but it does not make much sense anymore today. For example, it is impossible to discuss the Europeanisation of private law without asking the question at what level of governance private relationships are best regulated or how legitimate the rulemaking by European institutions or private regulators actually is. These are questions that directly touch upon discussions in other disciplines. In the same vein, similar developments in different fields are now too often seen as isolated because of too little contact among academics working in different fields.[78] Therefore, I do not believe that the common

74 On which the special issue of *American Journal of Comparative Law*, 41, 1993, p. 351 *et seq.*

75 The importance of international cooperation is emphasised by Akkermans 2009, p. 803 *et seq.* and Del Duca 2001, at p. 7.

76 Cf. Samuel 1992, p. 171-184.

77 Although the dichotomy of public and private law can already be found in Roman sources (D. 1.1.1.2), its importance as an epistemological categorisation is much more recent and directly related to the emergence of the nation-state.

78 An example is the discussion about comparative inspiration in private law and about 'constitutional dialogue' in constitutional law.

departmental structure in continental universities, with its sharp distinction between departments of private law, public law, criminal law, European law and legal theory, is conducive to promote high quality teaching and research. It is a much better strategy to form interdisciplinary groups in which academics of different backgrounds work together, also because the more creative research is often at the intersection of disciplines.

Bibliography

Akkermans 2009
Akkermans, B., 'Challenges in Legal Education and the Development of a New European Private Law', *German Law Journal*, 2009, No. 10, p. 803-814.

Akkermans 2011
Akkermans, B., 'The Development of European Private Law and its Challenges on the Law School Curriculum', in Heringa, A.W. & Akkermans, B. (eds.), *Educating European Lawyers*, Antwerp: Intersentia, 2011, p. 159-178.

Arthurs 2009
Arthurs, H.W., 'Law and Learning in an Era of Globalization', *German Law Journal*, 2009, No. 10, p. 629-639.

Atiyah & Summers 1987
Atiyah, P.S. & Summers, R.S., *Form and Substance in Anglo-American Law*, Oxford: Oxford University Press, 1987.

Becker 1992
Becker, G.S., *The Economic Way of Looking at Life*, Nobel Lecture in Economics, Stockholm, Noble Foundation, 1992.

Bell 2003
Bell, J., 'Legal Education', in Cane, P. & Tushnet, M. (eds.), *The Oxford Handbook of Legal Studies*, Oxford: Oxford University Press, 2003, p. 901-919.

Boele-Woelki 2004
Boele-Woelki, K. (ed.), *Principles of European Family Law*, various volumes, Antwerp: Intersentia, 2004.

Cappelletti 1978
Cappelletti, M. (ed.), *New Perspectives for a Common Law of Europe*, Florence: European University Institute, 1978.

Catá Backer 2007
Catá Backer, L., 'Global Law in American Law Schools: Prospects and Difficulties of Incorporating a Transborder Element in Legal Education', 2007, available on SSRN, <http://papers.ssrn.com/sol3/papers.cfm?abstract_id=969870> (last consulted 8 January 2011).

De Búrca 2009
De Búrca, G., 'Developing Democracy Beyond the State', *Columbia Journal of Transnational Law*, 2009, Vol. 46, p. 101-158.

Dedek & de Mestral 2009
Dedek, H. & de Mestral, A., *'Born to be Wild:* The 'Trans-systemic' Programme at McGill and the De-Nationalization of Legal Education', *German Law Journal*, 2009, No. 10, p. 889-911.

Del Duca 2001
Del Duca, L., 'Cooperation in Internationalizing Legal Education in Europe - Emerging New Players', *Penn State International Law Review*, 2001, Vol. 20, p. 7-14.

Del Duca 2007
Del Duca, L.F., 'The importance of understanding the role of statutes, regulations, and cases in legal practice and legal education in the United States legal system', in *IALS Conference Learning from each other: enriching the law school curriculum in an interrelated world*, Washington, IALS, 2007, p. 21-29.

De Witte 2011
De Witte, B., 'European Union Law: A Common Core or a Fragmented Academic Discipline?', in Heringa, A.W. & Akkermans, B. (eds.), *Educating European Lawyers*, Antwerp: Intersentia, 2011, p. 19-41.

De Witte & Forder 1992
De Witte, B. & Forder, C. (eds.), *The Common Law of Europe and the Future of Legal Education*, Deventer: Kluwer, 1992.

Dunkin 1983
Dunkin, M.J., 'A Review of Research on Lecturing', *Higher Education Research and Development*, 1983, Vol. 2, p. 63-78.

European Group on Tort Law 2005
European Group on Tort Law, *Principles of European Tort Law*, Vienna: Springer, 2005.

Glenn 2003
Glenn, H.P., 'A Transnational Concept of Law', in Cane, P. & Tushnet, M. (eds.), *The Oxford Handbook of Legal Studies*, Oxford: Oxford University Press, 2003, p. 839-862.

Glenn 2006
Glenn, H.P., 'Aims of Comparative Law', in Smits, J. (ed.), *Elgar Encyclopedia of Comparative Law*, Cheltenham: Edward Elgar, 2006, p. 57-65.

Hage 2011
Hage, J., 'Comparative Law and Legal Science', in Heringa, A.W. & Akkermans, B. (eds.), *Educating European Lawyers*, Antwerp: Intersentia, 2011, p. 65-77.

Hayton *et al.* 1999
Hayton, D.J. *et al.* (eds.), *Principles of European Trust Law*, Deventer: Kluwer, 1999.

Heringa 2002
Heringa, A.W., 'Towards a European Law School! A Proposal for a Competitive Diversified Model of Transnational Co-operation', in Faure, M. & Smits, J. (eds.), *Towards a European Ius Commune in Legal Education and Research*, Antwerp: Intersentia, 2002, p. 3-13.

Heringa 2010
Heringa, A.W., 'European Legal Education: The Maastricht Experience', *Penn State International Law Review*, 2010, Vol. 29, p. 81-94.

Husa 2009
Husa, J., 'Turning the Curriculum Upside Down: Comparative Law as an Educational Tool for Constructing the Pluralistic Legal Mind', *German Law Journal*, 2009, Vol. 10, p. 913-926.

Jansen 2010
Jansen, N., *The Making of Legal Authority*, Oxford: Oxford University Press, 2010.

Jansen & Michaels 2007
Jansen, N. & Michaels, R., 'Private Law and the State', *Rabels Zeitschrift*, 2007, Vol. 71, p. 345-397.

Jestaz & Jamin 2004
Jestaz, Ph. & Jamin, Ch., *La doctrine*, Paris: Dalloz, 2004.

Junker 2005
Junker, R., 'Where Law and Pedagogy Meet in the Transsystematic Contracts Classroom', *McGill Law Journal*, 2005, Vol. 50, p. 789-808.

Kennedy 1990
Kennedy, D., 'Legal Education as Training for Hierarchy', in Kairys, D. (ed.), *The Politics of Law: A Progressive Critique*, New York: Pantheon, 1990, p. 38-58.

Kornet 2011
Kornet, N., 'Building a European-Oriented Law Curriculum', in Heringa, A.W. & Akkermans, B. (eds.), *Educating European Lawyers*, Antwerp: Intersentia, 2011, p. 101-120.

Kötz 1992
Kötz, H., 'A Common Private Law for Europe: Perspectives for the Reform of European Legal Education', in De Witte, B. & Forder, C. (eds.), *The Common Law of Europe and the Future of Legal Education*, Deventer: Kluwer, 1992, p. 31-41.

Kronman 2007
Kronman, A., *Education's End*, New Haven: Yale University Press, 2007.

Lando & Beale 2000
Lando, O. & Beale, H. (eds.), *Principles of European Contract Law*, Boston: Kluwer, Vols. I and II, 2000.

Lando *et al.* 2003
Lando, O. *et al.* (eds.), *Principles of European Contract Law*, Boston: Kluwer, Vol. III, 2003.

Legrand 2003
Legrand, P., 'The Same and the Different', in Legrand, P. & Munday, R. (eds.), *Comparative Legal Studies: Traditions and Transitions*, Cambridge: Cambridge University Press, 2003, p. 240-311.

Levitt & Dubner 2009
Levitt, S.D. & Dubner, S.J., *Superfreakonomics*, New York: William Morrow, 2009.

Lipstein 1992
Lipstein, K., 'European Legal Education in the Future: Teaching the "Common Law of Europe"', in De Witte & Forder (eds.), *The Common Law of Europe and the Future of Legal Education*, Deventer: Kluwer, 1992, p. 255-263.

Mattei, Ruskola & Gidi 2009
Mattei, U., Ruskola, T. & Gidi, A., *Schlesinger's Comparative Law*, New York: Foundation Press, 7th ed., 2009.

Michaels & Jansen 2006
Michaels, R. & Jansen, N., 'Private Law Beyond the State? Europeanization, Globalization, Privatization', *American Journal of Comparative Law*, 2006, Vol. 54, p. 843-890.

Mincke 1992
Mincke, W., 'Practical and Propositional Knowledge as the Basis of European Legal Education', in De Witte, B. & Forder, C. (eds.), *The Common Law of Europe and the Future of Legal Education*, Deventer: Kluwer, 1992, p. 285-294.

Moens 2007
Moens, G.A., 'The Mysteries of Problem-Based Learning: Combining Enthusiasm and Excellence', *University of Toledo Law Review*, 2007, Vol. 38, p. 623-632.

Morisette 2002
Morisette, Y.-M., 'McGill's Integrated Civil and Common Law Program', *Journal of Legal Education*, 2002, Vol. 52, p. 12-28.

Nussbaum 1997
Nussbaum, M.C., *Cultivating Humanity: A Classical Defense of Reform in Liberal Education*, Cambridge Mass.: Harvard University Press, 1997.

Nussbaum 2003
Nussbaum, M.C., 'Cultivating Humanity in Legal Education', *University of Chicago Law Review*, 2003, Vol. 70, p. 265-279.

Posner 1990
Posner, R.A., *The Problems of Jurisprudence*, Cambridge Mass.: Harvard University Press, 1990.

Rakoff & Minow 2007
Rakoff, T.D. & Minow, M., 'A Case for Another Case Method', *Vanderbilt Law Review*, 2007, Vol. 60, p. 597-607.

Ramsden 2003
Ramsden, P., *Learning to Teach in Higher Education*, London: Routledge, 2nd ed., 2003.

Rubin 1988
Rubin, E.L., 'The Practice and Discourse of Legal Scholarship', *Michigan Law Review*, 1988, Vol. 86, p. 1835-1905.

Samuel 1992
Samuel, G., 'What is it to have knowledge of a European public law?', in De Witte, B. & Forder, C. (eds.), *The Common Law of Europe and the Future of Legal Education*, Deventer: Kluwer, 1992, p. 171-184.

Sen 2009
Sen, A., *The Idea of Justice*, Cambridge Mass.: Harvard University Press, 2009.

Smits 2000
Smits, J., 'A Principled Approach to European Contract Law?', *Maastricht Journal of European and Comparative Law*, 2000, Vol. 7, p. 221-223.

Smits 2009
Smits, J., *Omstreden rechtswetenschap*, Den Haag: Boom, 2009.

Smits 2010a
Smits, J.M., 'The Complexity of Transnational Law', in Van Erp, J.H.M. & Van Vliet, L.P.W. (eds.), *Netherlands Reports to the Eighteenth International Congress of Comparative Law*, Antwerp: Intersentia, 2010, p. 113-130.

Smits 2010b
Smits, J., *Rechtstoerisme: Burgerlijk Wetboek en Grondwet voorbij de Staat*, Tilburg: Tilburg University, 2010.

Stigler 1963
Stigler, G., *The Intellectual and the Marketplace and Other Essays*, London: Free Press of Glencoe, 1963.

Strauss 2006
Strauss, P.L., 'Transsystemia - Are we Approaching a New Langdellian Moment? Is McGill Leading the Way?', *Journal of Legal Education*, 2006, Vol. 56, p. 161-171.

Tzannes 1997
Tzannes, M., 'Problem-based learning in legal education: intentionally overlooked or merely misunderstood?', *The Law Teacher*, 1997, Vol. 31, p. 180-197.

Valcke 2004
Valcke, C., 'Global Law Teaching', *Journal of Legal Education*, 2004, Vol. 54, p. 161-182.

Von Bar & Clive 2009
Von Bar, Chr. & Clive, E. (eds.), *Principles, Definitions and Model Rules of European Private Law: Draft Common Frame of Reference*, München: Sellier, 2009.

Von Jhering 1852
Von Jhering, R., *Geist des Römischen Rechts*, Leipzig: Keip, Vol. I, 1852.

Wade 1990
Wade, J.H., 'Meet MIRAT: Legal Reasoning Fragmented into Learnable Chunks', *Legal Education Review*, 1990, Vol. 2, p. 283-297.

Jaap Hage

COMPARATIVE LAW AND LEGAL SCIENCE

1. Introduction

In many comparative and European teaching programmes, such as the European Law School at Maastricht University, much attention is devoted to comparative law. This raises the questions what makes comparative law so important, and why law students should devote a considerable part of their time to the law of different Countries and to the similarities and differences between these different legal systems. To answer these questions, we take a closer look, both at the different ways in which comparative law can be useful for legal scientists, and at the way in which the study of comparative law should benefit law students.

If we want to know why the study of comparative law is useful, the first thing we should be clear about is the *nature of comparative law*. Zweigert and Kötz characterise it as the description of the law of different legal systems for the purpose of 'comparative reflections'. They also seem to assume that these comparative reflections should end up with conclusions about the proper policy for the law to adopt.[1] This is rather vague, but a more specific characterisation of comparative law would run the risk to exclude valuable types of research which are generally classified as comparative law, such as the study of legal transplants.[2] In the following we will encounter different useful forms of 'comparative reflection'.

The focus in this contribution will be on the use of comparative law for legal science in a broad sense. This does not imply that comparative law has no use in *legal practice*. Law students who have familiarised themselves with the law of different legal systems are less likely to experience the threshold of the unfamiliar when they encounter in their practical work cases or situations which have points of contact with more than one legal system. For instance: a legal practitioner who works in a law firm in either Dutch or Belgian Limburg (provinces of respectively the Netherlands and Belgium) is likely to encounter cases for which familiarity with both Dutch, federal Belgian and Flemish law is crucial. Experience with

1 Zweigert & Kötz 1997, p. 6.
2 Cf. Fedtke 2006.

comparative law facilitates the search for law in foreign legal systems and prepares the lawyer for the possibility that what seems obvious in, for instance, the Netherlands, may nevertheless be different in Flanders.[3] On a less mundane level we see that legal decision makers, such as judges, occasionally base their decisions on comparative considerations.[4] Legal counsels are therefore well-advised to take this into account.

Apart from applicability in legal science and legal practice, the study of comparative law brings the advantage of broadening one's view of the law. Without comparative insight, the law may seem to consist of the rules that govern a number of situations and cases; it seems to be the fixed structure of society. After familiarisation with comparative law, the law of a legal system - notice the relativisation - has become one of several possible ways of dealing with societal situations. Comparative insight makes it possible to take a less committed stance towards one's own law and thereby creates the opportunity to use one's parochial law more creatively.[5]

2. Method

Comparative law can play a role in legal science, both as a scientific method and as a heuristic tool. To obtain a clear view of what these uses amount to, it is necessary to delve a little deeper into the nature of scientific research.

Science in general, and therefore also legal science, is a social phenomenon, a cooperative enterprise aimed at the acquisition, accumulation and systematisation of knowledge. The advantage of science over individual acquisition of knowledge is that scientists can build on the results of their colleagues and predecessors. To quote Newton: 'If I have seen further it is only by standing on the shoulders of giants'.[6] Science is a way in which people collaborate in the pursuit of knowledge.

Here is where method enters the picture, for what is a scientific method? A scientific method indicates what count as good reasons for adopting or rejecting a potential piece of knowledge. Take for instance two lawyers. One of them thinks that the contents of the law can be determined through the study and interpretation of authoritative texts such as statutes, treaties, guidelines, and case law. The other one thinks that the contents of the law should be determined by empirical research aimed at the discovery of which rules would make human beings most happy if

3 An example would be that family allowances, which are granted in The Netherlands on territorial basis, are granted in Belgium on the basis of one's labour contract.

4 A brief discussion of this phenomenon can be found in Smits 2006.

5 The author of the present contribution experienced this opportunity himself when he used the common law construction of economic property (trust) to deal with some problematic cases concerning the use of marital dwellings after divorce (Hage 1979). At that time only to receive the learned comment that this was not Dutch law….

6 Original Latin: '*Pigmaei gigantum humeris impositi plusquam ipsi gigantes vident*'. Letter to Robert Hooke of 15 February 1676. Source: <http://en.wikiquote.org/wiki/Isaac_Newton> (last consulted on 15 December 2009). The phrase 'standing on the shoulders of giants' appears to stem from Bernard of Chartres (twelfth century). See <http://en.wikipedia.org/wiki/Standing_on_the_shoulders_of_giants> (last consulted on 25 April 2010).

they were enforced by collective means. These two lawyers would disagree fundamentally on what are good reasons in a discussion about the contents of the law, and most probably they cannot cooperate in legal research.

The adoption of a particular method boils down to agreement on what count as good reasons. Since such an agreement is a precondition for science as collaborative knowledge acquisition, a shared method is almost by definition a precondition for science.[7] Reasons in general, and therefore also reasons for accepting or rejecting a particular piece of potential knowledge, are facts that are *relevant* for what they are reasons for or against.[8] The adoption of a method is a choice for what counts as relevant in selecting the right answer to a research question.

The adoption of a method is also a choice concerning the kind of data that must be collected in order to argue for or against a potential piece of knowledge. For instance, on a hermeneutic method for legal science the relevant data that justify a particular legal conclusion might include that this conclusion is supported by the literal interpretation of a statute. The proper way of performing legal research, method in the derived sense, is to a large extent[9] determined by method in the primary sense, the recognition of particular kinds of data as relevant for answering a particular kind of research question. A method is therefore always related to a research question, because the research question, in combination with a view as to which data are relevant for answering this type of question, together determine which information should be collected.[10]

There are different kinds of science, which can be distinguished on basis of the kinds of knowledge pursued in them. In the *physical sciences* we look for the explanation (and prediction[11]) of physical phenomena. The phenomena are explained by bringing the facts of a particular case under a lawlike generalisation and by deriving the facts that need to be explained from these facts and the law. An example would be the explanation why a rod of iron expands, from the fact that the rod was heated and the law that metals expand when heated. The physical sciences aim to explain facts through the discovery of the laws which make explanations possible. Their method is, amongst others, to test hypothetical laws against empirical data.

7 That science requires a shared method does not exclude that this method is mostly implicit, or that it changes in the course of time. If such a change is drastic, for instance if physics comes to be based on experiments rather than on interpretation of authoritative texts, the nature of the science changes too.

8 An extensive discussion of the nature of reasons can be found in Hage 1997, Chapter 2.

9 Other factors might be conventions on how results are to be published, and restrictions on how research may be financed.

10 This is essentially the point that Toulmin made with his claim that warrants (the standards that determine which data are relevant, which also function as inference rules) are field dependent. Cf. Toulmin 1958, Chapter 1.

11 On the so-called 'covering law model' the only difference between explanation and prediction is that explanation deals with phenomena from the past, while prediction deals with phenomena in the future. See Hempel 1965.

In psychology and sociology we try to explain human behaviour by showing how this behaviour made sense in the eyes of the persons who exhibited this behaviour.[12] The method is then to test hypotheses against data concerning the beliefs and attitudes of the acting persons. There are also sociologists and psychologists who try to give causal explanations of human behaviour, analogous to the way in which phenomena are explained in the physical sciences.[13] On this view of the humanities, the method is to test hypothetical laws against actual data concerning human behaviour. Notice, by the way, how these different methods lead to completely different versions of psychology or sociology.

In the *historical sciences* we aim to describe and explain events and facts from the past. The method is in part the same as that of the (other) humanities, including the battle of methods. In the *moral sciences*, we aim to discover which behaviour is good or bad, right or wrong. Here we have a battle of methods too, especially concerning the correct way to establish moral standards. Utilitarians postulate a standard (maximisation of happiness) and thereby turn most of moral science into a matter of psychology.[14] Kantians try to base the ultimate moral standard on the free and rational nature of moral creatures (human beings).[15] Aristotelians aim to derive moral standards from human nature,[16] and coherentists seek the justification of moral standards in the coherency of, amongst others, general moral standards and moral intuitions.[17] In *mathematics* we try to discover what follows from a given set of axioms (deductive science), and to find axiom sets from which a number of attractive theorems can be derived (axiomatisation).[18]

The precise nature of *legal science* is disputed.[19] Some believe that legal science aims to describe the positive law that 'follows from' a set of legal sources such as legislation, treaties, and case law. The nature of legal science is then the establishment of the proper meaning of these texts, and the relevant method is hermeneutic.[20] Others believe that legal science aims to systematise the legal materials in order to obtain a coherent whole in which the concrete rules follow from legal sources and a set of principles and values, while the principles and values can be induced from the concrete rules. On this view, legal science would have a lot in common with mathematics.[21] Again others take it that the primary task of legal science is to discover what the best law is, and on this view legal science is

12 See for instance Dray 1994.
13 See for instance Kincaid 1994.
14 De Geest has proposed the same move in order to transform doctrinal legal science into a 'real' science. Cf. De Geest 2004.
15 An influential recent exposition of Kantian ethics is Korsgaard 1996.
16 A modern representative of this view is Finnis 1980.
17 The *locus classicus* here is Rawls 1971.
18 Cf. Beerling *et al.* 1970.
19 At present we deal only with traditional, doctrinal legal science. Other sciences that have the law as their object, such as legal history and sociology of law will later be discussed briefly.
20 The hermeneutic nature of doctrinal legal science was emphasised in Smith 2009 and in Van Hoecke 2010, p. 43.
21 In different ways, this view is exposed in Dworkin 1986, Chapter 6; Van Rhee 2004, and Mackor 2011.

similar to the moral sciences.[22] The practice of doctrinal legal science seems to consist of a mixture of these three approaches.

3. Heuristics and Comparative Law

Although there are many different kinds of science, with different research questions and different methods, at a more abstract level they are all similar. Science has to do with answering research questions. The potential answers are hypotheses, and these hypotheses are tested against other information, such as empirical evidence, moral intuitions, and the derivability of theorems, and they are compared to each other. In this 'struggle for life'[23] the hypotheses which seem best should be[24] accepted provisionally, until even better hypotheses become available.

Within this process, two aspects can be discerned. One is the testing of hypotheses against the available information, including the gathering of information against which the hypotheses are to be tested, and the mutual comparison of available hypotheses to determine which one deserves to survive. For the comparison and testing of hypotheses, a science has a method in the form of a set of standards that determine which evidence counts as relevant for a particular kind of hypothesis and what makes that one hypothesis is preferable above another one. Through the application of these standards the adoption of a particular hypothesis as the answer to a research question is provisionally justified.

The second aspect of the process of science is the generation of hypotheses. Scientific method has to do with the testing and selection of hypotheses, and requires a set of pre-existing hypotheses as the fuel on which to run. Scientific method does *not* generate the hypotheses itself; there is no method for framing correct hypotheses.[25] Still the availability of good hypotheses is crucial for science, because scientific method consists of selecting the best hypothesis from the available ones. Without good 'fuel' the process of generating good scientific knowledge does not fly. Although there is no method which can guarantee the production of good hypotheses, there are techniques to increase the chance that good hypotheses are generated. Such techniques are called 'heuristics'.[26] Heuristics can take many forms, varying from having a good night sleep, via taking some alcoholic drinks to increase inspiration, to studying the already available hypotheses and their shortcomings.

22 This view is, in different versions, defended in Smits 2010 and in Hage 2011.

23 This biological metaphor stems from Popper 1972.

24 'should be' because our discussion deals with what should rationally be accepted and not with the actual practice of science, which does not always satisfy the highest standards of rationality.

25 As outflow of the logical-empirist movement in the thirties of the previous century, there have been attempts to develop an inductive method for theory *confirmation* (for the *corroboration* of hypotheses). Not much has come out of these attempts. Cf. Howson 2000.

26 The idea of heuristics was elaborated in Lakatos 1970. More recently it has gained widespread popularity in artificial intelligence, in connection with intelligent search. Cf. Haugeland 1989, p. 176-179. In Dutch legal science, the role of heuristics was emphasized in Nieuwenhuis 1976.

In particular this last heuristic is often very fruitful. Indeed, it is seldom possible to devise fruitful hypotheses as potential answers to research questions if one is not familiar with the problem field and the theories (that is: as yet non-refuted hypotheses) circulating in it.[27] Here lies an important role for comparative law, because it is possible to view the law of different legal systems as so many hypotheses about the most viable solution for some societal problem.[28] The experiences with these regulations provide indications about the quality of the solutions, and suggest what should be maintained and where improvement is desirable. In other words, *the study of comparative law can be a valuable heuristic tool.*

It should be noted, however, that it does not follow that comparative law can tell us what is the most viable solution for a problem. The selection of the best of hypotheses from a set of viable ones is a matter of scientific *method*. Therefore the next issue to be addressed is whether comparative law is also (part of) a method for legal science. This issue can only be dealt with by a more detailed analysis of the kinds of research questions that are asked in legal science.

4. Legal Sciences

There are many different research questions that can be asked about the law, but most of them can be categorised under one of the following three headings:

1. Explanation of the law's contents;
2. Evaluation of the law;
3. Description of the law.

4.1. *Explanation*

Explanation of the law's contents can both be logical/systematic, historical and sociological. A logical/systematic explanation shows on the hand how concrete rules and decisions 'follow' from underlying principles, values and policies. On the other hand – but this is more or less the same thing approached from a different angle – it shows which principles, values and policies are apparently presupposed by the rules and decisions of positive law. This type of explanation is advocated by Dworkin, Van Rhee, and Mackor.[29]

A historical explanation explains the contents of positive law through earlier versions of the positive law, and the internal legal events that deal with it, such as legislation, judicial decision-making and doctrinal discussions. A sociological explanation focuses on the effects which the contents and – even more importantly – the operation of positive law (law in action) has on society, and how the feedback

27 Too extensive familiarity may be a problem, though, because it may tie the researcher to the trodden paths and prevent him or her from developing bold new ideas.
28 This is also stressed in Smits 2006.
29 Dworkin 1977; Van Rhee 2004; Mackor 2011.

from society leads to changes or the lack thereof in the contents of the positive law. Examples of topics that may ask for explanation are:

- that different legal systems that started from the same foundation (e.g. Roman Law) have developed into different directions, and
- that systems with different starting points have nevertheless developed similar legal institutions.

If comparative law is to play a role in the method of explanatory legal science, comparative data should be relevant for the selection of the best explanatory hypothesis. The subfield of comparative law that deals with so-called 'legal transplants'[30] illustrates that this is indeed the case. Legal transplants are pieces of law from one legal system that are adopted in another legal system. The phenomenon that Belgian private law is similar to French private law can be explained from the fact that the Belgian civil code was a local adaptation of the French civil code of 1804. The fact that the private law of many countries on the European continent exhibits large structural similarities can be explained from the large-scale reception of Roman law in the late Middle Ages. In general, the study of legal transplants provides valuable data that are useful for explaining the contents of a particular regulation.

4.2. *Evaluation*

Evaluative legal science can take the shape of passing value judgements on actual or hypothetical (proposed) regulations, or of the selection of the 'best' regulation from a set of alternatives. In both cases a standard is needed that specifies under which conditions a regulation can be perceived as good, or as better than some other regulation. These standards tell us which facts about the regulations are relevant for assessing them as good or bad, right or wrong, or as better or worse than some other regulation. The evaluative judgement will be based on the application of these standards to the data about the regulation. A relatively simple standard would be that a regulation is the better, the more happiness it produces. For practical purposes, this very abstract standard would have to be replaced by more concrete ones. For instance competing possible regulations in the field of criminal law might be evaluated by means of the standard that rules are better, the more they succeed in reducing crime. The underlying assumption would then be that the reduction of crime is good because it produces more happiness. The relevant data for assessing a regulation would then concern the effects of the regulation, in the first place on the level of crime, and ultimately on the total amount of happiness.

The battle of methods that exists in the moral sciences would occur here too, because there is no broad agreement on the proper standard for evaluating legal regulations. However, although there is no agreement on the appropriate standard, according to most standards the effects of rules on society are relevant for the

30 Cf. Watson 1993; Fedtke 2006 and Graziadei 2006.

evaluation. Although comparative law in the strict sense of comparing the contents of laws from different legal system does not provide the relevant information, comparative law in a broader sense, which also takes into account what the practical effects of regulations are, does provide information that is relevant for evaluative purposes. It should be noted, however, that only comparative law in a broad sense can provide the relevant information and that even that form of comparative law cannot decide on the standard for evaluation.

4.3. *Description of the Law*

The possible role of comparative law in connection with the description of the law depends on one's conception of the law and its contents. The contents of the law can either be taken as the content of the law

I. of a particular legal system, or
II. in general.

I. The former approach will be appropriate if one takes law to be *positive law*, law that was explicitly made by national or international legislatures or judges. If law is taken to be positive law, the contents of the law can, in theory, be determined by studying the legislation and case law that count as a source of the law at issue. The results of comparative law will then hardly count as reasons why a particular description is true.

However, this simple picture of positive law is not completely correct, amongst others because both legislation and case law require interpretation.[31] If there is disagreement about the proper interpretation of one or more relevant texts, at least two possibilities present themselves.

a. The first possibility is that we have run out of law, and that the choice between competing interpretations is from the legal point of view arbitrary. A legal decision maker must exercise, to use Dworkin's phrase, 'strong discretion'.[32] In theory it would then be possible to toss a coin, because the choice between the different interpretations is arbitrary. In practice some standard will be adopted, but the choice of the standard is again arbitrary from the legal point of view. One possible standard would be to prefer the interpretation which is best from the moral point of view. Another standard would be to adhere to the views of the majority. And again a different standard is to choose for an interpretation that was adopted in other legal systems. In the last case, comparative law provides essential information. In all of these cases, however, comparative law does not provide us with a reason why a particular description of the law is the

31 On interpretation from a comparative perspective, see MacCormick & Summers 1991 and MacCormick and Summers 1997.

32 Dworkin 1977, p. 32.

correct one, but at most why a particular regulation *should* be adopted to fill the gap that exists in positive law.

b. The second possibility is that the national law itself contains standards for making the choice between different interpretations,[33] and then there are again two possibilities:

   1. The standards refer to hard facts such as the intention of the historical legislature or the prevailing public opinion (if it exists), and can be applied without making any value judgements. Then the choice between the competing interpretations can be made on the basis of empirical data, e.g. by establishing the intention of the historical legislature. Another possibility, which seems to be realised mostly in cases where international private law is applicable, is that the standards provided by national law point to the law of foreign legal systems. If this is the case, the results of comparative law provide us with reasons why the national law has a particular content.
   2. The application of the standards for choosing between interpretations requires an evaluative judgment, e.g. a judgement about the purpose of the rule, or about the needs of society. In that case the content of the law can only be established by making value judgements.[34] What was written about the use of comparative law for evaluative legal science then becomes relevant for descriptive legal science too.

II. Nowadays it is less fashionable than it used to be a few centuries ago,[35] but the question after the contents of the law may also be interpreted as dealing not with the positive law of a particular legal system, but with the content of the law in general (*ius commune*, or *ius naturale*). This is a feasible approach if one takes the law to be the best regulation to be enforced by collective means, where the positive law of different legal systems is a body of rules that must seriously be taken into account for reasons of legal certainty.[36] If one takes law to be the best possible regulation, the determination of the contents of the law is essentially an evaluative matter. What was written about the use of comparative law for evaluative legal science is then also relevant for descriptive legal science.

33 The classic example in this connection is Art. 1 of the Swiss Civil Code, which tells the judge which sources to use if no relevant provisions can be found in the statutory text.

34 It may seem strange that the description of the law can be based on value judgements. That this is possible nevertheless is because the positive law refers to evaluative standards. This brings along that a description of the positive law in abstract must mention these standards and that a description of the implications of the positive law for concrete cases requires the application of these standards.

35 The idea that there was a *ius commune* a common law for continental Europe, had found wide acceptance at the end of the fiftheenth century. Cf. Stein 1999, p. 75. From a philosophical perspective, similar ideas gained adherence in the form of a natural law that could be known through reason. Cf. Kelly 1992, p. 186-189.

36 More on this approach in Hage 2011.

5. Conclusion

The study of comparative is useful for lawyers and law students for several reasons:

Practical reasons
1. A lawyer who has familiarised him or herself with the law of foreign legal systems is less likely to experience the 'threshold of the unfamiliar'.
2. Occasionally legal decision makers base their decisions on comparative considerations.
3. The study of comparative law broadens one's horizon and makes it easier to relativise one's parochial law. Thus, the national law can be seen as one possible solution to societal problems, and not anymore as the legal structure of human society.

Scientific reasons
4. Comparative law can be a useful heuristic tool, which allows legal scientist to generate valuable hypothetical answers to research questions both more easily and with a wider scope.
5. Depending on the type of research questions one tries to answer and on one's view of the law, comparative law can also play a role in scientific method.

   - Such a role is undisputable for some kinds of explanation of the law's contents (legal transplants).
   - Comparative law in a broad sense may provide data which are relevant for questions of evaluative legal science.
   - Comparative law can play a role in descriptive legal science too, for instance if one takes law to be the best possible regulation for collective enforcement.

This both explains and justifies the ample attention for comparative law in the curriculum of the Maastricht European Law School.

Bibliography

Beerling, Kwee, Mooij, Van Peursen 1970
Beerling, R.F., Kwee, S.L., Mooij, J.J.A. & Van Peursen, C.A., *Inleiding tot de wetenschapsleer*, Utrecht: Bijleveld, 1970.

De Geest 2004
De Geest, G., 'Hoe maken we van de rechtswetenschap een volwaardige wetenschap?', *NJB*, 2004, p. 58-66.

Dray 1994
Dray, W., 'The Rationale of Actions', in Martin, M. & McIntyre, L.C. (eds.), *Readings in the Philosophy of Social Science*, Cambridge: MIT Press, 1994, p. 173-180.

Dworkin 1977
Dworkin, R., *Taking Rights Seriously*, Londen: Duckworth, 1977.

Dworkin 1986
Dworkin, R., *Law's Empire*, Londen: Fontana, 1986.

Fedtke 2006
Fedtke, F., 'Legal Transplants', in Smits, J. (ed.), *Elgar Encyclopedia of Comparative Law*, Cheltenham: Edward Elgar, 2006, p. 434-437.

Finnis 1980
Finnis, J., *Natural Law and Natural Rights*, Oxford: Oxford University Press, 1980.

Graziadei 2006
Graziadei, M., 'Comparative Law as the Study of Transplants and Receptions', in Reimann, M. & Zimmermann, R. (eds.), *The Oxford Handbook of Comparative Law*, Oxford: Oxford University Press, 2006, p. 441-476.

Hage 1979
Hage, J.C., 'De echtelijke woning na echtscheiding', *WPNR*, 1979, No. 5502, p. 708-715.

Hage 1997
Hage, J.C., *Reasoning with Rules*, Dordrecht: Kluwer, 1997.

Hage 2011
Hage, J.C., 'The Method of a Truly Normative Legal Science', in Van Hoecke, M. (ed.), *Methodologies of Legal Research. Which Kind of Method for What Kind of Discipline?*, Oxford: Hart Publishing, 2011, p. 19-44.

Haugeland 1989
Haugeland, J., *Artificial Intelligence. The very idea*, Cambridge: MIT Press, 1989.

Hempel 1965
Hempel, C.G., 'Studies in the Logic of Explanation', in Hempel, C.G., *Aspects of Scientific Explanation and Other Essays in the Philosophy of Science*, New York: The Free Press, 1965, p. 245-290.

Howson 2000
Howson, C., 'Evidence and Confirmation', in Newton-Smith, W.H. (ed.), *Companion to the Philosophy of Science*, Oxford: Blackwell, 2000, p. 108-116.

Kelly 1992
Kelly, J.M., *A Short History of Western Legal Theory*, Oxford: Clarendon Press, 1992.

Kincaid 1994
Kincaid, H., 'Defending Laws in the Social Sciences', in Martin, M. & McIntyre, L.C. (eds.), *Readings in the Philosophy of Social Science*, Cambridge: MIT Press, 1994, p. 111-130.

Korsgaard 1996
Korsgaard, C.M., *Creating the Kingdom of Ends*, Cambridge: Cambridge University Press, 1996.

Lakatos 1970
Lakatos, I., 'Falsification and the Methodology of Scientific Research Programs', in Lakatos, I. & Musgrave, A. (eds.), *Criticism and the Growth of Knowledge*, Cambridge: Cambridge University Press, 1970, p. 91-196.

MacCormick & Summers 1991
MacCormick, D.N. & Summers, R.S. (eds.), *Interpreting Statutes: a Comparative Study*, Darthmouth: Ashgate, 1991.

MacCormick & Summers 1997
MacCormick, D.N. & Summers, R.S. (eds.), *Interpreting Precedents: a Comparative Study*, Darthmouth: Ashgate, 1997.

Mackor 2011
Mackor, A.R., 'Explanatory non-normative legal doctrine', in Van Hoecke, M., *Methodologies of Legal Research. Which Kind of Method for What Kind of Discipline?*, Oxford: Hart Publishing, 2011, p. 45-70.

Nieuwenhuis 1976
Nieuwenhuis, J.H., 'Legitimatie en heuristiek van het rechterlijk oordeel', *Rechtsgeleerd Magazijn Themis*, 1976, p. 494-515.

Popper 1972
Popper, K.R., 'Evolution and the Tree of Knowledge', in Popper, K.R., *Objective Knowledge. An Evolutionary Approach*, Oxford: Clarendon Press, 1972, p. 256-284.

Rawls 1971
Rawls, J., *A Theory of Justice*, Cambridge: Harvard University Press, 1971.

Smith 2009
Smith, C., 'Het normatieve karakter van de rechtwetenschap: recht als oordeel', *Rechtsfilosofie en Rechtstheorie*, 2009, No. 38, p. 202-225.

Smits 2006
Smits, J.M., 'Comparative Law and its Influence on National Legal Systems', in Reimann, M. & Zimmermann, R. (eds.), *Handbook of Comparative Law*, Oxford: Oxford University Press, 2006, p. 513-538.

Smits 2010
Smits, J.M., *Omstreden rechtswetenschap*, Den Haag: Boom Juridische uitgevers, 2010.

Stein 1999
Stein, P., *Roman Law in European History*, Cambridge: Cambridge University Press, 1999.

Toulmin 1958
Toulmin, S.E., *The Uses of Argument*, Cambridge: Cambridge University Press, 1958.

Van Hoecke 2010
Van Hoecke, M., *Is de rechtswetenschap een empirische wetenschap?*, inaugural address Tilburg 2010, Den Haag: Boom Juridische uitgevers, 2010.

Van Rhee 2004
Van Rhee, C.H., 'Geen rechtsgeleerdheid, maar rechtswetenschap!', *Rechtsgeleerd Magazijn Themis*, 2004, p. 196-201.

Watson 1993
Watson, A., *Legal Transplants. An Approach to Comparative Law*, London: University of Georgia Press, 1993.

Zweigert & Kötz 1997
Zweigert, K. & Kötz, H., *An Introduction to Comparative Law*, Oxford: Clarendon Press, 3rd rev. ed., translated by Tony Weir, 1997.

Sjef van Erp

TEACHING LAW IN EUROPE: FROM AN INTRA-SYSTEMIC, VIA A TRANS-SYSTEMIC TO A SUPRA-SYSTEMIC APPROACH

1. Introductory Remarks

One of the most fundamental questions legal theorists ask is undoubtedly: 'how do lawyers think?'[1] What, in essence, they want to know is which modes of thought and which thought patterns are characteristic of persons who deal with social conflicts in an institutionalised way. The archetype is usually the judge. The question then becomes: how do judges think? A very pragmatic answer to this question could be: they think as they were taught to think. In other words: legal thinking is the result of legal education. It is, therefore, legal education which should be analysed more thoroughly to track the various legal modes of thought and legal thought patterns.[2]

Since the end of the eighteenth century, with the rise of the nation-state, the codification movement on the Continent of Europe and the rise of the doctrine of precedent in the English legal tradition, the law was taught on the basis of a nationally oriented *curriculum*, stressing the uniqueness and importance of its own vision of law. As a consequence, everywhere a more dogmatic (perhaps one could better say: doctrinal) approach can be found, in which one's own values, legal

1 This contribution is based on my experience in setting up and teaching an English language Bachelor course on comparative property law and an English language Master course on European property law in the Maastricht European Law School Programme, setting up and teaching a Bachelor course on comparative property law in the Bremen/Oldenburg (Germany) and Groningen (Netherlands) Hanse Law School Programme and teaching a course on European property law in the Master Programme European Law of the China-EU School of Law in Beijing.

2 I therefore have grave doubts as to the functioning of the Socratic Method in American law schools. Any teacher asking questions will do this from his/her own background and what he/she considers the 'correct' answer. Except for fundamental human rights, I do not see how a student can give any 'true' or 'false' answers without a framework from which to decide what is true or false. The framework is the society in which teacher and student live and the legal system that has been inherited from previous generations. Cf. for Germany Esser 1972 and for the Netherlands Schoordijk 1972.

policies, principles, concepts and rules are only questioned on the basis of an intra-systemic analysis and not from a trans-systemic viewpoint. By intra-systemic analysis a study is meant that takes the national system as its starting point, including its legal values, policies, principles, concepts and rules, without questioning the correctness of all of these, except for lack of internal consistency or coherence. The result is a technocratic view of the law. This approach still prevails in most legal systems. A typical area where such a technocratic view can be found is private law, more particularly property law. Let me give an example from the civil law tradition. Any German law student can explain in great detail the highly complicated legal relationship between the owner and the possessor (*Eigentümerbesitzerverhältnis*). Whether this relationship is really of relevance for legal practice or perhaps nothing more than an intellectual tool to create a desired mind-set is not a part of the discussion at German law faculties. In the common law tradition any English law student can explain what is meant by 'consideration' as being a fundamental requirement for a legally binding contract. The same question as regarding the previous example can be asked. Is 'consideration' really of such great practical relevance as is argued in textbooks, or is its analysis a way to teach which economic values are important to common lawyers and thus - again - create the required mind-set? Such a technocratic view is introspective and not really intended to look further than what is being taught as acquired wisdom. A critical mind-set is not aimed for and sometimes even seen as pure ideology (either as too left wing or too right wing oriented), forgetting that technocratic thinking is an ideology in itself.

The above does not mean that intra-systemic legal thinking is not valuable. Looking for consistency and coherence makes a legal system more stable, not only in its formative stage, but particularly when it is applied. A legal system will gain strength when it is applied on a non-discriminatory basis and without at random decisions. Intra-systemic legal thinking should therefore remain a part of any law school *curriculum*. Teaching law at an academic level, however, should go further. Choices made in earlier periods (whether Roman times, the reign of the Tudors, the French Revolution or the Industrial Revolution) do not always provide a good platform for the solution of modern day problems, arising from such phenomena as globalisation or the Information Revolution. These new phenomena demand a rethinking of earlier choices and therefore an open mind and the courage to reject such earlier solutions and enter uncharted waters.

Teaching law therefore can no longer merely focus on intra-systemic analysis - although, let me again be very clear about this, such analysis should not be forgotten! - but must concentrate on trans-systemic and even supra-systemic examination of the various legal traditions.[3] By trans-systematic analysis I mean the

[3] On the relevance of dogmatic legal thinking see for the Netherlands Vranken 2006, p. 122 *et seq*. On p. 123 he argues that there is 'room for a less legal-technical style of argument', adding: 'Comparative law makes an important contribution here, because applied correctly it can focus all attention on the heart of the matter instead of on the details, and therefore on the underlying values of rules, principles, precedents and doctrines.' This leaves the question open how the comparative legal method can be 'applied correctly'. As Vranken focused on →

same as Dedek and De Mestral when they describe the famous McGill Programme trans-systemic courses, as courses 'in which an area of law is treated as a unified field across the divide of different legal traditions.'[4] Trans-systemic analysis uses the functional method to discover how legal traditions solve particular problems, discovering the underlying values, policy choices, leading principles, concepts, ground rules and more specific technical rules. Through trans-systemic analysis the groundwork (perhaps one could say: the matrix) of legal systems can be found. From this perspective two goals can be reached. A return to an intra-systemic analysis, but now realising upon which choices the system's foundations were built and the creation of a supra-systemic approach to law to solve today's problems which arise from globalisation of the economy and the Information Revolution. A supra-systemic approach looks for solutions which are acceptable within diverging legal traditions, but cannot be traced back to one particular legal tradition. An example is the development of 'autonomous' European law.[5] In my view, a good law school *curriculum* should combine these three approaches.

In the following paragraphs I will further elaborate upon the trans-systemic and supra-systemic analysis of the law. Teaching comparative law will be at the heart of those paragraphs. First of all, the more classical approach to comparative law will be dealt with.[6] Remarkably enough - although upon further reflection, not really surprising - the classical approach is highly technocratic. One would expect that comparative law might resist technocratic legal thinking, but this is only the case if comparative law is an essential part of a law school *curriculum* from the very beginning and is integrated in the whole programme. If not, comparative law is only a tool to see how other legal systems may be the same or, as the case may be, different. It is nothing more than '*Auslandsrechtskunde*', the art to explain what others - but not you! - think. The very moment the comparative law adds a *tertium comparationis* to actually learn from the analysis, the stage of trans-systemic analysis is entered and the first steps towards supra-systemic analysis can be made. This will be discussed in the final paragraphs.

2. Teaching Comparative Law: the Classical Approach

Comparative law presupposes that (a) separate legal systems exist, which (b) are different from one's own legal system (and therefore 'foreign') and which (c) can be 'compared'. This is typically a nineteenth century approach, as before the codification era and the petrification of the common law as a result of the rules of precedent, mainly developed in the nineteenth century, legal systems were uncodified, fluid and therefore more receptive to the influence of legal thinking as developed elsewhere. A major example is the reception of Roman law by the

the role of legal scholarship and not on the role of comparative law *per se*, this question was left unanswered.

4 Dedek & De Mestral 2008.

5 Cf. Van Erp 2010a.

6 Cf. for the term 'classical' in relation to comparative law also Dedek & De Mestral 2008, p. 891.

continental legal systems, resulting in the mixture of local and Roman laws called the *'ius commune'*. In English law until the rise of the declaratory theory of the judicial function (courts pronounce the law as it has always existed), the growing importance of the principles of judicial consistency and legal certainty, the establishment of the Incorporated Council of Law Reporting in 1865 and the restructuring of English courts as a result of the Judicature Acts 1873-1875 no strict rules of precedent were applied.[7] This changed in 1898 with the House of Lords decision in *London Tramways Co.* v. *London County Council*.[8] It is remarkable to see that the development of the doctrine of precedent runs parallel to the codification movement on the Continent of Europe. It seems as if the fragmentation of legal systems on the Continent following the rise of the nation-state and the ensuing enactments of 'national' codes is reflected in the growing divide between the Continent and England following from the rules of precedent and an increasing focus by English lawyers on legal developments within the common law tradition worldwide. Each separate legal tradition and each separate legal system was looking for its own interpretation of what consistency and certainty demanded. The civil law retreated behind its codes, the common law behind its rules of precedent.

Comparative law - for some time on the Continent even regarded as merely comparison of legislation - required an educated legal mind.[9] It was therefore an area which could only be entered by those who already had received their legal education and training. In fact, it was an area for a distinct group of specialists, who could understand foreign languages and would accompany their intellectual travels with physical travel by visiting foreign countries. In the words of Mirow:

> 'The jurist recognizes the source as foreign, and brings out special interpretive tools to apply the source. This intellectual act, as the comparative legal moment, is the birth of comparative law.'

He then continues:

7 Cf. Hood Phillips & Hudson 1988, p. 211 *et seq.*

8 [1898] AC 375. In the words of Earl Halsbury L.C.: 'My Lords, for my own part I am prepared to say that I adhere in terms to what has been said by Lord Campbell and assented to by Lord Wensleydale, Lord Cranworth, Lord Chelmsford and others, that a decision of this House once given upon a point of law is conclusive upon this House afterwards, and that it is impossible to raise that question again as if it was *res integra* and could be reargued, and so the House be asked to reverse its own decision. That is a principle which has been, I believe, without any real decision to the contrary, established now for some centuries, and I am therefore of opinion that in this case it is not competent for us to rehear and for counsel to reargue a question which has been recently decided.' This should now, of course, be read in the light of the 1966 Practice Statement, [1966] 3 ALL ER 77, by Lord Gardiner, L.C., in which the House of Lords reserved the right to overrule its own previous cases. See also Hondius 2007, p. 31 *et seq.*, p. 38.

9 Cf. the establishment in 1869 of the French *Société de Législation Comparée*.

> '(...) there is a moment, an intellectual moment, when comparative law is born in the minds of judges and lawyers, and this moment can only occur when a legally trained mind is confronted with foreign law.'[10]

This approach to comparative law I would like to call 'classical comparative law'. I call it 'classical' in the sense as contract lawyers discuss 'classical contract law' when they mean contract law as it developed in the nineteenth century and I refer to 'classical property law' when discussing property law as it evolved in that same century.[11] It was a period of thinking in terms of separation to create clarity and legal certainty (a good example is the famous German *Trennungsprinzip*, separating the law of obligations from the law of property), defining clear cut concepts, legal positivism and creating national law as a means to develop a nation's identity. In such a climate comparative law can only be done once when the legal mind is ready for it; especially a jurist should be able to distinguish what is foreign and intrusive from what is national and 'ours'. The leading theme underlying this classical approach is, in the words of Lee: 'Comparative law should begin at home'.[12] First analyse your own legal system and perhaps the divergence which can be found there (from the perspective of the United Kingdom: the different legal systems which exist in England & Wales, Scotland, Northern Ireland, the Isle of Man and the Channel Islands) and, only after you have understood your own system, an examination of foreign systems can follow.

The classical approach can thus be characterised by formalism and distance. Foreign law is studied from codes, text books and, in the common law tradition, cases without taking into account the history that preceded this nineteenth century formalism and the underlying ideological, political and socio-economic circumstances. Although the liberal market ideology and the resulting *laissez-faire* economics had its followers all over Europe, still differences in ideology, politics and social-economic conditions could be found, but were ignored.

After the Second World War this began to change. Two world wars had brought the world – albeit through terrible conflicts – closer together. New means of communication were invented and used. Economic integration was seen as a way to prevent another devastating war. Economic interdependence would create political and military stability, so it was expected. In such an integrating world, a separating view on comparative law no longer fitted. Furthermore awareness arose that 'law in action' was to be distinguished from 'law in the books'. This reflected the growing consciousness that law should be seen in context, as no legal system functions in a vacuum and consequently no comparison can take place in a vacuum. Comparison is not a formal exercise, but demands a contextual inquiry into the 'foreign' legal

10 Dauchy, Bryson & Mirow 2010, p. 229 *et seq.*, p. 234.

11 See Kennedy 2006, p. x *et seq.* and Kennedy 2010, p. 811 *et seq.* Cf. also Atiyah 1979, reprint, 1985), p. 681 *et seq.*; Van Erp 2009a, p. 1517 *et seq.*

12 Lee 1990, p. 116.

system as well as a contextual analysis of your own legal system. It even requires an analysis of how the legal mind thinks.[13]

Still, classical comparative law does not fade away that quickly. A striking example is the leading English case of *Aluminium Industrie Vaassen BV* v. *Romalpa Aluminium Ltd.*[14] Of course, the application of foreign (in this case: Dutch) law was limited by the rule that if foreign law is not argued and explained, it is presumed to be the same as English law.[15] Nevertheless, particularly Roskill, L.J. must have sensed that something was going very wrong in this case. It looks as if he had wanted to examine Dutch law before adjudicating the case on the basis of English law, but the procedural stance taken by the parties, combined with formalism and distance, the two characteristics of classical comparative law, prevented him from intervening in the thought process leading to the decision. See e.g. the following remark by Roskill, L.J.:

> '(...) it would have been interesting to have known what the position was under Dutch law, as indeed it would have been interesting to know how a Dutch lawyer would have construed some of those express terms.'[16]

The facts of the Romalpa case are fairly straightforward. Aluminium Industrie Vaassen (AIV) had sold aluminium foil to Romalpa. The sale was governed by Dutch law, as applied under the old Netherlands Civil Code. Clause 13 of the general conditions, which had been translated from the original Dutch into English, stipulated (1) a reservation of ownership of any foil delivered, but not yet paid, (2) a transfer of ownership of any products made with the foil and (3) a transfer of claims on third parties if the foil or the products made from that foil were sold to third parties. Such sale was allowed in the ordinary course of business. The clause stated that Romalpa would hold the products made from the foil for AIV, as AIV was the 'fiduciary owner'. Under the old Netherlands Civil Code case law had accepted a transfer of ownership for security purposes, inspired by German law. Following terminology from Roman law this transfer was called fiduciary, as the new owner – the '*zekerheidseigenaar*' (owner for security purposes), also called '*fiducaire eigenaar*' (owner fiducia) – was entrusted with the property for a particular purpose, in this case: security. Only if the transferee would not pay his debts to the transferor would the transferor use his right of ownership. In other words: fiduciary ownership meant ownership for security purposes. Any connection whatsoever with the English concepts of trust or 'fiduciary relationships' (e.g. between principal and agent, bailor and bailee) was absent, as Dutch law does not know the English trust

13 It can, therefore, be no surprise that the Essays for Tony Honoré on the occasion of his 65th birthday are called 'The Legal Mind', with, among others, a contribution by P. Atiyah on Form and substance in legal reasoning: the case of contract. MacCormick & Birks 1986. Atiyah's contribution can be found on p. 19 *et seq*.

14 [1976] 1 WLR 676.

15 *Ibidem*, p. 688.

16 *Ibidem*, p. 684.

or the English law of equity.[17] Nevertheless it was decided that equity governed, although particularly Roskill L.J. not only had certain doubts about how the case would have been decided by a Dutch court, but also about the adequacy concerning the English translation of the applicable general conditions. He remarked:

> 'Those conditions were in Dutch, but there was what one might describe as an authentic and specially prepared, though not perhaps very well expressed, English translation of the Dutch conditions.'

A few sentences further on in the judgment he reinforced his remark by stating that:

> 'it cannot be said that the English translation is happy.'[18]

Indeed, the English translation was quite unhappy, because as a consequence of the translation of '*fiduciaire eigenaar*' into 'fiduciary owner' the civil law unitary concept of ownership was lost in translation and the equitable concept of tracing was found to apply.[19]

3. Trans-systemic and Supra-systemic Comparative Law

Although classical comparative law is now generally rejected and replaced by a more context driven approach, it is usually still classical in the sense that legal systems are compared. Students are confronted with comparative law after they have been trained to apply a particular legal system. Comparison will be starting from what might be called the 'home' system and, consequently, the other system will be 'foreign'. This approach is strengthened by the classical approach to private international law. Even today the starting point in this area of the law often is that it is a national area of law, which deals with what municipal law to apply in an international case, i.e. a case which has connections with more than one legal system. Not only is private international law still too frequently seen as 'national' and does private international law analysis consequently start from the 'home' system while cautiously watching other 'foreign' systems, it also presupposes that legal systems are separate and that a choice between those systems has to be made as being unavoidable. Growing market integration, both regional and global, does however provoke a twofold transformation of perception and consequently a change in perspective, perhaps even a paradigm change. First of all a growing realisation that legal systems are sometimes far more alike than previously thought, at least at the level of values, leading principles, policy choices, fundamental concepts and ground rules. Secondly, the rising awareness that the differences between legal systems, at least within particular regions such as the European Union or the United States of America, are not so fundamental that these cannot be

17 Such a transfer of ownership for security purposes is no longer allowed under the present Civil Code, which contains an explicit 'fiducia ban': Art. 3:84(3) Netherlands Civil Code.

18 *Ibidem*, p. 684.

19 See on the Romalpa case Fentiman 1998, p. 159 *et seq*. and p. 166 *et seq*.

overcome in the interest of further market integration, which may lead to more economic prosperity. It has rightly been argued by Fauvarque-Cosson that this latter perception may change the relationship between comparative law and private international law from allies to enemies.[20] Comparative law was an ally of private international law when legal systems were seen as separate from one another, comparative law becomes an enemy of private international law when it results in harmonisation or unification of the law and thus leads to private international law becoming irrelevant.[21] Fauvarque-Cosson expects comparative law and private international law to become 'bound by a common transnational destiny' when looking at the enormous impact of human rights on both areas of law. Comparative law will be more and more focussed on international, transnational and supranational sources of law, whereas private international law will see a strengthening of the *ordre public* exception to protect the values as expressed in charters protecting fundamental human rights.[22]

The views as developed by Fauvarque-Cosson find increasing support. More and more attention is being paid to how law school *curricula* should and could react to the growing importance of teaching law as a comparative mode of thought, although not everyone seems to be convinced. In this respect interesting proposals to restructure American law school *curricula* should be mentioned. They can be found in two reports written under the auspices of the Carnegie Foundation. The more recent of the two is a report of 2007, drafted by a team of 5 authors.[23] This 2007 report is the sequel to a report from 1914, drafted by Redlich.[24] Remarkably enough, but the reason probably has to do with the background of its authors (Redlich was an Austrian law professor, who later taught at Harvard; the authors of the 2007 report all are deeply embedded in American society), the 1914 report sometimes compares civil (Roman) law with common law, whereas the 2007 report is more inward looking. The 1914 report focuses on the success of Langdell's case method, but also wants to broaden the *curriculum* with institutional lectures at the beginning of the *curriculum* and two encyclopaedic series of lectures at the end, a series on jurisprudence (theory of law) and a series on Roman law. His view as to including comparative law – but what else could be expected in the beginning of the twentieth century? – is, however, to some extent limited. Not only is it rather classical, but, more particularly, what Redlich understands as comparative law is rather

20 Fauvarque-Cosson 2001, p. 407 *et seq.*

21 On the concepts of 'harmonisation' and 'unification' see Boele-Woelki 2010, p. 32 *et seq.*

22 Fauvarque-Cosson 2001, p. 427. See also on a developing transnational private law Callies & Zumbansen 2010, p. 27 *et seq.*

23 Sullivan, Colby, Welch Wegner, Bond & Shulman 2007.

24 Redlich 1914, republished in 2008. Redlich was a remarkable person, as can be read in Maxeiner 2008, p. 2: 'Professor Redlich was one of the foremost jurists of his day. When commissioned to write the report he was professor of law in the University of Vienna, author of books in English as well as in German on the common law world, and member of the Austrian parliament. He later became Finance Minister of Austria, Charles Stebbins Fairchild Professor of Comparative Public Law at Harvard Law School, first head of the Harvard Institute of Comparative Law, and deputy judge of the Permanent Court of International Justice.'

comparative legal history than the comparative study of (modern) law.[25] The 2007 report has a very different focus. It examines how to integrate the cognitive, practical and ethical-social, what the report calls, 'legal apprenticeship'. The 2007 report therefore deals with the on-going debate on what is 'academic' about teaching law and to what degree teaching law should be aimed at preparing students for a legal practice in which they act while conscious about the broader aims of law than just the particular interests of an individual (e.g. a client). Still, even in the model in which teaching national (U.S. wide) law is replaced by teaching transnational (i.e. global) law - the so-called 'integrative method' - the case method is at the heart of legal education. It is interesting to read in the 2007 report how the case method, as developed by Langdell at Harvard law school in the second half of the nineteenth century, was taken over by the Harvard business school and then the model 'migrated again' into medical schools, such as McMaster in Canada and Michigan State in the United States and was then called 'problem-based learning'.[26] It is this latter teaching method that was chosen by the Maastricht law faculty as its basic teaching technique, from the very moment it was founded, adopting the approach selected by the Maastricht faculty of medicine, which, in its turn, had taken over this method from McMaster. So when the Maastricht law faculty - as the only faculty in the Netherlands and perhaps even the European Union - introduced problem-based learning as its basic teaching method, in fact this faculty returned to Langdell's method of teaching law at Harvard law school in the nineteenth century. This method is also used in its European Law School programme. This proves that the case method, as implied by Redlich, is not specific for law *curricula* in common law jurisdictions, but can also be used in *curricula* aimed at studying other traditions than those essentially based on case law. In his comments on the 2007 Carnegie report, this is also argued by Backer.[27] After having remarked that the legal *curriculum* cannot escape from internationalisation, but that also the relationship with the bench and the bar should not be forgotten he states:

> 'Many law schools have already begun to respond to this change in the environment in which lawyers must be trained. On the academic side, research that remains tied to a particular locale will be marginalized as increasingly parochial in the coming decades. Likewise, law schools that ignore the needs of the practising bar will find themselves cut off from the profession.'[28]

25 On p. 45 of his report Redlich writes: 'If the student has mastered all essential institutions and doctrines of the common law during his three years' course, through the analysis of countless cases, he will certainly now be sufficiently matured to undertake, with full understanding, tow important tasks. First, he should be able to grasp the general scientific theory of the law as one of the great dominating phenomena of human civilization and human thought. Secondly, he should now be fully prepared to cast to great advantage a comparative glance at that second mighty system of law which has shaped the history of humanity, namely the Roman law.'

26 Redlich 2008, p. 199.

27 Backer 2008, p. 49 *et seq.*

28 Backer 2008, p. 112. See also Vai Lo Lo 2010, p. 117 *et seq.*

He does, however, express clear doubts about applying the case method to the teaching of European law and civil law, although he admits that the case method might be a supplementing teaching approach. In his own words:

> 'Though possible, it is not clear that the case dialogue method is the most suitable for conveying the essence of European Union law, though its insights might to some extent translate. The case dialogue method itself, as signature pedagogy, becomes more problematic when applied to instruction in civil law. Yet even there the reality of changes in civil law suggest a place for case dialogue instruction as a lens through which the codes are understood. On the other hand, problems as a lens through which to understand the workings of a code might be suitable. (...) The important lesson, though, is that international and foreign law can be taught using American pedagogical instruments without losing the power of instruction.'[29]

Backer's observations are, certainly from a European viewpoint, interesting and instructive to read. From the perspective of European law faculties the most problematic aspect of teaching law on a comparative and European basis is not the teaching methods as such, but its content: what 'law' should be taught at a trans-systemic and, with regard to European law, supra-systemic level?

The 2007 Carnegie Foundation report proposes to replace the 'additive' model with an, already mentioned, 'integrative' model, by which the authors mean that particularly legal practice should not be added to a programme as an extra, but should be fully integrated. An integrative approach can, however, also include the cognitive side of 'legal apprenticeship'. This is done in the so-called 'McGill Programme', which follows a trans-systemic approach, in which the teaching of civil and common law is to be fully integrated. The difficulty with regard to this approach is that it borders upon leaving the teaching of law as a system and embarking upon the teaching of a theory of law. Dedek and De Mestral make this very clear when they discuss how the McGill trans-systemic teaching method could overcome the problems that European law faculties face when integrating European law in their standard courses:

> 'Taken seriously, the promotion of the 'European dimension' calls not only for the addition of more EU-related content to an already content-laden *curriculum*; it also calls for a paradigm shift away from the study of law as the study of a 'system' of positive law of a certain jurisdiction, and towards a de-contextualized, maybe more abstract study of the questions that reach beyond jurisdictional boundaries.'[30]

Or even more direct:

> 'The ultimate aspiration of this programme, (...), is to transcend the fixation on the study of law as the study of 'legal systems'- hence the label 'trans-systemic' legal education.'[31]

29 Backer 2008, p. 107.
30 Dedek & De Mestral 2008, p. 896.
31 Dedek & De Mestral 2008, p. 897.

That the trans-systemic approach is more about a theory of law than law itself, defined as a system of rules applied in an institutionalised way, can also be seen in Glenn's analysis, although it seems as if he does not go as far as Dedek and De Mestral.[32] According to Glenn trans-systemic teaching

> 'cannot involve inventing the law to be taught, nor concentrating exclusively on law known as international. It should rather involve the teaching of law which is more deeply rooted or profound than the law of legal systems, that which underlies and pervades all of them. This, it will be suggested here, involves reinvigoration of the idea of legal tradition as the necessary foundation of legal systems and as the necessary means of teaching across, through, and beyond them. Reinvigoration of the idea of legal tradition provides benefits, however, beyond those of legal education. It also allows a larger and more convincing explanation of the normativity of law and of the relations between the laws of the world.'[33]

In Glenn's view a legal tradition is, in essence, information about how certain problems were resolved in the past. This information is the foundation upon which (groups of) legal systems are built.[34] This certainly is also a trans-systemic approach, but not so completely severed from legal systems as Dedek and De Mestral argue.

It cannot be denied that teaching law from a trans-systemic perspective demands more and broader knowledge than understanding only one legal system. However, we should never forget why we teach our students: we want them to become lawyers, who can practice not only across legal systems, but also (and even for most of them) within a particular legal system. Radically disconnecting the teaching of law from analysis of legal systems will result in a programme that is no longer interesting for the bar and the bench. They will, no doubt, react with setting up their own - supplementary - programmes and exams, as is done in the United States with the bar exam. This is not, of course, in itself a bad development, but it should be realised that this might happen. It can be avoided, if teaching trans-systemically is not completely cut off from analysis of positive legal systems. What I find almost astonishing about the analysis by Dedek and De Mestral is what they implicitly remark as to the limits of the trans-systemic approach. After having described some of the core courses that are taught on a trans-systemic basis they add:

> 'In first year, Civil Law Property is the one private law course that is not taught trans-systemically because of its systemic development and its cultural specificity, and in order to give students an opportunity to experience the internal 'logic' of either system.'[35]

Is property law really so different from other areas of private (or public) law that it cannot be taught trans-systemically?

32 Glenn 2005, p. 864 *et seq.*
33 Glenn 2005, p. 867.
34 Glenn 2005, p. 872 *et seq.*
35 Dedek & De Mestral 2008, p. 905.

In the European Law School *curriculum* of Maastricht University we now teach 2 courses on property law. The European Law School offers a programme of Bachelor and Master courses, on a comparative and European (therefore: non-domestic) basis. Originally, when the programme still was a mixture of Dutch law (in Dutch) and comparative law (in English) I developed and taught an (obligatory) English language Bachelor course on European property law. Later, when the English Language Track was introduced, this course became an (optional) part of the Master programme and for the Bachelor programme a new obligatory course was developed. When a student chooses the European Law School programme – English Language Track 'Comparative Property Law' and 'European Property Law' are the only property law courses offered. Let me describe both courses briefly.

The Bachelor course, taught in the second year of the *curriculum*, has the following basic objectives: (1) Basic knowledge of the historical development of property law in Europe, (2) fundamental comparative knowledge of leading property law values and principles, policy choices, basic concepts, ground rules and technical rules in French, German, Dutch and English law, (3) basic comparative knowledge of leading principles and ground rules in mixed legal systems, such as Scotland and South Africa and (4) basic knowledge of the current developments in comparative and European property law. The course has a double focus. First of all, it aims to introduce students to the underlying values, policy choices, leading principles, basic concepts and ground rules of major property law traditions in Europe. In the second place it introduces students to the '*mentalité*' (the legal culture) of a particular tradition. The latter is done by discussing basic concepts within the setting of a major legal tradition in which this concept has been developed more explicitly than in other legal traditions. As a teaching method both overall lectures are given next to small seminar groups, following the case method. The course starts, to give but an example, with a discussion of property in Roman law; students are asked to reflect upon the Roman law concepts of '*possessio*', '*dominium*' and what it means if someone claims '*meum esse*'. Then French law is discussed, with an emphasis on the consequences of the French Revolution and the impact on what constitutes a property right (principle of *numerus clausus*), followed by German law, discussing limited property rights and 'expectation rights' such as preliminary registration of a sales agreement in a land register together with a discussion of land registration systems. After this, Dutch law with its ban on fiduciary transfer is dealt with. Having the students thus introduced to the civil law, using a historical-comparative approach, we then cross the Channel and devote a relatively large amount of time to English law. Finally, mixed legal systems are discussed to show how civil law and common law can come together, followed by an introduction into European property law (emanating from the European institutions: European Union, European Economic Area and the Council of Europe) and an overview of modern developments in property law as a result of, e.g., information technology, such as 'virtual property'.

The Master course builds upon the Bachelor course, but, because it is also open to students with a different bachelor's degree than law, starts with a brief introduction into comparative property law. In this introduction legal history and the leading principles of *numerus clausus* and transparency (specificity and publicity) are analysed, followed by a discussion of property security rights. The latter topic might seem rather specific and even random. Security rights, however, are being discussed, because it is in particular with regard to these rights that in Europe efforts are made towards harmonisation or unification. Further development of European property law will largely depend on the success of harmonising or unifying security rights.[36] The weeks after this comparative introduction are devoted to property law as developed by the European Union (regulations, directives, case law created by the European Court of Justice) and within the Council of Europe (protection of ownership as a fundamental human right), followed by a prognostic analysis of the possible future impact of the European internal market on property law. Part of the first mentioned topic is a general analysis of difficulties and opportunities to create a European property law, focussing, of course, on the Draft Common Frame of Reference and taking as examples the introduction of the English trust in civil law systems, such as France and Germany and the proposal to introduce a law on euro-mortgage (a uniform type of non-accessory mortgage, based upon German and Swiss law).[37] Under the heading of internal market and property law the impact of the European treaties on property law is being analysed. The so-called 'four freedoms' (free movement of people, goods, services and capital) are at the heart of this final part of the course.[38]

When looking at the programme of the two courses, the difference in focus is that the Bachelor course uses the trans-systemic method, whereas the Master course follows a more European supra-systemic approach. The European Union is an autonomous legal order and concepts of European law, for that reason, have to be developed autonomously. The difficulty, of course, is what 'autonomy' means. In order to start answering the question how in European law autonomous concepts can be developed a purely trans-systemic method will be insufficient. In essence, this method still is based on comparative legal research and any conclusion as to a shared framework or shared building blocks will, consequently, be based on elements coming from all the examined legal systems. To develop autonomous European concepts we need a supra-systemic technique, aimed at developing a common frame of reference, which takes as its starting point terminology as can be found in the European treaties and European legislation and only uses the outcome of trans-systemic analysis as far as the shared framework or shared building blocks are concerned. Upon this foundation a new, European autonomous legal terminology and an autonomous legal system can be built. As I wrote in another contribution:

36 Cf. Van Erp 2009b, p. 3 *et seq.*

37 See Study Group on a European Civil Code and Research Group on EC Private Law (Acquis Group 2009.

38 See on this also the contribution of B. Akkermans to this volume.

> 'In this way, European concepts will not be totally disconnected from the laws of the Member States, and at the same time Member States will not be able to 'claim' the concept as 'their own' for originating in their national legal tradition. Proceeding in this way, Europe could (and in my view: will) develop into a mixed legal system, or to be more precise: a mixed system sui generis.'[39]

This is the final aim of the Master course on European property law, which follows a supra-systemic approach: to develop a truly European law of property, inspired by a trans-systemic analysis of the various European legal traditions, but developed from within the framework of the European treaties and the *acquis communautaire*.

4. Concluding Remarks

We have come a long way from teaching comparative law as a separate last year subject for a small group of interested students to a full Bachelor and Master programme with only trans-systemic and supra-systemic courses. Even if a law *curriculum* is still more domestically oriented than non-domestically, the nineteenth century classical comparative law method is abandoned everywhere. This is partly due to the influence of European law on the national legal systems. Since the first European treaties were concluded - the Treaty establishing the European Coal and Steel Community (1951), the Treaty establishing the European Atomic Energy Community (1957) and the Treaty establishing the European Economic Community (1957) - the growing European Union more and more has become the fabric within which the laws of the Member States develop. The result is - as I have argued for the area of property law - a growing osmosis of European and national law.[40] More recently, it has also sometimes led to antagonism and a resulting propensity towards thinking in terms of national instead of European interests, forgetting that in today's world economies are so intertwined that the once perhaps clear borderline between national and foreign is becoming increasingly vague. In my view, such antagonism can, at least in part, be countered by teaching how various layers of law - in other words: how complexity of legal sources - in the modern world governs our relationships. This will also show that a comparative legal analysis concentrating on black letter law (e.g. merely on legislation in civil law systems) is now a phenomenon of the past.

Today a contextual understanding of foreign law is generally accepted as the proper way to examine and understand foreign law. Even the concept of 'foreign' law itself can be questioned, also in cross-border common law - civil law relations. If 'foreign' law is applied, following a European (or even a national) rule of private international law, is this law than still so foreign, one may ask? Furthermore, recognition of foreign law may result in adaptations in the law that recognises foreign solutions when these diverge from those in the receiving system. In this way unification of private international law my result indirectly in unification or harmonisation of substantive law.

39 Van Erp 2010b.
40 Van Erp 2006.

A good example to show this is, again, a leading English case, but this time a very recent decision by the United Kingdom Supreme Court in the case of *Radmacher (formerly Granatino)* v. *Granatino*.[41] The case is about a pre-nuptial agreement concluded between a husband from France and a wife from Germany. The husband came from a well-to-do family and the wife came from a family that was extremely wealthy. The wife's father urged his daughter to conclude a pre-nuptial agreement, to be drawn up by a German notary and governed by German law, to safeguard her present and future property interests. The wife followed her father's advice and the agreement was drawn up and signed in Germany. The husband had not received any independent advice, did not understand German (the agreement was read out in German and then translated by the notary in English) and no negotiations had preceded the agreement. They married in 1998 in London where they established their matrimonial home. Two children were born. The husband was an investment banker, but after the marriage he decided to follow a full time study in Oxford for a D Phil in biotechnology. In 2006 the marriage broke down and the couple divorced, the husband asking for ancillary relief under Section 25 of the Matrimonial Causes Act 1973 and claiming a part of his wife's property. Under English law, as it stood before this case, the possible impact of a pre-nuptial agreement on the decision of the court was that it was one, but certainly not a decisive, factor. The final decision was within the court's discretion. The main question to be decided by the Supreme Court was whether this approach should still be followed. The majority (Lord Phillips, Lord Hope, Lord Rodger, Lord Walker, Lord Brown, Lord Collins and Lord Kerr) referred to solutions in other legal systems as follows:

> '3. The approach of English law to nuptial agreements differs significantly from the law of Scotland, and more significantly from the rest of Europe and most other jurisdictions. Most jurisdictions accord contractual status to such agreements and hold the parties to them, subject in some cases to specified safeguards or exceptions. Under English law it is the court that is the arbiter of the financial arrangements between the parties when it brings a marriage to an end. A prior agreement between husband and wife is only one of the matters to which the court will have regard. The uncertainty as to the weight that the court will attach to such agreements has led to calls for reform. The history of steps taken towards the reform of our law is set out in the judgment of Thorpe LJ in this case in the Court of Appeal [2009] 2 FLR 1181, paras 16-23.'

Nevertheless the Supreme Court decided that, while reiterating that in spite of the choice of law clause English law applied, the agreement should be followed, if entered into freely unless this would be unfair under the circumstances. Even Baroness Hale of Richmond, JSC, although she dissented as to several parts of the majority decision, could not ignore the international elements in this case and the fact that the agreement was, according to unquestioned evidence before the judge in first instance, valid according to the laws of Germany and France.[42] She stated:

41 [2010] UKSC 42; [2010] WLR (D) 260.

42 *Radmacher* v. *Granatino*, majority decision, No. 101.

'181. In strict legal terms the so-called 'foreign element' is irrelevant. If the proceedings take place in England and Wales, the applicable law is that of England and Wales, irrespective of where the parties come from, how long they have been here, or how close their connection is with this jurisdiction. The United Kingdom has made a deliberate choice not to adopt the Hague Protocol on the law applicable to maintenance obligations and has only agreed to participate in the Council Regulation (EC) No 4/2009 on the basis that it would not be required to do so. English family lawyers seem to have a horror of having to apply foreign law which must appear strange to European lawyers who are quite used to doing so. Anyone who chooses to divorce here must be advised that the court will apply English law and not the law of the country which the parties have chosen or with which the marriage has the closest connection.

182. In another sense, however, the foreign element cannot be totally irrelevant. It may affect the relevant considerations in a number of ways. It may be a crystal clear indication that the parties intended their agreement to be legally binding, not only upon themselves, but also on the court. On the other hand, a foreign couple may have been warned, as this couple were warned, that their agreement might not have the same effect in other countries as it did in the country where it was made. But it means that their expectations may have been very different. The agreement may also have affected their later behaviour to a greater extent than it would have done had they not regarded it as legally binding.

183. None of this is to suggest that evidence of foreign law will be necessary in a foreign case. The relevance is not as to the effect of a foreign agreement in English law because, by the time the case gets to the divorce court, it has none. The relevance is as to the parties' intentions and expectations at the time when they entered into it.'

What we see here is what may be called harmonisation or unification of the law 'through the backdoor'. As a result of a rule of private international law, either directly demanding the application of foreign law or indirectly by demanding that a legal act governed by foreign law is to be taken into account, foreign law is made a part of the domestic legal system. In this way foreign law is no longer 'foreign', as, one way or the other, it has been adopted by the receiving legal system. Such a process requires more than a nineteenth century classical comparative analysis; it requires at least a contextual awareness. In this case, it is submitted, the leading view was that in Europe generally, also in matrimonial matters, party autonomy prevails and not the views of a single judge or a panel of judges.[43] The *Radmacher* v.

43 See Van Erp 2010c, p. 8. See also the majority decision in *Radmacher* v. *Granatino*, No. 78: 'The reason why the court should give weight to a nuptial agreement is that there should be respect for individual autonomy. The court should accord respect to the decision of a married couple as to the manner in which their financial affairs should be regulated. It would be paternalistic and patronising to override their agreement simply on the basis that the court knows best. This is particularly true where the parties' agreement addresses existing circumstances and not merely the contingencies of an uncertain future.'
Cf., however, also the critical remarks by Baroness Hale of Richmond, JSC: '137. Above all, perhaps, the court hearing a particular case can all too easily lose sight of the fact that, unlike a separation agreement, the object of an ante-nuptial agreement is to deny the economically weaker spouse the provision to which she – it is usually although by no means invariably she – would otherwise be entitled: see, for example, Gail Frommer Brod, 'Premarital Agreements
→

Granatino case shows that even when under its rules on private international law a Member State of the European Union, such as in this case the United Kingdom, is forced to apply its own domestic law in an international - intra Member State - situation, comparative legal analysis has become unavoidable.[44]

A law *curriculum* completely devoted to the study of comparative and European law should no longer be looked at with admiration by those who favour the education of European (and no longer: purely national) lawyers or, as the case may be, with suspicion by those who feel themselves threatened by foreign (non-national) influences out of their control. If such a programme combines intra-systemic, trans-systemic and supra-systemic legal teaching it will prepare students for a legal practice which will only become more complex, given the increasing economic (and the resulting legal) integration. Such a practice may be local or international, but in both cases the comparative and European study of law will be a *conditio sine qua non* for becoming a reliable lawyer.

and Gender Justice' (1994) 6 Yale Journal of Law and Feminism 229. This is amply borne out by the precedents available in recent textbooks: see, for example, Harris & Spicer, Prenuptial Agreements: A Practical Guide (2008), Appendix D, or Wood, Lush, Bishop & Murray, Cohabitation: Law, Practice and Precedents, 4th ed (2009), pp 583–592. Would any self-respecting young woman sign up to an agreement which assumed that she would be the only one who might otherwise have a claim, thus placing no limit on the claims that might be made against her, and then limited her claim to a pre-determined sum for each year of marriage regardless of the circumstances, as if her wifely services were being bought by the year? Yet that is what these precedents do. In short, there is a gender dimension to the issue which some may think ill-suited to decision by a court consisting of eight men and one woman.'

44 In the United States a reverse trend may be found. Oklahoma, followed by other states, is introducing legislation that would ban the application by courts of international and foreign (more explicitly: sharia) law. It is unclear what the outcome of this trend could be. However, in a global economy, in which the United States is playing a leading role, international and foreign law can simply not be ignored. What would happen if the European Union would forbid its courts to apply non-European law? See: <http://conflictoflaws.net/2010/the-battle-between-oklahoma-and-foreign-law/>.

Bibliography

Atiyah 1979
Atiyah, P.S., *The Rise and Fall of Freedom of Contract*, Oxford: Oxford University Press, 1979, reprint 1985.

Backer 2008
Backer, L.C., 'Internationalizing the American Law School Curriculum (in Light of the Carnegie Foundation's Report)', in Klabbers, J. & Sellers, M. (eds.), *The Internationalization of Law and Legal Education. Ius Gentium: Comparative Perspectives on Law and Justice 2,* Dordrecht: Springer, 2008, p. 49-112.

Boele-Woelki 2010
Boele-Woelki, K., *Unifying and Harmonizing Substantive Law and the Role of Conflict of Laws,* Law Lectures Hague Academy of International Law, Leiden/Boston: Nijhoff Publishers, 2010.

Callies & Zumbansen 2010
Callies, G.-P. & Zumbansen, P., *Rough Consensus and Running Code. A Theory of Transnational Private Law*, Oxford/Portland, Or.: Hart Publishing, 2010.

Dauchy, Bryson & Mirow 2010
Dauchy, S., Bryson, W.H. & Mirow, M.C., *Ratio Decidendi, Guiding principles of judicial decisions, Vol. 2 'Foreign' Law, Comparative studies in Continental and Anglo-American legal history/Vergleichende Untersuchungen zur kontinentaleuropäischen und anglo-amerikanischen Rechtsgeschichte*, Berlin: Duncker & Humblot, 2010.

Dedek & De Mestral 2008
Dedek, H. & De Mestral, A., 'Born to be Wild: The 'Trans-Systemic' Programme at McGill and the De-Nationalization of Legal Education', to be found electronically at the German Law Journal: *German Law Journal*, 2008, Vol. 9, p. 889-912, available at: <http://www.germanlawjournal.com/index.php?pageID=11&artID=1128> and the Social Science Research Network (SSRN): <http://ssrn.com/abstract=1488265>.

Esser 1972
Esser, J., *Vorverständnis und Methodenwahl in der Rechtsfindung: Rationalitätsgrundlagen richterlicher Entscheidungspraxis*, Frankfurt am Main: Athenäum Fischer Taschenbuch Verlag, 1972.

Fauvarque-Cosson 2001
Fauvarque-Cosson, B., 'Comparative Law and Conflict of Laws: Allies or Enemies? New Perspectives on an Old Couple', *American Journal of Comparative Law*, 2001, Vol. 49, p. 407-428.

Fentiman 1998
Fentiman, R., *Foreign Law in English Courts. Pleading, Proof and Choice of Law*, Oxford: Clarendon Press, 1998.

Frommer Brod 1994
Frommer Brod, G., 'Premarital Agreements and Gender Justice', *Yale Journal of Law and Feminism*, 1994, Vol. 6, p. 229-296.

Glenn 2005
Glenn, H.P., 'Doin'the Transsystemic: Legal Systems and Legal Traditions', *McGill Law Journal*, 2005, Vol. 50, No. 4, p. 863-898.

Harris & Spicer 2008
Harris, I. & Spicer, R., *Prenuptial Agreements: A Practical Guide*, London: Hammicks Legal Publishing, 2008.

Hondius 2007
Hondius, E., 'Precedent and the Law', in Boele-Woelki, K. & Van Erp, S. (eds.), *General Reports of the XVIIth Congress of the International Academy of Comparative Law*, Brussels/Utrecht: Bruylant and Eleven International Publishing, 2007, p. 31-50.

Hood Phillips & Hudson 1988
Hood Phillips, O. & Hudson, A.H., *First Book of English Law*, London: Sweet and Maxwell, 1988.

Kennedy 2006
Kennedy, D., *The Rise and Fall of Classical Legal Thought*, Washington D.C.: Beard Books, 2006.

Kennedy 2010
Kennedy, D., 'Savigny's Family/Patrimony Distinction and its Place in the Global Genealogy of Classical Legal Thought', *American Journal of Comparative Law*, 2010, Vol. 58, No. 4, p. 811-841.

MacCormick & Birks 1986
MacCormick, N. & Birks, P., *The Legal Mind, Essays for Tony Honoré*, Oxford: Clarendon Press, 1986.

Plender 1990
Plender, R. (ed.), *Legal History and Comparative Law. Essays in Honour of Albert Kiralfy*, London: Frank Cass, 1990.

Redlich 1914
Redlich, J., 'The Common Law and the Case Method in American University Law Schools: A Report to the Carnegie Foundation for the Advancement of Teaching', *Bulletin*, 1914, No. 8.

Redlich 2008
Redlich, J., 'The Common Law and the Case Method in American University Law Schools', in Maxeiner, J.R., *Educating Lawyers now and then: an Essay Comparing the 2007 and 1914 Carnegie Foundation Reports on Legal Education*, Lake Mary: Vandeplas Publishers, 2008.

Schoordijk 1972
Schoordijk, H.C.F., *Oordelen en Vooroordelen*, Deventer: Kluwer, 1972.

Study Group on a European Civil Code and Research Group on EC Private Law 2009
Study Group on a European Civil Code and Research Group on EC Private Law (Acquis Group), *Principles, Definitions and Model Rules of European Private Law. Draft Common Frame of Reference. Outline Edition*, Munich: Sellier European Law Publishers, 2009.

Sullivan, Colby, Welch Wegner, Bond & Shulman 2007
Sullivan, W.M., Colby, A., Welch Wegner, J., Bond, L. & Shulman, L.S., *Educating Lawyers: Preparation for the Profession of Law*, The Carnegie Foundation for the Advancement of Teaching, Preparation for the Professions Program, San Francisco: Jossey-Bass, 2007.

Van Erp 2006
Van Erp, S., *European and National Property Law: Osmosis or Growing Antagonism?*, Sixth Walter van Gerven Lecture, Groningen: Europa Law Publishing, 2006, also to be found electronically at the website of the Social Science Research Network (SSRN): <http://papers.ssrn.com/sol3/papers.cfm?abstract_id=1372166>.

Van Erp 2009a
Van Erp, S., 'From "classical" to modern European property law?', *Essays in honour of Konstantinos D. Kerameus/Festschrift für Konstantinos D. Kerameus*, Athens/Brussels: Ant. N. Sakkoulas/Bruylant, 2009, p. 1517-1533, available at SSRN: <http://ssrn.com/abstract=1372166>.

Van Erp 2009b
Van Erp, S., 'Security Interests: A Secure Start for the Development of European Property Law', in Hinteregger, M. & Boric, T. (eds.), *Sicherungsrechte und Immobilien in Europa*, Vienna/Berlin: Lit Verlag, 2009, p. 3-39.

Van Erp 2010a
Van Erp, S., 'The Methodological Impossibility to Create 'Autonomous European' Law', editorial *Electronic Journal of Comparative Law*, 2010, Vol. 14, No. 2, available at: <http://www.ejcl.org/142/editor142.html>.

Van Erp 2010b
Van Erp, S., 'Editorial - The Methodological Impossibility to Create "Autonomous European" Law', *Electronic Journal of Comparative Law*, 2010, Vol. 14, No. 2, available at: <http://www.ejcl.org/142/editor142.html>.

Van Erp 2010c
Van Erp, S., 'Matrimonial Property Regimes and Patrimonial Aspects of Other Forms of Union: what Problems and Proposed Solutions?', (Proposal for Rome IV Regulation), Directorate General for Internal Policies, Policy Department C: *Citizens' Rights and Constitutional Affairs. Legal Affairs. European Parliament Briefing Note for Inter-Parliamentary Committee Meeting* - Workshop on civil justice: 'How to Facilitate the Life of European Families and Citizens?', Brussels 30 November 2010.

Vranken 2006
Vranken, J.B.M., *Exploring the Jurist's Frame of Mind*, Deventer: Kluwer Law International, 2006.

Wood, Lush, Bishop & Murray 2009
Wood, H., Lush, D., Bishop, D. & Murray, A., *Cohabitation: Law, Practice and Precedents*, Bristol: Jordan Publishing Ltd., 4th ed., 2009.

Vai Lo Lo 2010
Vai Lo Lo, 'The Internationalisation of Legal Education: a Road Increasingly Travelled', in Hiscock, M. & Van Caenegem, W. (eds.), *The Internationalisation of Law. Legislating, Decision-making, Practice and Education*, Cheltenham/Northampton, MA: Edward Elgar, 2010, p. 117-134.

Nicole Kornet

BUILDING A EUROPEAN-ORIENTED LAW CURRICULUM

1. Introduction

Today's law graduates are facing a world in which the law and the practice of law are undergoing constant transformation as a result of European integration and globalisation. These developments inevitably raise new challenges for legal education. The Europeanisation of law and legal practice calls for the education of a new generation of law graduates. Law graduates who are less dependent on a single legal system and with the know-how to operate in a European and global legal environment. With its focus on national law, the traditional law curriculum is ill-suited to educating such 'European law graduates'. Legal education therefore will need to undergo transformation to become progressively 'Europeanised'.

To respond to not only European developments in legal education, but also to the expansion of European law and the ever-increasing harmonisation of law, it has become increasingly necessary to develop a truly European-oriented law curriculum. An innovative example of such a curriculum is provided by the European Law School - English Language Track at Maastricht University. This European-oriented law curriculum not only recognises the European origin of, and expanding influence of EU law on, national law, it also fundamentally integrates European and comparative law into the curriculum, dislodging the study of law from its focus on a single legal system.

In this contribution discusses the nature and set up of such a European-oriented law curriculum. First, some comments will be made on the need to adapt the law curriculum from its current national orientation towards a European orientation (2). This is followed by a discussion of the nature and possible content of a European-oriented law curriculum (3). Finally, as a case study, a brief overview of Maastricht University's European Law School will be given as an example of how such a European-oriented law curriculum could be implemented (4).

It is noted from the outset that a European-oriented law curriculum as proposed in this contribution and as implemented at Maastricht University is not without obstacles and is controversial since it remains necessary to train lawyers who are qualified according to national standards which are generally focused on the acquisition of knowledge of national law. Nevertheless, it represents an attempt to meet the challenges that the Europeanisation of law, legal practice, legal scholarship and legal culture raises for legal education.

2. Europeanisation of Law, Legal Practice and Legal Education: The Need for European Law Graduates

European integration and globalisation have a significant impact on the law legal practice, legal scholarship and legal culture. These developments, in particular the Europeanisation of law and legal practice, raise new challenges for legal education.

The harmonisation and unification of law as a result of ever-deepening European integration has led not just to the expansion of EU law but also to the Europeanisation of national law. The influence of European law – in its broadest sense, also including for instance the European Convention on Human Rights – on the constitutional, administrative, private and criminal law of the Member States cannot be denied,[1] and a cursory look at, for instance, the company, competition, public procurement and consumer law of Member States of the European Union further demonstrates the depth of the influence of European law on national legal systems and the gradual development of a supranational European legal system. There are few areas of law these days that are entirely free from European influence. Consequently, the study of law cannot be confined to the study of national law and one or two individual and separate courses on EU law that focus on the institutional aspects and EU substantive law. These developments demand a more integrated approach, which gives attention to the European and international origins of national law as well as the influence of European integration and globalisation processes on national legal systems and the complex interrelationship between the two.

European integration has led to the Europeanisation of legal practice. In particular, as a consequence of secondary legislation concerning the legal profession, legal practitioners can avail themselves of their free movement rights to practice a legal profession in another Member State.[2] EU Member States are required to recognise qualifications obtained by their citizens in another Member State. Furthermore, the Establishment directive for lawyers entitles a lawyer to practice the legal profession under his home title on a permanent basis in another Member State and lays down a procedure whereby the migrant lawyer can integrate into the profession of the host state. It is therefore no longer the case that a law graduate who studied law in one country is limited to practising law in that country. European integration has thus led to the Europeanisation of the labour market for legal practitioners; it has also necessitated it. Through the creation of the internal market, legal problems are becoming all the time more transnational, which demands lawyers who are capable of thinking across jurisdictional boundaries. This

1 See for example, Curtin *et al.* 2006.

2 Council Directive 77/249/EEC *OJ* L 78, 26 June 1977, 17 (Lawyers Services Directive); Council Directive 89/48/EEC *OJ* L 19, 24 January 1989, 16 (Recognition of Diplomas Directive); Directive 98/5/EC *OJ* L77, 14 March 1998, 36 (Lawyers Establishment Directive). See Claessens 2008; Schneider 2002, p. 15-38; and Claessens and Schneider 2011.

has led to the Europeanisation of (commercial) legal practice, which can also be evidenced by the intensified collaboration between law firms in European networks, mergers between law firms in different countries and the establishment of large international law firms.[3] It should be observed that these developments are not limited to the European Union; there is an internationalisation of commercial legal practice.[4]

The constant expansion of EU law has led to the emergence of a new discipline, distinct from national legal scholarship: European legal scholarship, which focuses not just on the law of the European Union, but also on the influence of EU law on national law, the necessity, desirability and feasibility of harmonisation, comparative law, and the divergence and convergence of national legal systems. The development of truly European legal scholarship is particularly strong in the field of private law, nevertheless it is growing fast in other fields as well. Furthermore, as a result of these interconnected developments (Europeanisation of law, scholarship and practice), it is possible to observe a new European legal culture emerging.[5] Since law is embedded in culture, European law must be embedded in an evolving European legal culture. Through the growing body of European law, a common European legal identity, European values and principles, a European legal methodology and mode of legal reasoning will gradually emerge, unavoidably affecting national legal culture.

The Europeanisation of law, legal scholarship, legal practice and legal culture must inevitably have an important impact on legal education.[6] This has two dimensions: the Europeanisation of higher education systems and the Europeanisation of the law curriculum.

With respect to the influence of the EU on higher education, initiatives have been taken at a European level to stimulate and facilitate student mobility. For example, through the Erasmus programme students are able to study a semester abroad, and higher education institutions are encouraged to cooperate through intensive programmes, networks and multilateral programmes.[7] In the 1999 Bologna Declaration, the Ministers of Education from 29 European countries jointly declared that a European Higher Education Area would be created by 2010, 'in order to enhance the employability and mobility of citizens and to increase the international competitiveness of European higher education.'[8] Through the Bologna

3 See e.g. Glenn 2001, p. 982.

4 See for example, Bernabe-Riefkohl 1995, p. 137-162; Von Mehren 2001, p. 1215-1224.; Glenn 2001; Roorda 1993, p. 141.

5 See e.g. Hesselink 2002, Chapter 2, p. 11-71; also see Fauvarque-Cosson 2007, p. 13.

6 Also see e.g. the contributions in De Witte & Forder 1992; and Faure, Smits & Schneider 2002; Akkermans 2009, p. 803-814; Chesterman 2009, p. 879; Storme 2001, p. 135-145; Schlechtriem 2001, p. 531-538. Also see the contribution of Smits 2011.

7 See <http://ec.europa.eu/education/lifelong-learning-programme/doc80_en.htm>.

8 See the Bologna Declaration of 19 June 1999, available at: <http://www.ond.vlaanderen.be/hogeronderwijs/bologna/documents/MDC/BOLOGNA_DECLARATION1.pdf> (last visited on 26 October 2010). Today the Bologna Process involves 47 countries, all parties to the European Cultural Convention 1954 of the Council of Europe. For up-to-date information →

process greater transparency and comparability of educational systems in Europe through, for example, the introduction of a bachelor-master structure throughout Europe, is pursued. The creation of a European Higher Education Area is also directed at promoting the attractiveness and competitiveness of higher education institutions in Europe. Through the creation of new courses and programmes responding to Europeanisation and globalisation, universities are able to compete for foreign students. Consequently, in response to increased mobility of students as well as teaching staff, universities increasingly offer courses with European or comparative elements. Furthermore, it is possible to observe a veritable explosion of LL.M. programmes in European and comparative law aimed at attracting students from around Europe, if not the world, as well the emergence of double degree programmes.[9]

These initiatives reflect steps in the direction of Europeanising higher education systems in response to European integration; but they only represent a small-scale Europeanisation of the law curriculum. The impact of European integration has not yet led to a general overhaul of the law curriculum to integrally adapt it to the Europeanisation of law and legal practice. A European curriculum for legal education does not exist. New developments aimed at responding to the ever-expanding European law are typically embedded in the traditional national law curriculum or follow on from a bachelor programme oriented on national law. These courses necessarily remain embedded in the traditional national law curriculum because law is still primarily viewed as a national product, and legal education is consequently circumscribed by national borders. Not only is the subject-matter of the law curriculum regarded as 'national', the subsequent practice of law is also dependent on the national legislature and/or legal profession. It must be kept in mind that admission to the bar, and therefore access to the legal professions (lawyer, judge, prosecutor and in some countries even legal advisor), remains subject to national regulation. As long as the requirements to enter the profession remain national, the study of law will remain oriented on national law and will consequently remain affected by national borders. This in turn renders the achievement of the Bologna objectives particularly difficult for legal education.[10] Unlike other academic disciplines such as the natural sciences, medicine, economics, psychology, and other social sciences, which are not restricted by national borders in the knowledge required or to be acquired, or the language in which it is studied, law remains embedded in a national legal system, a national legal culture and a national (legal) language.

This national orientation of the law curriculum renders it difficult to respond adequately to the need for a new generation of law graduates who are less dependent on a single legal system. To practice law in this European legal environment, legal practitioners need to be capable of crossing national borders, not only physically but also intellectually. They must be able to adjust to ever-changing

on the Bologna process and the European Higher Education Area, see the official website: <www.ehea.info>.

9 See Klebes-Pelissier 2007, p. 173-180.

10 Also see Bortoluzzi 2010.

(European) law, to understand the European origins of an ever-expanding body of national law, and to communicate effectively with legal practitioners in other jurisdictions. Educating this new generation of law graduates requires reconsideration of the law curriculum and ever more calls for a European-oriented law curriculum.

A glimpse of a European approach to legal education can be caught from the past. National laws were not the central focus of university education until the nineteenth century. The 'reception' of Roman law from the twelfth century led to the development of a common law - *ius commune* - for continental European countries.[11] Received Roman law did not replace local and national customs and laws, rather it was supplementary; it was followed where no local or national rules existed, but it was also used to interpret local and national rules. This *ius commune* formed the basis for legal education and legal scholarship. Students and professors travelled from one country to another in order to study at different universities, basic scholarly works were written in one common language - Latin - and were used throughout the continent and the qualifications obtained by law graduates were recognised in all countries.[12] With the rise of the nation state and the codification of law as a means to unite the nation in the second half of the eighteenth century, law and legal education became nationally oriented and studying abroad became an extravagance.[13] Yet, looking to the future, law will increasingly be based on a new-style *ius commune* comprising principles and rules that are common to EU Member States as a consequence of harmonisation and unification measures.[14] This must inevitably have consequences for legal education, calling for a reorientation.

3. Building Blocks of a European-Oriented Law Curriculum

This evolving European legal environment calls for 'European' law graduates. Since European integration and the globalisation of legal practice requires lawyers to increasingly deal across borders, they must be flexible enough to think across jurisdictional boundaries to become 'interpreters' of legal systems and traditions.[15] They must be comfortable to work with divergent national legal systems or at least be capable of collaborating effectively with their counterparts in other jurisdictions. To be able to communicate effectively with each other, they must be able to understand each other's legal backgrounds, including its traditions, concepts, institutions and style of legal reasoning as well as each other's legal language. This profile of a 'European law graduate' calls for a different type of law curriculum. Rather than focusing on the laws peculiar to an individual national system, it

11 On the history private law see for instance, Van Caenegem 1992.
12 *Ibidem*, p. 76 *et seq.*; De Groot 1992, p. 14-15.
13 See De Groot 1992, p. 15.
14 Also see Fauvarque-Cosson 2007, p. 11.
15 Bernabe-Riefkohl 1995, p. 149, who also writes that these lawyers have the 'responsibility for bridging the gulf of disparate national experiences, traditions, institutions and customs' (p. 153); Von Mehren 2001; Glenn 2001.

requires a European-oriented law curriculum that combines the comparative study of national legal systems with an intensified study of European law in all fields of law. A European-oriented law curriculum trains these European law graduates' to swiftly understand new legal systems, identify the common European or international origins of divergent national laws and solve transnational legal problems. One way to provide such a European-oriented curriculum is to dislodge the study of law from a single national legal system and to study the law on a comparative and European basis.

A core component of a European-oriented law curriculum is the comparative study of law.[16] However, before commencing the actual comparative study of the various fields of law, such as contract, tort, property, constitutional, administrative and criminal law, a foundational course would elaborate on the functions, aims and methodology of comparative law, as well as provide an introduction into the legal systems that form the basis for the comparative study during the curriculum. This gives rise to five further aspects to be discussed: (i) the selection of the relevant legal systems, (ii) the nature and content of the introduction into those legal systems, (iii) the comparative teaching methodology, (iv) the content of the comparative law study, and (v) the relationship between the comparative law study and European law.

The choice of legal systems is a difficult task. With a European-oriented law curriculum, the focus is on the legal systems of the European Union which currently has 27 Member States. It would obviously be unrealistic to base a European-oriented law curriculum on all these legal systems. A restriction of the number of national legal systems to be compared should consequently be made. This is also practical from an educational point of view, since there is little added value in educating students in all European legal systems. A curriculum in which all the legal systems of the Member States of the EU are addressed in all fields of law would be impossible to teach within the standard three-year bachelor degree structure. Furthermore, it is not the aim of a European-oriented curriculum to train law graduates with detailed knowledge of all EU national laws. Instead, the focus is on training law graduates who are capable of adjusting to different legal systems and who can think across national jurisdictional boundaries. Comprehensive knowledge of all national legal systems of the European Union is not necessary to achieve that objective. A selection of legal systems should therefore be made. But which legal systems should be selected as the primary focus of the comparative curriculum? In broad lines, it is generally accepted that the major European legal systems broadly representing the major legal families (the Romanistic, Germanic and Anglo-American common law legal families) must be addressed in comparative law courses, which would suggest at least focusing on French, German and English law as representatives of those legal families in Europe.[17] There may be good arguments to also include a Nordic legal system which is positioned between the

16 On the role of comparative law, also see the contribution of Hage 2010.

17 On legal families, see e.g. Zweigert & Kötz 1998; Glenn 2007; Husa 2006, p. 382-392. Also, Storme 2001.

major legal families,[18] Scots law as a mixed legal system, and possibly a system from central or Eastern Europe. The question is whether such systems should be integrated comprehensively in the curriculum or included where they provide significant insights. Depending on the structure of the programme, the latter approach may be more feasible.

Having selected the legal systems that will form the focus of the comparative study, it is necessary to provide a basic introduction into these legal systems. A foundational course should provide an introduction into the historical background, development and structure of the legal systems being studied, their sources of law and the relationship between them, their legal style including the 'distinctive mode of thinking'[19] reflected in the nature and style of its legislative system and the style and reasoning of the courts,[20] as well as the role given to legal scholarship.[21] Such a course should provide the foundations for the comparative courses to follow and an elementary understanding and explanation of the commonalities and differences in the solutions to be found in those legal systems.

With respect to the comparative law methodology, although there are various approaches to comparative law and the methodological debate is a flourishing one, the method chosen here is to adopt a functional, problem-oriented comparative approach.[22] In contrast to many conventional law curricula, in which comparative law is a course often offered to students as an elective towards the end of a comprehensive education in the own legal system,[23] in the European-oriented law curriculum expounded here, comparative law should be viewed as a teaching method: law is taught comparatively.[24] One way to integrate comparative law in the teaching method is to adopt a functional, problem-oriented approach.

In this functional, problem-oriented approach to teaching law, students are presented with hypothetical scenarios which involve various concrete legal problems. Students are then challenged to discover how the legal problems are dealt with in different legal systems. This focus on concrete problems is well-suited to a European-oriented law curriculum. By studying the legal rules, concepts and institutions in different systems relevant to the legal issues raised by the hypothetical scenario, students can discover that all legal systems are confronted with the task of creating rules to deal with particular problems and protect certain

18 See e.g. Zweigert & Kötz 2001.

19 Zweigert & Kötz 2001, p. 69.

20 For example, Markesinis 2000, p. 294-309, who highlights the differences between the English and German judicial style and technique which is very insightful for understanding the legal systems at hand, but also illustrates where legal systems can learn from each other, suggesting for instance that German legal academics and practitioners could benefit from studying how English judges 'craft' their judgments and how English judges could benefit from looking at German substantive law and its techniques of controlling litigation.

21 Also see e.g. Von Mehren 2001, p. 1219.

22 On comparative law and methodology in general see, for instance, contributions in Reimann & Zimmermann 2006, and Smits 2006. For more on the functional method of comparative law see e.g. Michaels 2006, p. 339-382; Zweigert & Kötz 1998, p. 32-47.

23 See Gordley 2001, p. 1003; Husa 2009, p. 913-926.

24 See also Heringa 2002, p. 8.

interests, but that the choices they make and the solutions they adopt might differ significantly. Since the study of law has been dislodged from a particular legal system, students will not be clouded by preconceptions from their own national legal system which often leads them to believe that the particular solution provided by the 'own' legal system is the only and right solution to a certain problem. By focusing on concrete legal problems it is possible to see how they are dealt with in various legal systems, comparing the concepts, rules and institutions of those legal systems to search for a common core, to uncover and attempt to explain their similarities but also the differences. Progressing through the curriculum, the problems can become ever more complex. This comparative law teaching method should lead to law graduates who are more creative and open-minded since they have learnt to appreciate that there are many approaches to dealing with a particular problem, sometimes leading to different results and sometimes leading to similar results except by following a different path.

Turning to the content of the comparative law study, a European-oriented law curriculum provides comparative courses in the main fields of law, including at least the core areas of private law (contract, tort, property), constitutional and administrative law and criminal law. As the curriculum progresses, the focus of the courses would shift from comparing the national legal systems to a greater emphasis on the European dimension of law in these various areas.

To provide an example: a comparative and European approach to teaching contract law would commence with an introduction to the law of contract from a comparative perspective, analysing how the different national contract laws regulate contractual relations, including the sources and structure of contract law, the concept of a contract, fundamental principles, and how for instance contract formation, validity, content and effects of the contract, (non-) performance and remedies are dealt with. The rules, concepts, principles and institutions and the similarities and differences between the national laws would be analysed. The analysis could then develop to consider whether the similarities reflect a common core of rules and principles that could for instance constitute a basis for harmonisation or unification of the law, or whether the differences are so fundamental that they stand in the way of convergence between the systems, therefore requiring choices to be made should harmonisation or unification be pursued. Further consideration would clearly need to be given to the necessity, desirability and feasibility of harmonisation of contract law. This could be followed by a study of the measures taken in the field of contract law at a European (and international) level and the direct and indirect impact these have on national legal systems. Returning to a comparative approach, it is then possible for instance to compare how the harmonisation measures have been transposed in national legal systems and the effects this has had on the national legal system, since national legal systems often struggle to fit European rules into their national contracts laws without this leading to fragmentation, inconsistencies and disruption of the system. In this way, a European-oriented curriculum aims to integrate the comparative and European dimensions, leading to a greater understanding of the complexity of the inter-relationship between national and European law.

Before being able to address the interplay between European law and national law, it would be necessary to gain an in-depth understanding of EU law, including its foundations, institutions, law-making procedures, competences etc., as well as its substantive law.[25] This focus constitutes nothing new or innovative in legal education, since these days the national-oriented law curriculum in EU Member States addresses these elements of European law to one degree or another. Nevertheless, it forms the fundamental groundwork that is necessary for the remainder of the European-law oriented law curriculum. The innovative aspect of the European dimension of a European-oriented law curriculum is to move beyond the traditional content of courses focusing on European law to look at the interplay between European law and national law. This means looking at the influence and impact of European law on the various fields of (national) law, including a critical evaluation of the desirability, necessity and feasibility of harmonisation, convergence or unification of laws these fields. This goes beyond simply looking at the differences and similarities between legal systems and the instruments that aim to harmonise such national legal systems, but includes also addressing for instance the legal, political, sociological, economic arguments for deciding to adopt measures and the direct and indirect impact of such measures on the various fields of national law. Although such focus in the area of private law has become well-established due to the far-reaching development of scholarship in the area of European private law, in other areas, this focus is new. Nevertheless, in all fields of law these days it is possible to observe a complex inter-relationship between national and European law.

A European-oriented law curriculum would also provide students with a foundation in jurisprudence (legal theory and philosophy) to provide students with a deeper understanding of the nature of law, legal reasoning and methodology. In addition, knowledge of the legal history and development of legal systems in Europe is also important. When comparing legal systems, in particular those on the continent, an understanding of the historical development of those systems and the common legal heritage shared by many countries through the reception of Roman law can be enlightening to explain the similarities and parallel developments. In this way, legal history can complement the comparative study of law and add to the understanding by revealing common foundations, and also show the different routes taken where this common heritage does not exist and the challenges this presents for European integration.[26] At the same time, it is necessary to gain an understanding of the historical, economic and political developments that form the driving force behind European integration process and the development of law in Europe.

It is important to note at this point what a European-oriented law curriculum does not aim to do. It does not aim to create specialists in EU law, nor is the aim to create experts on all the national legal systems studied. After all, this would be

25 See the contribution of Bruno de Witte, "European Union Law: A Common Core or a Fragmented Academic Discipline?" in this book.

26 Also see Schrage & Heutger 2006, p. 393-406; Kötz 1992, p. 31-41; and Gordley 2001.

impossible in a three-year bachelor programme, since each national law curriculum devotes an entire bachelor and master programme to teaching such detail. It is clearly not possible to achieve the same depth of knowledge of the law in a European-oriented law curriculum as a national-oriented law curriculum is able to achieve with respect to the national legal system. In this way, the focus of a European-oriented law curriculum is different from the 'ordinary' law curriculum since the primary aim is not to teach comprehensively details of the national, positivistic law.[27] The relativity of knowledge of positive law is becoming increasingly apparent with changes in law occurring at an every-increasing pace. This different focus of a European-oriented law curriculum is related to the different profile of a 'European law graduate', who should be adept to deal with law that is undergoing constant transformation as a result *inter alia* of European integration and globalisation.

4. Case Study: The European Law School

In advance of general trends in Europe today, Maastricht University launched the concept of a European Law School already in 1991.[28] In contrast to the national orientation of the traditional law curriculum, the European Law School aims to bring together students from various European countries with a view to teaching them an innovative curriculum with a European and comparative law focus. At the time, a fully-fledged European-oriented law curriculum was considered to be still too ambitious, since European law was not yet sufficiently developed to form the foundation of a law curriculum. Nevertheless, a first step in the direction of such a European-oriented law curriculum was taken by introducing a post-graduate LL.M. programme in 1992, the *Magister Iuris Communis* (Master of European and Comparative Law). With the knowledge and experience gained from this LL.M. programme, it proved possible to set up the European Law School, which welcomed its first cohort of students in 1995.

The European Law School combines traditional legal education in the national law of the Netherlands with courses that approach the study of law from a comparative and European perspective, looking for a common core and the developing European law. At that time, it was still thought that it would be 'unworkable and unwise' to introduce a truly European-oriented law curriculum, as

27 Also see De Witte & Forder 1992, p. viii-ix, who write that such a curriculum aims to foster the necessary 'dexterity of thinking across jurisdictional boundaries', albeit 'to the detriment of encyclopaedic knowledge of one single legal system'.

28 The Faculty of Law of the then Rijksuniversiteit Limburg, now Maastricht University, organised a conference on the occasion of its tenth anniversary on 'Legal Education in the Future' with the purpose of exploring the possibility of developing a wholly new curriculum in legal studies based on European and comparative law, the results of the conference can be found in De Witte & Forder 1992. Also see the contribution of Aalt Willem Heringa, 'Towards a Truly European Legal Education: An Agenda for the future', to this book.

the state of European law had still not ripened or developed enough to form the basis for such a curriculum.[29]

By 2006, however, the richness of European law in its broadest sense could no longer be denied, leading to the introduction of an English language track in the European Law School. This entirely English-taught programme is detached from any one national legal system and provides a truly European-oriented law curriculum, teaching law entirely from a comparative and European perspective. Consequently, within the European Law School, there are now two tracks: the regular track that combines traditional legal education in the national legal system of the Netherlands with courses adopting a comparative and European perspective (ELS-regular), and an innovative, fully-fledged comparative and European law curriculum (ELS-ELT).

This development of first creating an LL.M. programme in comparative and European law, followed by the establishment of the European Law School which combines national legal education with comparative and European courses before creating a fully-fledged European-oriented law curriculum was necessary. It was necessitated by the pace of development of the law, since at the time the concept of a European-oriented law curriculum was launched, the state of the law in Europe was not quite ripe enough for such a curriculum.

Further factors necessitating such a phased introduction of a European-oriented law curriculum relate to the need to develop expertise in all areas of the curriculum. This has two important dimensions. In the first place, it is important to ensure that faculty staff are specialised to teach this new curriculum in the sense that they have conducted comparative law research in their fields into the national legal systems to be studied, the developments of European law, and the interaction between national and European law. It is evident that the interaction between the Europeanisation of legal scholarship and the Europeanisation of legal education is essential in this context. In the second place, it is necessary to develop appropriate teaching materials which have a European and comparative law focus. Although the past decades have been marked by a Europeanisation of legal scholarship, which has led to a vast array of eminent comparative law treatises, monographs, encyclopaedias, and academic journals devoted to European and comparative law only a few of these publications can be used for teaching purposes. Much of what is written is not directed at the undergraduate student population, but is written by scholars for postgraduate students and academics. For this reason, it has become necessary to develop new teaching material that provides general comparative introductions into the various fields of law. However, developing these new textbooks is not without challenges of its own, as they need to find a common language, common legal foundations and principles in which to discuss the law.

That the development of European law can form the basis for an entire curriculum can be seen from the programme's curriculum. The overall aim of the programme is to provide a balanced programme that teaches students law from a comparative and European perspective.

29 Heringa 2002, p. 5.

The curriculum commences with a foundational course which focuses on teaching fundamental concepts and principles underlying various legal systems to allow students to understand what law is, how different societies establish law, what the law should include and why, as well as teaching them the language of the law - its legal terms of art - in various legal fields. This is followed by courses on in two core fields of law: contract law and constitutional law. These courses adopt a functional, problem-oriented comparative methodology which is reinforced by the general teaching method at Maastricht University, which can be characterised as being problem-based, small-scale and skills oriented.[30] These courses introduce students to the basic features, concepts, principles and rules in the fields of constitutional and contract law. The overarching concepts of constitutional law learnt from a comparative perspective will also provide a foundation for the subsequent study of the basic features of the European Union. In their first year, students are given a foundational course addressing the core issues of international law and EU law, including its nature, sources, and institutions as well as extra-legal elements including the history of international law, European integration and political science.

Students are also introduced to the historical, economic and political background necessary to understand the legal systems they are studying, the European integration process and the development of law in Europe. They take a course on legal history, which introduces them to European legal history, from Roman Antiquity to the present days, facilitating the understanding of the differences and similarities between legal systems.[31] Following on from the historical perspective, students are given a political, economic and theoretical view of the process of European integration and the development of the European Union, offering the necessary knowledge for a good understanding of the law of the European Union and the development and convergence of law in Europe at present.

The second and third years of the programme are characterised by their continuation of the comparative study of law in core fields and an in-depth focus on European law. The knowledge of private law is expanded with the study of comparative property and tort law,[32] company law,[33] as well as with civil procedure.[34] Students are also grounded in the history and general principles of private international law, its general structure, sources and topics. The second year also contains three courses focusing on different the comparative study of aspects of criminal law, criminal procedure and criminal justice.

Following on from the foundational course on international and European law, the second year provides in-depth knowledge of the European Union and EU law. Courses are devoted to a thorough study of institutional EU law and the

30 It should be observed that Maastricht University is unique in that the educational model of problem-based learning (PBL) has been at the core of teaching at Maastricht University since it was founded.

31 On teaching legal history, see the contribution of Van Rhee & Van der Meer in this book.

32 On teaching European private law, see the contribution of Akkermans 2011.

33 On company law, see the contribution of Olaerts 2011.

34 On teaching European civil procedure, see the contribution of Verkerk & Van Rhee 2011.

internal market, in particular the free movement of persons, goods and services, as well as the basic rules of free and fair competition which are necessary to ensure its smooth operation. These two courses form a central core in the European Law School curriculum. What is discussed and learnt in these courses provides the basis for subsequent courses that look at the influence of European law on particular fields of law.

It should be noted that up until this point in the curriculum, most courses in particular fields of law (contract, tort, property, constitutional, criminal law etc) have been approached from a comparative perspective. Only later in the curriculum does the focus shift towards the developments at a European level and the interplay between European law and national law. For instance, students are first introduced to the law of contract from a comparative perspective. Only after they have acquired in-depth knowledge of EU law do they follow a course which addresses the growing influence of EU law on national contract law. It addresses the harmonisation debate, looking at what form a future European contract law should take; the difficult interrelationship between European law and national law; the influence of EU law on particular areas of national (consumer) contract law, such as contract formation, standard terms, withdrawal, sale of goods, financial services, etc.[35]

This pattern of comparative law followed by the focus on the European influence on national law can be seen throughout the curriculum. This shift to addressing the European influence also can be seen, for instance, in the fields of criminal law and administrative law. Whereas students first study these fields of law from a comparative perspective, they subsequently approach them from a European perspective. In the context of criminal law, following a comparative study of substantive and procedural criminal law, students follow a course addressing the cooperation between EU Member States in criminal matters, through the establishment of the European Criminal Justice Are and the emergence of common European institutions in the field of criminal law: Europol, Eurojust, Euronetwork, and the European Public Prosecutor. Similarly, following the comparative study of administrative law, students can follow a course on European administrative law, which addresses *inter alia* the development of principles of administrative law at a European level, as well as the influence of European law on national administrative law.[36]

An important component throughout the first two years of the curriculum is the skills training programme which focuses on teaching students the skills law students and graduates need, for instance, analysing and applying legislative provisions, case law, conducting legal research and legal writing skills. The skills training aims to integrate the European-oriented character of the ELS-ELT. Legal skills are taught in a European and comparative way by showing students, for instance, the difference between civil law and common law legislative provisions, the differences in style of judicial decisions in different legal systems, the differences

35 On teaching European contract law and private law in general, see Akkermans 2011.

36 On teaching European public law, see the contribution of Kiiver & Eliantonio 2011.

in the hierarchy of sources in various legal systems. One module within the skills training focuses in particular on the nature of the common law systems and aims to teach students for instance how to analyse common law judgments and work with the doctrine of precedent. Students are also confronted with legal translation exercises to demonstrate to them the difficulty of translating concepts from one legal system to another. Wherever possible, the skills training modules are linked to the substantive courses being followed at the time. For example, whilst following courses on comparative contract law and comparative constitutional law, the examples used in the skills training to teach students the skills needed, for example, to analyse for legislative provisions will be taken from the contract laws and constitutions being studied at that time. This reinforces and facilitates the acquisition of substantive knowledge being studied at that time. The second and third years include a continuation of the skills training with two main components: legal writing and moot court training. Although legal research and writing are an integral part almost all courses in the ELS-ELT programme, the legal writing course in the second year in particular focuses on improving students' technical writing skills and research techniques which prepares them for writing a final essay in the third year. The second year concludes with a moot court training which aims to develop students' written and oral pleading skills.

Following the second year, the basic, mandatory programme of the ELS-ELT is completed, and students are given various options. The basic idea behind the third year is specialisation. ELS-ELT students have vastly divergent ambitions, interests, and future career perspectives. Not all students aim to enter into the legal profession. In the third year, students can opt to continue studying law from a comparative and European perspective, follow a minor in Dutch law which gives them the opportunity to obtain civil effect to allow them to enter the legal profession in the Netherlands, study abroad, do an internship, participate in moot court competitions, or follow a minor at a non-law faculty (e.g. business and economics, political sciences).

Particular attention should be given to the minor in Dutch law. The European Law School aims to graduate students who can also work in the legal environment of larger companies and specifically the larger law firms as well as the government ministries. Nevertheless, national law sets up a significant barrier to achieving the goal of educating truly 'European' law graduates since to be admitted to the bar, a law graduate must meet the national requirements for admission. In the Netherlands, this means that to practice law in the Netherlands, a law graduate must be admitted to the Dutch bar which necessitates educating students in Dutch law. In essence, this means that students must study the private law, constitutional law, administrative law and criminal law of the Netherlands, as well as Dutch civil and criminal procedural law. For students in the ELS-regular track, these civil effect requirements are not problematic; the mandatory courses in the first two and a half years of their bachelor programme ensure that provided the student completes a master's degree in law, resulting in civil effect. To facilitate access to the legal profession for ELS-ELT students, a minor in Dutch law was developed. In the third year of the bachelor programme, those students who choose to obtain civil effect follow a mandatory programme comprising the essential courses on Dutch law in the Dutch language. In the second half of the second year, they are prepared for studying Dutch law in Dutch by means of three introductory courses on Dutch private law, Dutch administrative law and Dutch criminal law and criminal procedure. Students who follow this Dutch law minor obtain civil effect once they have completed a master in law. This need to create a Dutch law minor to give students access to the legal profession demonstrates that in the absence of a European system of legal education and European standards of access to the legal profession, the need to educate law graduates in national law to give them access to the European labour market for legal services remains.

5. Conclusion

Legal education in Europe has not remained unaffected by the Europeanisation of law and legal practice, this is apparent from the inclusion of courses on EU law and comparative law in many law curricula and the sudden increase of master programmes in European and comparative law. However, these developments are often piecemeal and are typically embedded in the traditional national law curriculum or follow on from a bachelor programme oriented on national law. They only represent a small-scale Europeanisation of legal education. In addition to specialists in national law, it is also necessary to educate 'European' law graduates who are comfortable with different jurisdictions, who are flexible enough to adapt to and find their way around different legal systems, who can identify the European or international origins of laws, and identify legal issues and provide solutions to transnational legal problems. This calls for innovative programmes in which the law curriculum is overhauled and integrally adapted to the Europeanisation of law and legal practice. This calls for a reorientation of the law curriculum. These developments call for a European-oriented law curriculum in which the law is taught from a comparative and European perspective. Such a European-oriented law curriculum aims to provide students with an understanding of the historical background, development, structure and legal style of the major national legal systems, to identify the common principles and concepts underlying national legal systems as well as the fundamental differences between them. In searching for the reasons for similarity or difference, a European-oriented law curriculum will confront students with the common legal heritage shared by many countries as well as the European origins of much of today's national law. It will look both at the top-down, supranational influence coming from the European Union and its impact on the legal systems of the Member States, as well as the convergence of legal systems from the bottom-up. That legal education in Europe cannot remain unaffected by the Europeanisation of law and legal practice is apparent, however, progress to integrally adapt the law curriculum to the Europeanisation of law and legal practice is lagging behind. There are many ways in which the Europeanisation of legal education can be achieved; this contribution has aimed to identify some of the building blocks of a European-oriented law curriculum and to illustrate how it can be implemented by looking at Maastricht University's European Law School – English Language Track.

Bibliography

Akkermans 2009
Akkermans, B., 'Challenges in Legal Education and the Development of a New European Private Law', *German Law Journal*, 2009, Vol. 10, p. 803-814.

Akkermans 2011
Akkermans, B., 'The Development of European Private Law and its Challenges on the Law School Curriculum', in Heringa, A.W. & Akkermans, B. (eds.), *Educating European Lawyers*, Antwerp: Intersentia, 2011, p. 159-178.

Bernabe-Riefkohl 1995
Bernabe-Riefkohl, A., 'Tomorrow's Law Schools: Globalization and Legal Education', *San Diego Law Review*, 1995, Vol. 32, p. 137-162.

Bortoluzzi 2010
Bortoluzzi, C., 'A New European Model of Legal Education as One of the Institutional Elements of the New European Common Law', *Global Jurist*, 2010, Vol. 10, available at: <http://www.bepress.com/gj/vol10/iss1/art3> (last visited on 26 October 2010).

Chesterman 2009
Chesterman, S., 'The Evolution of Legal Education: Internationalization, Transnationalization, Globalization', *German Law Journal*, 2009, Vol. 10, p. 877-888.

Claessens 2008
Claessens, S., *Free Movement of Lawyers in the European Union*, Nijmegen: Wolf Publishers, 2008.

Claessens & Schneider 2011
Claessens, S. & Schneider, H., 'Legal Education and Free Movement of Lawyers in the European Union', in Heringa, A.W. & Akkermans, B. (eds.), *Educating European Lawyers*, Antwerp: Intersentia, 2011, p. 121-156.

Curtin *et al.* 2006
Curtin, D.M. *et al.* (eds.), *European Integration and Law*, Antwerp: Intersentia, 2006.

De Groot 1992
De Groot, G.-R., 'European Education in the 21st Century', in De Witte, B. & Forder, C. (eds.), *The Common Law of Europe and the Future of Legal Education*, Deventer: Kluwer, 1992, p. 7-29.

De Witte 2011
De Witte, B., 'European Union Law: A Common Core or a Fragmented Academic Discipline?', in Heringa, A.W. & Akkermans, B. (eds.), *Educating European Lawyers*, Antwerp: Intersentia, 2011, p. 19-41.

De Witte & Forder 1992
De Witte, B. & Forder, C. (eds.), *The Common Law of Europe and the Future of Legal Education*, Deventer, Kluwer, 1992.

Faure, Smits & Schneider 2002
Faure, M., Smits, J. & Schneider, H. (eds.), *Towards a European Ius Commune in Legal Education and Research*, Antwerp: Intersentia, 2002.

Fauvarque-Cosson 2007
Fauvarque-Cosson, B., *The Rise of Comparative Law: A Challenge for Legal Education in Europe*, Walter Van Gerven Lectures, Groningen: Europa Law Publishing, 2007.

Glenn 2001
Glenn, H.P., 'Comparative Law and Legal Practice: On Removing the Borders', *Tulane Law Review*, 2001, Vol. 75, p. 977-1002.

Glenn 2007
Glenn, H.P., *Legal Traditions of the World*, Oxford: Oxford University Press, 3rd ed., 2007.

Gordley 2001
Gordley, J., 'Comparative Law and Legal Education', *Tulane Law Review*, 2001, Vol. 75, p. 1003-1014.

Hage 2011
Hage, J., 'Comparative Law and Legal Science', in Heringa, A.W. & Akkermans, B. (eds.), *Educating European Lawyers*, Antwerp: Intersentia, 2011, p. 65-77.

Heringa 2002
Heringa, A.W., 'Towards a European Law School! A Proposal for a Competitive, Diversified Model of Transnational Co-Operation', in Faure, M., Smits, J. & Schneider, H. (eds.), *Towards a European Ius Commune in Legal Education and Legal Research*, Antwerp: Intersentia, 2002, p. 3-13.

Heringa 2011
Heringa, A.W., 'Towards a Truly European Legal Education: An Agenda for the Future', in Heringa, A.W. & Akkermans, B. (eds.), *Educating European Lawyers*, Antwerp: Intersentia, 2011, p. 3-18.

Hesselink 2002
Hesselink, M.W., 'The New European Legal Culture', in *The New European Private Law. Essays on the Future of Private Law in Europe*, Deventer: Kluwer Law International, 2002, p. 11-71.

Husa 2006
Husa, J., 'Legal Families', in Smits, J. (ed.), *Elgar Encyclopedia of Comparative Law*, Cheltenham: Edward Elgar Publishing, 2006, p. 382-392.

Husa 2009
Husa, J., 'Turning the Curriculum Upside Down: Comparative Law as an Educational Tool for Constructing the Pluralistic Legal Mind', *German Law Journal*, 2009, Vol. 10, p. 913-926.

Kiiver & Eliantonio 2011
Kiiver, Ph. & Eliantonio, M., 'Teaching European and Comparative Constitutional Law', in Heringa, A.W. & Akkermans, B. (eds.), *Educating European Lawyers*, Antwerp: Intersentia, 2011, p. 209-217.

Klebes-Pelissier 2007
Klebes-Pelissier, A., 'Double degrees in the context of the Bologna process', *European Journal of Legal Education*, 2007, Vol. 4, p. 173-180.

Kötz 1992
Kötz, H., 'A Common Private Law for Europe: Perspectives for The Reform of European Legal Education', in De Witte, B. & Forder, C. (eds.), *The Common Law of Europe and the Future of Legal Education*, Deventer: Kluwer Law and Taxation Publishers, 1992, p. 31-41.

Lando 2001
Lando, O., 'Nordic Countries, a Legal Family? A Diagnosis and a Prognosis', *Global Jurist Advances*, 2001, Vol. 1, available at: <http://www.bepress.com/gj/advances/vol1/iss2/art5> (last visited on 26 October 2010).

Markesinis 2000
Markesinis, B.S., 'Judicial Style and Judicial Reasoning in England and Germany', *Cambridge Law Journal*, 2000, Vol. 59, p. 294-309.

Michaels 2006
Michaels, R., 'The Functional Method of Comparative Law', in Reimann, M. & Zimmermann, R. (eds.), *The Oxford Handbook of Comparative Law*, Oxford: Oxford University Press, 2006, p. 339-382.

Olaerts 2011
Olaerts, M., 'Teaching European and Comparative Company Law', in Heringa, A.W. & Akkermans, B. (eds.), *Educating European Lawyers*, Antwerp: Intersentia, 2011, p. 179-193.

Reimann & Zimmermann 2006
Reimann, M. & Zimmermann, R. (eds.), *The Oxford Handbook on Comparative Law*, Oxford: Oxford University Press, 2006.

Roorda 1993
Roorda, P., 'The Internationalization of the Practice of Law', *Wake Forest Law Review*, 1993, Vol. 28, p. 141-160.

Schlechtriem 2001
Schlechtriem, P., 'The Growing Importance of European Law and How It Affects Teaching and Research in the Field of the Private Law of Obligations (Torts, Contracts and Restitution)', *Texas International Law Journal*, 2001, Vol. 36, p. 531-538.

Schneider 2002
Schneider, H., 'The Free Movement of Lawyers in Europe, and Its Consequences for the Legal Profession and the Legal Education in the Member States', in Faure, M., Smits, J. & Schneider, H. (eds.), *Towards a European Ius Commune in Legal Education and Research*, Antwerp: Intersentia, 2002, p. 15-38.

Schrage & Heutger 2006
Schrage, E. & Heutger, V., 'Legal History and Comparative Law', in Smits, J. (ed.) *Elgar Encyclopedia of Comparative Law*, Cheltenham: Edward Elgar Publishing, 2006, p. 393-406.

Smits 2006
Smits, J. (ed.), *Elgar Encyclopedia of Comparative Law*, Cheltenham: Edward Elgar Publishing, 2006.

Smits 2011
Smits, J., 'European Legal Education, or: How to Prepare Students for Global Citizenship?', in Heringa, A.W. & Akkermans, B. (eds.), *Educating European Lawyers*, Antwerp: Intersentia, 2011, p. 43-64.

Storme 2001
Storme, M., 'The Consequences of European Unification for Legal Education in the Member States', *European Review*, 2001, Vol. 9, p. 135-145.

Van Caenegem 1992
Van Caenegem, R.C., *An Historical Introduction to Private Law*, trans. D.E.L. Johnston, Cambridge: Cambridge University Press, 1992.

Van Rhee & Van der Meer 2011
Van Rhee, C.H. & Van der Meer, T., 'Teaching European Legal History', in Heringa, A.W. & Akkermans, B. (eds.), *Educating European Lawyers*, Antwerp: Intersentia, 2011, p. 247-260.

Verkerk & Van Rhee 2011
Verkerk, R.R. & Van Rhee, C.H., 'Teaching Comparative Civil Procedure', in Heringa, A.W. & Akkermans, B. (eds.), *Educating European Lawyers*, Antwerp: Intersentia, 2011, p. 195-208.

Von Mehren 2001
Von Mehren, A.T., 'The Rise of Transnational Legal Practice and the Task of Comparative Law', *Tulane Law Review*, 2001, Vol. 75, p. 1215-1224.

Zweigert & Kötz 1998
Zweigert, K. & Kötz, H., *An Introduction to Comparative Law*, Oxford: Clarendon Press, 3rd ed., 1998.

Sjoerd Claessens
Hildegard
Schneider

LEGAL EDUCATION AND FREE MOVEMENT OF LAWYERS IN THE EUROPEAN UNION

1. Introduction

Ever since the deadline for implementation of the lawyers' Establishment Directive passed on 14 March 2000,[1] it is safe to say that within the territory of the European Union there is a true free movement of lawyers.[2] After the implementation of that Directive it is now possible for every professionally fully qualified lawyer in the European Union to move to another Member State and exercise the relevant legal profession in that state, albeit for the first three years under his home country professional title.[3] In earlier secondary legislation it was already established that lawyers could provide cross-border services[4] and that lawyers could integrate fully in the legal profession of another Member State by having their professional qualifications recognized, which in many cases involves compensatory measures such as taking an aptitude test.[5]

This development with regard to the free movement of lawyers in Europe might lead to the idea that the legal profession is truly Europeanized, or in other words: that the traditional 'national' lawyer is replaced, or at least supplemented,

1 Directive 98/5/EC of the European Parliament and the Council of 16 February 1998 to facilitate the practice of the profession of lawyer on a permanent basis in a Member State other than that in which the qualification was obtained. [1998] *OJ* L 77/36, amended by Directive 2006/100/EC, *OJ* L 363.

2 See further: Claessens 2008. More recently Lubina & Schneider 2011.

3 This period can be shortened by applying the system of the Diploma Recognition Directive 2005/36/EC that in almost all cases will lead to an aptitude test, the successful passing of which leads to the right to practice under the professional title of the host Member State.

4 Directive 77/249/EEC of 20 March 1977, [1977] *OJ* L 78, lastly amended by Directive 2006/100/EC, *OJ* L 363.

5 Directive 89/48/EEC, [1989] *OJ* L 19/16 nowadays incorporated in Directive 2005/36/EC, [2005] *OJ* L 255/22, lastly amended by Directive 2006/100/EC, *OJ* L 363. See further to the implementation of Directive 89/48/EEC for lawyers, Schneider 1995.

by a species of 'European' lawyers.[6] That idea is also corroborated by the fact that the ministers of education of a large number of European states (including the Member States of the European Union) have created over the past 12 years and recently declared the European Area for Higher Education, better known as the 'Bologna Process'.[7] This process, that among other things created the bachelor master system and that heavily relies on the 1997 Lisbon Recognition Convention in laying down intentions for the academic recognition of diplomas, strengthened the impression that we now live in a European Union where both academic and professional qualifications are interchangeable, and any citizen of the European Union can exercise any profession for which he is qualified in any Member State of the European Union. But is that really the case?

In this chapter we shall show that at least for lawyers, or more importantly, those that aspire to become lawyers in the future, life is not that simple. In the following we shall closely examine the problems that prospective lawyers encounter when they seek to qualify as a lawyer in more then one Member State, or follow at least part of the qualification track in another Member State. Possible solutions to these problems and consequences for the legal education shall be discussed.

2. Identifying the Problem

In the introduction of this chapter it was mentioned that there was a 'true' free movement after the implementation of the Establishment Directive back in 2000. With that statement in mind the question might be posed why this image of 'European' lawyers is a mirage and why it is still difficult for prospective lawyers to choose to train in another Member State than their own.

The short answer to this question is that the system of free movement of lawyers as it was created over the past four decades is not concerned with the qualification track that must be followed in order to become a lawyer in any of the Member States' jurisdictions. Two out of the three pieces of secondary legislation that ensure the free movement of lawyers, the Services Directive and the Establishment Directive work in such a manner that only specific persons fall within the scope *ratione personae* of the Directives. In the Articles 1 of both Directives 77/249/EEC and 98/5/EC a list of professional titles is included[8] that defines the

6 This is corroborated by the fact that many implementation mechanisms for Directive 98/5/EC create a 'European Lawyer' for example the United Kingdom and Germany.

7 See further Claessens 2008. More recently to the Bologna process see Garben 2011; Garben & Schneider 2011. Concerning the impact of the Bologna Process for lawyers see Terry 2006, 2007 and 2008.

8 In the latest consolidated versions of the Directives that include the changes made by the expansion of the European Union in 2004 and 2007 the table in both Directives reads as follows:
- Belgium: Avocat/Advocaat/Rechtsanwalt
- Bulgaria: Адвокат
- Czech Republic: Advokát
- Denmark: Advokat
- Germany: Rechtsanwalt

→

scope *ratione personae* of the Directives, i.e. any EU national that is allowed to carry one of the titles mentioned in the tables can benefit from the rules laid down in the Directives. When, and under what circumstances an EU national is allowed to carry such a professional title is not regulated by the Directives, and is, at least in principle, a matter of the national authorities that convene the rights to carry such a title. Or, in other words, the Directives are not concerned with the question how one can obtain one of the professional titles mentioned in those Directives. Moreover, the table of professional titles also shows that this notion of a 'European lawyer' is not a legal reality. There is no separate category of 'European lawyers', any lawyer seeking to embark on European adventures must still be firmly rooted in one of the national professions in order to be able to carry one of the titles mentioned in the two Directives. The designation 'European lawyer' can at best be used for lawyers that are active in a Member State by virtue of these Directives in order to distinguish them from the lawyers that were purely domestically trained and qualified and never crossed borders. But next to being classed as 'European lawyers', these mobile lawyers are fully qualified national lawyers in at least one Member State of the European Union.

As stated above, the two Directives that are specifically addressed to lawyers are not concerned by the method how one becomes a lawyer. That was, and still is a matter of the Member States themselves. In all Member States the profession of lawyer is a so-called regulated profession[9] implying that all Member States have

- Estonia: Vandeadvokaat
- Greece: Δικηγόρος
- Spain: Abogado/Advocat/Avogado/Abokatu
- France: Avocat
- Ireland: Barrister/Solicitor
- Italy: Avvocato
- Cyprus: Δικηγόρος
- Latvia Zvērināts advokāts
- Lithuania: Advokatas
- Luxembourg: Avocat
- Hungary: Ügyvéd
- Malta: Avukat/Prokuratur Legali
- Netherlands: Advocaat
- Austria: Rechtsanwalt
- Poland: Adwokat/Radca prawny
- Portugal: Advogado
- Romania: Avocat
- Slovenia: Odvetnik/Odvetnica
- Slovakia: Advokát/Komerčný právnik
- Finland: Asianajaja/Advokat
- Sweden: Advokat
- United Kingdom: Advocate/Barrister/Solicitor

9 Using the definition of a regulated profession as used in Art. 3(1a) of Directive 2005/36/EC: 'a professional activity of group of professional activities, access to which, the pursuit of which, or one of the modes of pursuit of which, is subject, directly or indirectly, by virtue of legislative, regulatory or administrative provisions to the possession of specific professional qualifications; in particular, the use of a professional title limited by legislative, regulatory or →

laid down specific rules, i.e. qualifications tracks, that govern the access to and the exercise of the profession of lawyers in their territory. These rules are basically untouched by European law, which means that Member States were, and to a certain extent still are, fully free to determine the criteria that have to be fulfilled by a prospective lawyer. It would go far beyond the scope of this chapter to give a detailed overview of all the different criteria in place in the different Member States[10] but there are a number of general remarks that can be made. A number of phases in the qualification process can be distinguished. Firstly, nearly all Member States require prospective candidates to have a law degree. The only exception is the United Kingdom where any academic degree will suffice to start a qualification track, albeit a longer one, for the legal profession. The second element that almost all the qualification tracks for lawyers have in common is that they will also have to complete a professional education that is concluded in some way with an exam, normally called a Bar exam. Only in Spain the passing of a Bar exam after a professional training period was not necessary until very recently.[11] The extent of the Bar training and the Bar exam is different in the various Member States and so is its mode of application in the sense that some Member States apply a system where a candidate needs to pass an extensive exam at the end of the professional training while others, like the Netherlands, apply a system where prospective lawyers pass modules, and thereby 'collect' their Bar exam throughout their professional education. Only after these two elements - university education and professional training - are fulfilled a candidate qualifies for the legal profession and is allowed to carry one of the professional titles indicated above, and become a 'subject' of the European directives that specifically apply to lawyers.

This two-fold division of the qualification track also provides for two distinct entry points for Union nationals who seek to enter into the qualification process (and therewith seek to enter the legal profession) of another Member State. The first point of entry is after a candidate has finished his secondary education and seeks to follow a university education. In this case, a prospective candidate can move to another Member State and start his or her university education in that State in order to obtain a law degree. Students that are Union nationals have a (conditional) right to free movement on the basis of Directive 2004/38/EC.[12] They are therefore entitled to enter and reside in other Member States in order to follow their studies there. In addition, students will need to have their secondary education qualifications recognised. There are no European Union rules on the recognition of secondary education qualifications for the benefit of access to university education,

administrative provisions to holders of a given professional qualification shall constitute a mode of pursuit'.

10 For a detailed overview of at least the pre-2004 Member States see Claessens 2008.

11 Case C-119/09 *Robert Koller* v. *Rechtsanwaltsprüfungskommission beim Oberlandesgericht Graz* – Reference for a preliminary ruling from the *Oberste Berufungs- und Disziplinarkommission* (Austria) lodged on 1 April 2009, nyr.

12 Directive 2004/38/EC of the European Parliament and the Council of 9 April 2004 on the right of citizens of the Union and their family members to move and reside freely within the territory of the Member States. [2004] *OJ* L 158/77. See for students specifically Art. 7(1c) Directive 2004/38/EC. See also the decision of the Court in the case C-73/08 *Bressol* nyr.

so from a European Union point of view this competence remains primarily with the Member States.[13] The Member States, at least most of them, have committed themselves, already at a very early stage, to facilitate entry of their nationals into each others universities. In 1953 a Council of Europe Convention was concluded, which stated in a very concise manner that members shall recognise the equivalence of qualifications that give access to university education.[14] This has come to be known as the Paris Equivalence Convention, and has now been largely replaced by the Lisbon Recognition Convention (discussed below) but the latter has not been ratified by all Member States yet. As a result, the Paris Equivalence Convention is still relevant for those Member States who have not ratified the Lisbon Recognition Convention (also in relation to States that have ratified the Lisbon Recognition Convention themselves). Recognition on the basis of the Paris Equivalence Convention is unconditional and does not provide for exceptions on differences in content. The only negative side to entrance at this point is the fact that prospective candidates are still very young and it is not as evident that many candidates who are on the verge of adulthood, are ready to take such a decision, to move away to another Member State in order to start a legal career there. One can recently, however, notice an increasing willingness of students to study from there very beginning abroad.

How the assessment of equivalence takes place is up to the Member States, and it falls outside the scope of this chapter to review all the mechanisms in place. It suffices to state at this point that the Dutch agency *Nuffic* has gained a reputation in Europe for, among other things, the assessment of equivalence of secondary education qualifications. On its website is has a database that contains a wealth of information on this subject.[15]

The second point of entry for prospective lawyers is after the completion of university education. Candidates may ask for entry into the qualification track based upon the university education they enjoyed in their home Member State. Once again, for this eventuality, there is no European Union legislation that directly covers the situation of (prospective) lawyers in this respect. Generally, as was indicated above, competent authorities require a law degree from a domestic university. Sometimes requirements are even laid down by law, as is the case in Germany and the Netherlands. Access at this level is difficult because the national law degrees concentrate primarily on national law. So while substantial differences existing at secondary school level do not cause great concern, (i.e. explaining the more or less automatic recognition under the Paris Equivalence Convention), it becomes more difficult to disregard these differences for prospective lawyers after

13 See to the issue of EU competences in the area of education Garben & Schneider 2011, p. 410 *et seq.*

14 European Convention on the Equivalence of Diplomas leading to Admission to Universities, Paris 11 December 1953, CETS 015. The same subject matter is also covered by the Lisbon Recognition Convention (CETS 165) which will be addressed below, but which is not ratified by all Member States yet.

15 <www.nuffic.net/diplomawaardering/extranet/kenmerken.html>, last accessed 28 April 2011.

their university studies. It is for this reason that the Lisbon Recognition Convention also takes into account the possibility that there may be substantial differences between the university degrees in cases where recognition is requested.

Although there are recognition mechanisms in place in these two 'stages' they are not necessarily suited for persons who seek to become legal professionals in another Member State than where they have completed one of these stages. In practice it is relatively easy, language problems aside, for students to move to another Member State and study law there. It is the content of these studies that form the problem. Traditionally, academic education for lawyers if founded in the national legal system of the Member State where the university concerned is established. As a rule, such a curriculum is not helpful when such a student wants to move back to his or her Member State of origin in order to become a member of the legal profession there even if the national legal systems of the EU Member States are nowadays to a large extent based on EU legislation. Traditionally, there are exceptions like the uncomplicated mobility between Ireland and England due to the familiarity of the legal systems. Next to these problems that originate in the *content* of legal education in the different Member States (i.e. the focus on national law), there are also *legal* barriers that these students will have to conquer. Because of the fact that the relevant European directives only come into play when lawyers are already completely qualified, the stages of qualifications are governed primarily by national law. This leads to a phenomenon where Member States impose criteria for entering the second (professional) phase for qualifying as a lawyer. Generally Member States do not just require *a* law degree, but *the* law degree of that specific Member State, i.e. Member States require a domestic law degree (or an equivalent degree[16]) in order to enter a domestic professional legal qualification track. In some Member States, like the Netherlands, the law even lays down minimum requirements with regard to content of the curricula that give access to a qualification track for the legal profession. In the Netherlands this phenomenon is called *civiel effect* (civil effect). This civil effect or similar requirements exemplifies a real problem that law students have when they seek to qualify as a lawyer in another Member State, effectively barring either their qualification in that other Member State or effectively barring the possibility to study in another Member State and using the results of these studies when returning to the home country effectively.

It will be the purpose of the remainder of this chapter to explore possibilities to counter these problems.

3. Application of European Law?

One way to solve the problem identified in the previous paragraph might be to bring the problem as such under the scope of European Law. Recognition of the university qualifications at stake would no longer fall under the Lisbon Recognition

16 In this case 'equivalent' means equivalent on content. See the discussion concerning equivalence in the case *Peśla* as elaborated below.

Convention that still allows non-recognition as an outcome, but would be protected under the diploma recognition system in force in the European Union. This approach would at least safeguard the right to enter the qualification track in another Member State (albeit under application of the so-called compensatory measures that are allowed when substantial differences between the required qualifications in the host and home Member State have been established under the application of Directive 2005/36/EC. On first sight such a protection might be possible.

As was stated above, the secondary legislation of the European Union that applies specifically to lawyers, the Lawyers' Services Directive (Directive 77/249/EEC) and the Lawyers' Establishment Directive (Directive 98/5/EC) only apply to fully qualified lawyers, so they will be of no use to prospective lawyers that are still in the process of qualifying. This might however, not be the case for the Directive that lays down the *general* system for recognizing professional qualifications in the European Union, the Diploma Directive (Directive 2005/36/EC), previously Directive 89/48/EC. The part of the Directive that would be relevant in this case[17] is based on the premise of mutual recognition. In Article 13 of the Directive it is stated that if a person is allowed to exercise a *regulated* profession, or regulated professional activity, in one Member State, that person shall, in principle, be allowed to exercise that profession, or professional activity, in any of the other Member States, unless there are substantial differences between the professions or the professional activities in the host and the home Member State. In that case Article 14 of the Directive provides for the possibility that the host Member State may apply so-called compensatory measures. According to the article these measures may take the form of an adaptation period or an aptitude test to be chosen by the candidate who seeks entrance in a regulated profession in the host Member State. Only in situations where the profession requires a precise knowledge of national law, the host Member State may *impose* one of the modalities of compensatory measures. It may not be surprising that all Member States have opted for an aptitude test in case of the regulated legal professions, rather than an adaptation period.

In order for the Directive to apply in the situation of law students who seek to start their professional training in another Member States it must be checked whether the activity of being a trainee lawyer falls in the material scope of the Directive. The scope of the Directive is defined in Article 2 that states that the Directive shall apply to all European citizens who seek to pursue a *regulated profession* in another Member State. The definition of a regulated profession, in its turn, laid down in Article 3(1a) of the Directive reads as follows:

> 'a professional activity or group of professional activities, access to which, the pursuit of which, or one of the modes of pursuits of which is subject, directly or indirectly, by virtue of legislative, regulatory or administrative provisions to the possession of specific professional qualifications; in particular, the use of a professional title limited

17 It would go beyond the scope of this chapter to give an elaborate description of the Directive. See further Claessens 2008.

> by legislative, regulatory or administrative provisions to holders of a given professional qualification shall constitute a mode of pursuit'.

On first sight these conditions are fulfilled in the case of trainee lawyers. It was established above that in order to enter the professional qualification track for the profession of lawyer all Member States except the UK require a law degree. In addition, in many Member States trainee lawyers are designated with a professional title that is legally protected, like for example in Germany and Austria where trainee lawyers are designated as '*Referendar*' and '*Rechtsanwaltanwärter*'. Moreover, in Member States like the Netherlands and Belgium legal trainees use the same professional title (*advocaat*) as their fully qualified counterparts (albeit in a probationary manner).

3.1. *The Morgenbesser Case: A First Step towards Academic Recognition?*

In 2001 the European Court of Justice had an opportunity to rule on the applicability of the Directive 2005/36/EC predecessor, Directive 89/48/EEC in the case of trainee lawyers.[18] Ms. *Morgenbesser*, a French national, had studied law in France and obtained her degree there. After obtaining her degree, a *maîtrise en droit*, she started working at a Parisian law firm without further qualifying as a French *avocat*. After eight months, she moved to Italy and found a similar job with a law firm in *Genova*. One and a half year later, she filed a request with the Genovese Bar Association to be registered in the register of legal *practicanti*, i.e. the register for lawyers who are in the process of qualifying to become an Italian *avvocato*.

The *Genovese* Bar Association refused to register her, and so did the National Bar Association, on the ground of the fourth criterion of Article 17 of the *avvocato*-law which requires candidates to have a law degree conferred by an Italian university.[19] In reaction to these decisions Ms. *Morgenbesser* tried to have her French university diploma recognised in Italy.[20] The *Genova* University was willing to recognise her *Maitrîse* on the condition that Ms. *Morgenbesser* was to follow a two-year course in Italian law, passing thirteen exams and writing a dissertation. Ms. *Morgenbesser* kindly declined and appealed to the *Tribunale amministrativo regionale della Liguria*. The case eventually arrived at the *Consiglio di Stato*. Ms. *Morgenbesser* had in the meantime also applied for cassation of the National Bar Association's decision. It was the *Corta suprema di cassazione* which, in the end, filed the preliminary questions to the European Court of Justice in Luxembourg.[21]

The Supreme Court of Cassation asked the European Court of Justice whether a diploma conferred by a university in another Member State must be automatically valid for registering in a register of persons who follow a period of practical training

18 Case C-313/01, *Christine Morgenbesser* v. *Consiglio dell'Ordine degli avvocati di Genova*, [2003] ECR I-13467. See also Baas 2003, p. 973, and Timm & Kempter 2005, p. 2826-2828.

19 Paras. 25-27 Case C-313/01.

20 This form of academic recognition is generally seen as belonging to the competences of the Member States.

21 Paras. 28-31 Case C-313/01.

in order to enter in the legal profession of another Member State on the basis of the rules regarding free movement of services and freedom of establishment.[22] The European Court of Justice reformulated these questions and stated that the Supreme Court on the whole wanted to know whether a person who had a law degree from another Member State could be refused entry into a register of persons who follow practical training in order to enter in the legal profession of the Member State concerned on the sole ground that the individual did not have a law degree that was conferred, ratified or regarded as equal by a university from the Member State concerned.[23]

The European Court of Justice ruled that the status of *practicanti* could not be seen as a separate profession since being a *practicanti* is a necessary step in order to qualify as an *avvocato*. *Morgenbesser's* situation therefore did not fall according to the Court under the regime of Directive 89/48/EEC. The Court could have stopped there its reasoning since that was the extent of the question posed by the Italian court. However, it continued and ruled that even in the event where an activity was not caught by Directive 89/48/EEC (or any of the other Directives) the general rules covering the recognition of diplomas, as laid down in the established case law of the European Court of Justice, should apply. The Court then went on to refer to its *Vlassopoulou* ruling in which it was stated that a Member State impairs the free movement of persons in an unjustified manner if it fails to take in account knowledge and experience gained in another Member State (irrespective whether the situation concerned the free movement of workers or the freedom of establishment).[24] The Court came to the conclusion that the Genovese Bar Association could not refuse to register Ms. *Morgenbesser* as *practicanti* for the sole reason that she had no diploma conferred, ratified or recognised by an Italian university, and that her knowledge and experience gained in France (proven by her *maîtrise*) should be taken into account. The Court furthermore reiterated that when deciding upon the equivalence of diplomas the national authority could only look at the level of the qualification, except for diplomas concerning national law, whilst the national authority is allowed to compare taking into account established differences between the legal systems concerned.

It might be questioned why the Court did not rule that the activities of a *practicanti* constitute a regulated professional activity in the light of Directive 89/48/EEC. It seems obvious that Italy as a Member State applies rules that control the entry to the level of *practicanti* while training for the profession of *avvocato*. It should therefore not have been very difficult to rule that the professional activities exercised by a *practicanti* could be seen as a regulated professional activity. The Court could then have decided the case by referring to Articles 3 and 4 of the

22 The Supreme Court bases its question on Arts. 10, 12, 14, 39, 43, 49 and 149 EC, since Ms. Morgenbesser appealed on the basis of these articles. See paras. 31-32 case C-313/01.

23 Para. 33 Case C-313/01.

24 Doctrinally, the basis of the system lies in *Gebhard*. In that case the Court ruled that any hindrance to the free movement of person should be objectively justified. In this niche, objective justification could be obtained in adhering to the *Vlassopoulou*-doctrine.

Directive 89/48/EC,[25] now Articles 13 and 14 of Directive 2005/36/EC, and avoided the question of whether the system for the recognition of diplomas also applied to persons who were not considered as a fully educated professionals (*produit fini*) as the Court had done in the earlier case of *Neri*.[26]

The reason why the Court might have had difficulties to deal with the question in the light of a regulated profession, or a regulated professional activity, was, however, not so much because of the fact that the level of *practicanti* could not be seen as a regulated professional activity,[27] but more as a result of *Morgenbesser's* status in France. Ms. *Morgenbesser* did not have credentials that could be regarded as a diploma in the light of Article 1 of Directive 89/48/EEC. *Morgenbesser* only obtained her *Maîtrise en droit*, which did not give her direct access to the training for an *avocat*, since she did not pass her French CAPA yet. So even when the level of *practicanti* was seen as a '*semi produit fini*' then Directive 89/48/EEC could still not be applied to her since she did not qualify to participate in that similar level of training (*stagiaire*) in her home Member State, France yet.[28] The Court was therefore to some extent forced to deal with the question of recognition of diplomas outside the scope of Directive 89/48/EEC.

As stated above the Court referred to, and applied, the *Vlassopoulou* ruling to the problem posed by Ms. *Morgenbesser*. The application of the *Vlassopoulou* doctrine to situations that do not fall, or do not fall completely, under the system of diploma recognition laid down in secondary legislation is not new. In the earlier cases of *Aranitis*,[29] *Fernandez de Bobadilla*[30] and *Burbaud*,[31] the Court reached similar conclusions.

The case of *Morgenbesser* does have a revolutionary potential nevertheless. That potential does not lie in the application of the *Vlassopoulou* doctrine as such, but more in the facts to which the doctrine was applied. In *Morgenbesser*, the Court

25 It could have even been argued that in that case the situation of *Peros* and *Aslanidou* would have applied, since Italy had not implemented an aptitude test for *practicanti*. Morgenbesser could then have integrated without Italy being allowed to impose compensatory measures as it was late with implementation.

26 Case C-153/02, *Valentina Neri* v. *European School of Economics (ESE Insight World Education System Ltd.)*, [2003] ECR I-13555. This case revolved around the question whether Italy could refuse to recognize a diploma of an English University when the person in question had followed courses in an Italian establishment of that University, where the diploma would be recognized if she had studied in England. The Court avoided the question of diploma recognition by ruling that such a practice was an unjustified hindrance to the freedom of establishment of the school concerned.

27 The Court even implicitly acknowledged that a regulated professional activity was at stake (paras. 50-51 of *Morgenbesser*) and only denied explicitly that the level of *practicanti* was a regulated profession.

28 Para. 54 *Morgenbesser*. In this respect *Morgenbesser* can be distinguished from *Lubina*, discussed below, since Ms. Lubina did qualify for a position of *advocaat-stagiaire* in the Netherlands with her '*meester*' title.

29 C-164/94 *Aranitis* v. *Land Berlin*, [1996] ECR I-135.

30 C-234/97, *Teresa Fernández de Bobadilla* v. *Museo Nacional del Prado, Comité de Empresa del Museo Nacional del Prado, Ministerio Fiscal*, [1999] ECR I-4773.

31 Case C-285/01, *Isabel Burbaud* v. *Ministère de l'Emploi et de la Solidarité*, [2003] ECR I-08219.

first applied the *Vlassopoulou* doctrine to a situation that was concerned with a person who was not fully qualified to exercise a regulated profession in any of the Member States, including her home Member State, where she was not even qualified to enter the vocational training for the profession of *avocat*.[32] Ms. *Morgenbesser* could therefore not be regarded as a *produit fini* in the context of Directive 89/48/EEC. This is different from the cases described above which had all dealt with persons qualified to exercise a certain profession. Moreover the Court applied the ruling to a situation where the applicant wanted to enter a higher level in another Member State than the level which she had achieved in her home Member State.

In its judgment the Court never referred to the special circumstances of this specific case (i.e. the system of registers for *practicanti*) which ultimately brought the Court to this decision. It must therefore be assumed that the principle decision in *Morgenbesser*, i.e. the application of the *Vlassopoulou* doctrine to non-*produits fini*, is a rule that can be generally applied. It can furthermore be assumed that a person who is in the process of qualifying for a legal profession in one Member State, can move to another Member State and continue the process of qualification in that Member State. The host Member State may not impose its criteria for entering that qualification process *ipso facto* but must take into account any knowledge and experience that the candidate already gained in the qualification process in the other Member State, even where the candidate seeks entry in a level of the qualification process that has not been reached in the home Member State.

One might question what the difference is between the two regimes. It is clear, as was explained above, that the access to the level of trainee-lawyer is regulated in the Member States concerned, i.e. that it is a regulated professional activity in the light of the Directive. On the other hand the CJEU chose not to apply this Directive since the CJEU followed the argumentation of the governments involved in the procedure that the profession of trainee lawyer was a necessary step in the qualification as lawyer and not a separate professional activity. This decision is remarkable in the light of the *Kranemann*-case[33] that was decided a couple of years later in which the CJEU decided that a trainee lawyer (in this case a legal *Refendar* in Germany) was a worker in the light of article 45 TFEU. Apparently the court found there that the (professional) activity of a *Referendar* was not marginal and ancillary to the effect that the definition of worker would not be applicable to him. This is difficult to combine with the ruling in *Morgenbesser* were the ECJ decided that the period of traineeship was indivisibly connected with the profession itself. In addition, in *Morgenbesser* the CJEU did offer a way out of the problem by applying the *Vlassopoulou*-formula instead of the system of the Directive. In essence the Directive offers a right to diploma recognition albeit conditional on the basis of

32 In that sense the ruling of *Morgenbesser* even stretches beyond *Vlassopoulou* since Ms. Morgenbesser was able to use the *Vlassopoulou* comparison in a situation where she sought access to a stage of the qualification for a regulated profession that she was not entitled to enter in he home Member State because of the fact that she did not fulfil the criteria for entering that stage.

33 Case C-109/04, *Karl Robert Kranemann* v. *Land Nordrhein-Westfalen*, [2005] ECR I-02421.

possible compensatory measures (if a substantial difference between the host and home professional qualification is established), where the *Vlassopoulou*-formula guarantees at least an individual comparison between what is expected of the candidate and what the candidate can show in terms of professional qualifications and experience. Although the starting point is different, in the case of a recognition via the Directive and in the case of application of the *Vlassopoulou*-formula, the result will most likely be similar. Certainly in the case of lawyers where it is unlikely that the candidate fulfils the substantive requirements in one Member State with a law degree obtained in another Member State. Most probably the candidate in question will have to fulfil compensatory measures in order to have his or her qualifications (in this case a law degree) recognised in the host Member State. What the solution via the *Vlassopoulou*-doctrine lacks is the procedural and administrative safeguards (such as time limits on the decisions) that the Directive provides for. This might be a serious disadvantage when the Directive is not applied.

On the other hand the *Vlassopoulou*-formula provides for more flexibility than the pure application of the system of the Directive. Where the Directive starts from the premise of the qualifications acquired in the home state and how they compare with the qualifications required in the host Member State, the *Vlassopoulou*-doctrine compares what is required in the host Member State with which qualifications and professional experiences the candidate has (*n'importe quoi* whether these qualifications and/or experiences actually give access to a regulated professional activity in the home Member State). As is explained above, the CJEU, at least from this point of view, might not have been able to apply the system of the Directive in this very case since Ms. *Morgenbesser's* qualifications did not give her access to a regulated professional activity in France, at least not the regulated professional activity that she sought access to in Italy.

In other cases this position might have to be reviewed. Most recently the CJEU decided that the profession of notaries falls in the scope of the application of the Treaty.[34] Consequently, the recognition of notary qualifications might be an issue to be solved in the future. Contrary to advocate trainees who stay in this position only for a certain period of time until fully qualified as lawyers, candidate notaries might stay in this professional position for quite a long period and even for their full professional life in some of the Member States (e.g. the Netherlands). It will be very interesting in the future whether the Court would deny the application of Directive 2005/36/EC in the case of a recognition procedure concerning such a candidate notary. One has to admit, however, that the mobility of notaries across the European Union is perhaps at the moment more a hypothetical issue than a reality. Therefore one might have to wait quite for a long time until such a case might emerge.

It is hard to ascertain at the moment how similar cases for lawyers are dealt with on a day to day basis in the different Member States since the comparison, and

[34] Cases C-47/08 *Commission v. Belgium*; C-51/08 *Commission* v. *Luxembourg*; C-53/08 *Commission* v. *Austria*; C-54/08 *Commission* v. *Germany*; C61/08 *Commission* v. *Greece*; judgment of the CJEU from 24 May 2011, nyr. A similar procedure against the Netherlands C-157/09 has not been decided yet.

the ensuing decision, takes place on a very individual level. Only one Member State has decided to codify the CJEU's decision in national law, namely Germany, that has laid down the possibility to enter in the traineeship for the legal profession while having obtained a law degree in another Member State in paragraph 112a of the *Deutschen Richtergesetz*. In January 2007 a new paragraph 112a of the *Deutschen Richtergesetzes* (German Judges Law) entered into force.[35] The *Deutschen Richtergesetzes* mainly covers the profession of the judge in Germany, but it also contains the requirements necessary for entering the *Refendariat* since there exists only one German professional education for all the legal professions. The new paragraph 112a of the *Deutschen Richtergesetzes* seems a straightforward implementation of the *Vlassopoulou* comparison as mentioned in the *Morgenbesser* ruling. The paragraph states that any national of other Member States of the European Union who has a university diploma that gives him access to the professional training of the legal professions under Article 1 of Directive 98/5/EC may have his diploma checked by the German authorities in order to obtain a decision on equivalence. Paragraph 112a further states that where it is decided that the university diploma is not equivalent to the entrance requirements in Germany the candidate concerned may take an aptitude test in order to obtain entry in the profession of the *Referendar*. This aptitude test will cover civil law, penal law, administrative law and procedural law. It may be clear that in the majority of cases full equivalence will not be achieved as such and an aptitude test may be necessary. This paragraph 112a of the *Deutschen Richtergesetz* allows access to the qualification track of the profession of the *Rechtsanwalt* to those that can show that they have qualifications that are equivalent to the requirements for the First German State Exam. This legislation seems on first sight fully in line with the *Morgenbesser* ruling. However, the paragraph contains one additional requirement stating that assessment of equivalence is open only to those who are eligible to enter the qualification track in their home Member State. This leads to the conclusion that the German implementation goes beyond the limits set in the case law, since it makes the availability of the assessment of equivalence dependent on possession of a certain qualification. This might be problematic if one considers the case of Ms. *Morgenbesser* who was actually not yet qualified to enter directly the qualification track in France since she had not obtained her CAPA. Nevertheless she was still allowed the enjoyment of the assessment of equivalence in Italy. If the German provision were to be applied to her situation strictly she would not have been allowed an assessment of equivalence since she did not qualify for entrance into the qualification track in her home Member State. One might therefore conclude that the German implementation, or at least the attempt thereto, falls short of what the court guaranteed in *Morgenbesser* since the added flexibility of that ruling (i.e. the possibility to have all acquired qualifications and experiences compared with what is required in the host state even if these qualifications are not enough to enter the

[35] 'Deutsches Richtergesetz in der Fassung der Bekanntmachung vom 19. April 1972 (BGBl. I S. 713), zuletzt geändert durch Artikel 4 des Gesetzes vom 22. Dezember 2006 (BGBl. IS. 3416)'.

corresponding profession in the host Member State is not covered by the German provision.

3.2. *The Peśla Decision: in dubio pro mobilitate?*

Recently, the European Court of Justice had the opportunity to rule on the German implementation of *Morgenbesser* in the case of *Peśla*.[36] The case *Peśla* is a clear follow-up procedure of *Morgenbesser*. The applicant in the main proceeding is a Polish citizen, who has finished his legal education at the University *Poznań* with a Master degree. Furthermore, he had obtained a Bachelor and a Master degree at the University *Frankfurt (Oder)* in German and Polish Law. During this education, the applicant is obliged to pass certain university exams (*kleine and große Scheine*) in German private law, criminal law and public law. Furthermore, the applicant had proof of various internships at German law firms, post academic courses and other work-related activities in German law. The defendant is the Ministry of Justice of the German federal state of *Mecklenburg-Western Pomerania* (Mecklenburg-Vorpommern). In November 2005, the applicant filed a request for the admission to the judicial preparation training with reference to the judgment *Morgenbesser* and the submission of various qualifications at the regional Court of Appeal (*Oberlandesgericht/OLG*) in *Mecklenburg-Western Pomerania*. Based on the introduction of paragraph 112a DRiG from 31 December 2006, this had transferred the request to the defendant because the Ministry of Justice was in accordance with paragraph 112(a)(7) DRiG now competent to render a decision in the newly introduced assessment of equivalence (*Gleichwertigkeitsprüfung*). The defendant rejected the request on 27 March 2007, thus about one and a half years after the original application. According to the Ministry, the standard of assessment was the existence of such kind of knowledge, which is proven by passing the obligatory courses laid down in paragraph 5(1) DRiG. This knowledge encompasses the full range of German law on the level of the First State examination (*erstes juristisches Staatsexamen*). Given the difference to the German law, knowledge of foreign law could not be accepted as equivalent. Furthermore according to the Ministry, a prevention of reverse discrimination should be considered in the assessment of equivalence. Therefore, the documentary evidence, which entitles domestic students to attend the State examination, does not suffice for an EU foreigner, who has studied in another country, to acquire a finding of equivalence. The defendant argued that the presented documentary proof of the University *Frankfurt (Oder)*, which the applicant had acquired in the context of the Master programme, would not provide for the full spectrum of the First State examination. The Ministry of Justice granted the applicant in the decision the possibility, to attend on request an aptitude test (*Eignungsprüfung*) in accordance with paragraph 112a(3) DRiG.

Pursuant to subparagraph 3 of this provision the aptitude test is a State examination in the German language on the required knowledge in German law

[36] Case C-345/08, *Krzysztof Peśla* v. *Justizministerium Mecklenburg-Vorpommern*, [2009] ECR-I, nyp.

and the skill to successfully complete the legal preparation training (*Referendariat*). Courses, which may be tested, are civil law, criminal law and public law including the procedural laws. The written examination has to be drawn up in a way that they have not yet been attested in the context of the assessment of equivalence under paragraph 112a(1) and (2).

The applicant appealed against the decision from the Ministry of Justice at the administrative court in *Schwerin* on 27 April 2007 and claimed that the criteria of the aptitude test are in contradiction to those indicated by the Court of Justice. Furthermore, the applicant argued that his knowledge of German law in the context of his study, internships and at the work at two law faculties had not been taken into account sufficiently. The administrative court stayed the proceedings on 8 July 2008 and under Article 234 EC (now 267 TFEU) referred the following preliminary questions to the European Court of Justice.

> Is it compatible with Article 39 EC that a finding of equivalence under Paragraph 112a(1) and (2) of the *Deutsches Richtergesetz* (German Law on Judges) is made only if can be established on the basis of the documentary evidence submitted that the EU citizen has the knowledge and skills as tested in the (German legal) examination of mandatory subjects provided for in Paragraph 5(1) of the *Deutsches Richtergesetz*?
>
> If question 1 is to be answered in the negative: Does Article 39 EC require that the only criterion for an assessment of equivalence which is consistent with European law is whether the university diploma obtained by the EU citizen in the EU together with the additional evidence submitted by him of educational performance and experience is comparable from the point of view of the (intellectual) level of education and the extent of that education to the first German State examination in law?
>
> If question 2 is also to be answered in the negative: Is it compatible with Article 39 EC, if the finding of equivalence under Paragraph 112a(1) and (2) of the *Deutsches Richtergesetz* still takes the material examined in the mandatory subjects of the first (German legal) State examination as its reference point, but in the light of the legal education successfully completed elsewhere in the Union only somewhat 'lowered' requirements are imposed?

The question has been decided by the CJEU in December 2009. In this context, it is crucial to look in more detail at the national legislation. In doing so, a distinction and comparison has to be made between the quite recently introduced paragraph 112a DRiG and the other relevant national German provisions concerning the recognition of foreign university examinations. Relevant is here the already existing paragraph 112 DRiG. According to paragraph 112(1) DRiG, the federal provisions concerning the recognition of the university examination (*Schwerpunktbereichs-prüfungen*) are not touched by the DRiG. This reservation in favour of the federal legislation was put into the DRiG through Article 1 No. 8 of the Law to the reform of the legal education (*Gesetz zur Reform der Juristenausbildung*) from 11 July 2002. Since this time, the State examination consists of a university examination (*Schwerpunktsprüfung*) and the State examination of mandatory subjects (*Pflichtfachprüfung*). Paragraph 5a(1) second intent DRiG stipulates that at least two years of the education have to be followed at a Germany university. Thus, the regulation permits to study the remaining time at a foreign university. This poses the question, whether and to which extent successfully passed courses at foreign universities can account for the university part of the State examination, or even replace it. The German *Richtergesetz* answers this question only partially. It permits the recognition of courses passed at a foreign university, however, it does not regulate the conditions for recognition itself.[37] Based on paragraph 20 of the Framework Law on Higher Education (*Hochschulrahmengesetz/HRG*), this falls into the competence of the federal states. According to this law, courses passed at a foreign university, will be recognized, if their equivalence has been established. Paragraph 5(1) second intent and paragraph 112 DRiG remain untouched. The legislator expected from this construction explicitly a convergence of the legal education programmes in Europe.[38] In consequence, however, already before the introduction of paragraph 112a DRiG it was possible to profit from courses passed at foreign universities in the university part of the Final law examination and to complete the part of the exam organized as state exam (*staatlichen Pflichtprüfungsteil*) on the basis of the provisions of the German *Richtergesetz* in combination with the federal legislation on higher education.

The question is therefore, which value the introduction of paragraph 112a DRiG adds to the existing legal situation. The provision regulates the assessment of equivalence based on the standard of the *Morgenbesser* judgment for the admission to the professional trainings period (*Vorbereitungsdienst, Referendarzeit*) as well as, if necessary, an aptitude test. In this context, the question of equivalence is exclusively related to the state part of the examination. Recognition of the foreign university education as equivalent to the German university examination is thereby assumed.[39]

According to the wording of subparagraph 1 of this provision, applicants are admitted to the professional trainings period, if their knowledge and skills correspond to those in a successfully passed state examination of mandatory subjects (*Pflichtfachprüfung*) based on paragraph 5(1) DRiG. According to our view, this cannot mean that an equivalence in the sense of paragraph 112a DRiG can exclusively be established by a proof of the successful pass of the state examination. Otherwise, paragraph 112a(2) second indent makes no sense anymore, according to which in a case of the finding of no or only a partial equivalence, the applicant has to pass the aptitude test in accordance with paragraph 112 a(3) and (4).

In how far the documentary evidence of knowledge and skills in the German law as, for example, the proof of the various university exams (e.g. the *großen Scheine*) already establish equivalence, is disputed. However, they have to be taken into consideration in the assessment. The national authorities have this in our opinion insufficiently done in the case *Peśla*. *Schmidt-Räntsch* refer in their commentary on paragraph 112a explicitly to the German-Polish education as a possible proof of equivalence.[40] According to our view, the assessment of equivalence should not establish such a standard which would have as a consequence that in fact all candidates have to pass a full aptitude test. This would

37 See Schmidt-Räntsch & Schmidt-Räntsch 2009, para. 112, Rdnrs. 1 and 6 *et seq.*

38 *Ibidem*, Rdnr. 7.

39 *Ibidem*, para. 112a, Rdnr. 25.

40 *Ibidem*, Rdnr. 36.

contradict the goal of the *Morgenbesser*-principles. It would also not reflect the mutual trust in the quality of the educational system in other Member States that should determine the decision to recognize educational achievements according to the view of the European legislator and generally the case law of the CJEU.

In view of the decision of the Ministry of Justice *Mecklenburg-Western Pomerania,* one can expect a highly restrictive interpretation of the term 'equivalence' by the national authorities. This decision permits the presumption that also in the future the authorities will be of the opinion that candidates, qualified abroad, are only be admitted to the legal preparation training (*Vorbereitungsdienst*), if they successfully have passed the full aptitude test, which in fact more or less means the state examination part. In contrast, 'equivalence' in the sense of paragraph 112a(1) DRiG will categorically be rejected. Such a rejection of the equivalence can clearly not be seen as a reflection of the *Morgenbesser*- and *Vlassopoulou*-principles. Insofar it seems that even after the introduction of paragraph 112a DRiG the spirit of the originally established *Morgenbesser*-committee introduced in Germany directly after the judgment with its fact sheet and extensive checklist determines the decision practice.

According to our view, the proof of knowledge of German Law provided by *Peśla* should have been sufficient to consider equivalence according to paragraph 112a(1) or at least should have provided for a partial equivalence, if this provision should not just be regarded as an empty shell. Noteworthy is in this context that during the oral proceedings of the case *Peśla* before the Court of Justice, the representative of the defendant has admitted that on the basis of the facts and the appearance of the applicant during the proceeding, he assumed that the applicant would pass the aptitude test.[41] In such a case, would the standard of Articles 13 and 14 of Directive 2005/36/EC be applied, a direct or at least a partial recognition had to be rendered by the competent authorities. An aptitude test pursuant to Article 14 of Directive 2005/36 can only relate to the knowledge, which the candidate could not prove, but which is obligatory for his work-related activities.

Concerning the argument of reverse discrimination brought forward by the defendant, the CJEU has never accepted this argument for a justification of a restriction of the fundamental freedoms. Furthermore, the argument of reverse discrimination has to be questioned altogether. Pursuant to paragraphs 112 and 112a DRiG, already the education of the applicant abroad and his there acquired qualifications should be considered as equivalent to the German university exams (*Schwerpunktsprüfung*). The additional proof of study (*Studiennachweise*) and degrees acquired in Germany, inter alia, also the *großen* and *kleinen Scheine* in German law should be counted as an additional qualification, which has to be examined in the context of the assessment of equivalence. The situation is therefore different from a purely national educated candidate of the State examination. In this case the so-called *Scheine* are part of the university exam (*Schwerpunktsbereichprüfung*) and accordingly, cannot contribute again to the examination of mandatory subjects (*Pflichfachprüfung*) as proof of already acquired knowledge.

41 Decision of the Administrative Court Schwerin from 8 July 2008, 3 A 588/07.

The *Peśla* case could have turned into a boomerang for the national legislator, if the CJEU had used this opportunity to extend its existing case law and had further elaborated on the inherent obligation to recognize diplomas from other EU Member in the cases of admission to the professional legal education. With the judgment in *Peśla* the CJEU could have forced the national legislators or authorities to open up their professional training for young lawyers who have gained their academic legal training in another Member State. The CJEU did, however, not make use of this opportunity in its judgment from the 10th of December 2009. The Court clearly stressed, on the contrary, that Member States are under no obligation to accept candidates with a lower level of knowledge concerning the national law and only very cautiously repeated the obligation to take prior qualifications and acquired knowledge into considerations for a at least partial recognition. It is not very clear why the Court took this rather cautious position

Regrettably, there was no Advocate General's Opinion to the proceedings. Although this appears to have become more and more common in order to save time and to decrease the Advocates General's workload, the case of *Peśla* would have deserved more attention with respect to its legal and factual background. The national legislation, including the comparison between paragraph 112 and paragraph 112a DRiG as well as the context concerning the recognition of academic and professional qualifications in accordance with the provisions of Directive 2005/36/EC could have taken much more into consideration in the opinion of the Advocate General than it was done in the judgment.

What *Peśla* did not address at all was the problem identified above, namely the fact that the German rules contain a formal requirement with regard to the qualifications obtained in the home Member State namely the fact that the qualifications obtained in the home Member State must give access to the training stage in the home Member State. This formal requirement takes away the flexibility that was offered by the ruling in *Morgenbesser* and the *Vlassopoulou*-doctrine in comparison to the recognition system laid down in the Diploma Directive. Future case law will be necessary to challenge this problematic element in the German legislation.

Returning to the question whether European Law offers possibilities to those students that seek to switch Member States before they are fully qualified lawyers it must be concluded that on the basis of European Law, more specifically the *Morgenbesser* judgment, this possibility exist. It is however not an easy way to take in the light of the *Peśla* judgment. It can be expected that the many Member State relying on this judgment will require an entry level of national law knowledge that is precisely equal to the level required from national students without taking into account prior knowledge acquired concerning other legal systems. In addition, it has been shown that some Member States impose additional requirements that might, however, not be sanctioned by European Law as these requirements reduce the possibilities offered by the *Morgenbesser* judgment significantly. It will be up to new procedures to clarify this issue and whether the *Peśla* approach is the last word in this matter.

3.3. *The Koller Case: Right to Recognition or Abuse of Law?*

Noteworthy is already how the Court dealt with the Austrian proceedings of Robert Koller recently.[42] *Koller* is an Austrian national who has studied law in Austria. After having finalized his Austrian university education with the academic title '*Magister der Rechtswissenschaft*' he moved to Spain and started to study Spanish law there. Having passed some additional courses he acquired the title and qualification as *Licenciado en Derecho* after a homologation procedure in which his Austrian legal education was taken into account. This qualification gives until now direct access to the profession of *abogado* in Spain. As Spain does not have introduced yet a professional trainings period prior to be full qualification as lawyer the academic qualification as *Licenciado* is the only qualification necessary to enter the Spanish Bar and register as *abogado*. Having been registered as *abogado* in Spain for some weeks, *Koller* has returned home to Austria requiring from the competent authorities to be registered in Austria as *abogado* and to recognise his qualification according to the recognition procedure of Directive 89/48/EEC (now Articles 13 and 14 Directive 2005/36/EC).

The competent Austrian authorities *(Rechtsanwaltsprüfungskommission)* were not amused about this action and refused the recognition of *Koller´s* qualification as *abogado* in order to become an Austrian *Rechtsanwalt*. Advocate General *Trstenjak* published her opinion on 2 June 2010. According the Advocate General the recognition procedure of Directive 89/48/EEC (now Directive 2005/36/EC) clearly applies in this case. According to the Advocate General it must be presumed that the education or training in the context of the homologation procedure in Spain is an independent course of study. Non-recognition of the equivalence of the homologation procedure at European level would mean that achievement is not valued, but rather punished because applicants who pass the necessary examinations in less time than others would be worse off. That is according to her not appropriate, nor is it in accordance with European law as it stands at present. The Advocate Generals refers hereby explicitly to the Case C-286/06 Commission v Spain.[43] Nevertheless, *Koller* might according to her be obliged to pass an aptitude test in Austria in accordance with the Directive. However, the Advocate General also observed that Austria's additional requirement concerning a five years professional training as a prerequisite for admission to the aptitude test is contrary to the Directive. Furthermore, she rejected the assertion by the Austrian and the Greek government, that there is an abuse of law arguing that *Koller* was intending to circumvent national training rules concerning a profession.[44] Regarding the content of a possible aptitude test, the Advocate General referred to differences between *Koller´s* legal university studies completed in Austria and possible missing elements

42 Case C-119/09 *Robert Koller* v. *Rechtsanwaltsprüfungskommission beim Oberlandesgericht Graz* – Reference for a preliminary ruling from the *Oberste Berufungs- und Disziplinarkommission* (Austria) lodged on 1 April 2009, judgment from 22 December 2010, nyr.

43 Case 286/06, *Commission* v. *Spain*, ECR [2008], I- 2085.

44 The Advocate General refers clearly to the differences in Case C-311/06 *Cavallera* v. *Consiglio Nationale degli Ingegneri*, ECR [2009], I-415.

due to the lack of professional training, leading to the conclusion that an examination covering the regulations concerning the calculation of lawyers' costs and the rules of professional conduct for lawyers could be justified.[45]

The CJEU gave its ruling in the *Koller* case on 22 December 2010.[46] In its judgment, the Court essentially followed the Advocate General´s reasoning and confirmed the application of Directive 89/48/EEC (now Directive 2005/36/EC). Furthermore, the Court explicitly rejected Austria´s argument that the recognition could only follow, if the candidate provides proof of the required professional practical training. According to the CJEU, it is irrelevant for the classification of a diploma in the sense of Article 1(a) of Directive 89/48/ECC that the Spanish qualification degree does not certify a three or more year professional training. Important for the application of the Directive is, however, the fact that the Spanish authorities have admitted *Koller* to the Spanish Bar due to his full legal education in Austria and Spain after the homologation procedure.[47]

Consequently, according to the case-law of the Court, a citizen can in principle rely on the fundamental freedoms and secondary law against his own Member State.[48] This means however, that as long as in Spain the university education with the degree *'Licenciado en Derecho'* gives direct access to the profession of the *'abagado'*, the degree has to be classified as a diploma in the sense of Directive 89/48/EEC (and now 2005/36/EC).[49] Therefore, the Austrian authorities are obliged to conduct a recognition procedure pursuant to Articles 3 and 4 of Directive 89/48/EEC or now Articles 13 and 14 of Directive 2005/36/EC. Whether instead of an aptitude test in Austrian law an adaptation period could be required from Mr. *Koller*, depends on whether Austria has used this possibility when implementing Directive 89/48/EEC or 2005/36/EC. If this were the case, which actually is not to be expected, *Koller* could be obliged to take an adaptation period to become familiar with Austrian procedural law. Generally, Member States, according to Article 4 of Directive 89/48 and now Article 14 of Directive 2005/36 have the choice between an aptitude test and an adaptation period to compensate possible deficits in the education of the candidates. However, it has to be stated that the Member States in general have decided in favour of the aptitude test as an instrument for compensation. In the light of the judgments of the CJEU in the cases *Beutenmüller*

45 The Advocate General Conclusions in Case C-119/09 *Robert Koller* v. *Rechtsanwalts-prüfungskommission beim Oberlandesgericht Graz* – Reference for a preliminary ruling from the *Oberste Berufungs- und Disziplinarkommission* (Austria) lodged on 1 April 2009, para. 112.

46 Case C-119/09 *Robert Koller* v. *Rechtsanwaltsprüfungskommission beim Oberlandesgericht Graz* – Reference for a preliminary ruling from the *Oberste Berufungs- und Disziplinarkommission* (Austria) lodged on 1 April 2009, judgement of the Court of Justice on 22 December 2010 nyr.

47 The CJEU refers in this context to its ruling in the Case C-311/06, *Cavallera* v. *Consiglio Nationale degli Ingegneri*, ECR 2009, I-415 para. 50, and refers to the difference in the factual situation of this case from the facts in the *Koller* case.

48 See the ECJ judgments in Case 115/78 *Knoors* [1979] ECR 00399 and Case 246/89 *Broekmeulen* [1981] ECR 02311.

49 In Spain, the introduction of the practical education period as a requirement of admission for the Bar is discussed since decades. Currently, there is a transition regime until the practical part is finally introduced as an obligatory part of the professional legal education in Spain.

and *Peros*, a subsequent introduction of this possibility demanding an adaptation period particularly for the case *Koller* seems not acceptable.[50]

The comparison of the outcome in the *Peśla* and *Koller* cases show, however, clearly the thin line between academic and professional recognition. If Germany like Spain had recognised during a homologation procedure *Peśla's* Polish and German legal education he could have after completing the German professional training like his colleague *Koller* relied on Directive 89/48/EC (now 2005/36/EC) when returning to Poland. *Peśla* can now, however, after having finished his professional training in Poland rely on the Directives 2005/36/EC and 98/5/EC and return to Germany as fully qualified professional. He will have the right according to Directive 98/5/EC to practicing law there under his home professional title including actually German law. If he will practice German law there for a period of three years he will have to be admitted to the German Bar without any further aptitude test and be able to use the German title *Rechtsanwalt*. The results of both cases show how dubious and quite unsatisfactory it is that the recognition system of Directive 89/48/EC (now 2005/36/EC) has not been applied by the Court in cases like *Morgenbesser* and *Peśla*, while applying it without hesitation in a case such as *Koller*.

4. Possibilities in the Bologna System?

One reason for this different approach might be rooted in the fact that traditionally, the recognition of academic diplomas including university law degrees has been considered to fall outside the clear scope of EU law but was considered to take place on an intergovernmental level, nowadays mainly in the realm of the Bologna Process by applying the 1997 Lisbon Recognition Convention.[51] The Lisbon Recognition predates the Bologna Process as such and is based on a combined initiative of the Council of Europe and UNESCO. Both the Council of Europe and UNESCO were, throughout recent history, rather active in the field of academic recognition.[52] This activity, which for the Council of Europe mainly took place in the 1950s and 1960s, and for UNESCO in the 1970s, culminated in a joint Convention on the recognition of qualifications concerning higher education in the European region.[53]

The Convention covers both the recognition of qualifications giving access to higher education and the recognition of qualifications that are awarded after a period of higher education. The purpose of this paragraph will be to give a general overview of the workings of the Convention with the main emphasis being placed on the second part of the Convention, i.e. the recognition of qualifications that are awarded after a period of study. The 1997 Lisbon Recognition Convention does this

50 Case C-102/02 *Beutenmüller* [2004] ECR I-5405; Case C-141/04 *Peros* [2005] ECR I-7163.

51 Critically to this approach Garben & Schneider 2011.

52 Convention on the Recognition of Qualifications concerning Higher Education in the European Region, CETS No. 165, explanatory report, <conventions.coe.int/Treaty/en/reports/html/165.htm>.

53 CETS No. 165.

by declaring that everybody is entitled to an assessment of an application for recognition of qualifications solely on the basis of the knowledge and skills achieved.[54] In a very general fashion, it can be said that the signatories to the Lisbon Recognition Convention commit themselves to recognising higher education diplomas from other state parties.[55] This recognition may be withheld if there are substantial differences between the qualifications where recognition is sought and the qualification obtained. Apparently, although this does not become clear from the Convention itself, it is the national recognition authority that decides whether substantial differences exist.[56] States do not need, however, to create elaborated recognition mechanisms in order to fulfil the obligations of the Lisbon Recognition Convention if they at least provide for an assessment of the recognition concerned.[57]

On first sight, the essential elements of the Lisbon Recognition Convention entail nothing more than a very broad rule to recognise higher education qualifications accompanied with the possibility to make exemptions which is almost just as broad. Seen from the fact that this is an intergovernmental Convention this should come as no surprise. States are not willing to concede decision-making power to a supranational organisation, or to have their ability to take decisions limited by detailed treaty obligations, which is also apparent from their constant reluctance to cooperate on education matters in the framework of the European Community, or even now the European Union.[58]

What does this entail for those who aspire to become lawyers? It is likely that the Lisbon Recognition Convention is of little use to those who seek to become a lawyer in another Member State of the European Union after they finish their academic legal education. As stated above, it is possible under the Lisbon Recognition Convention to withhold recognition if there are substantial differences between the qualifications of the person seeking recognition, and the qualifications awarded in the Member State. It has been established earlier that the first step to becoming a lawyer in a Member State of the European Union is to study law at a university of that State. It can also be said that the curricula of those law faculties focus predominately on the national law of the respective State. It can therefore also be concluded that were a prospective lawyer seeks to have his law degree recognised under the Lisbon Recognition Convention he, or she, will almost always encounter the problem of substantial differences, and is therefore in no way assured of recognition. Moreover, to add to the recognition problem, the explanatory report to the Lisbon Recognition Convention states that in cases of regulated professions,

54 Art. III.1(2) Lisbon Recognition Convention CETS No. 165.

55 Art. VI.1 Lisbon Recognition Convention, CETS No. 165.

56 Convention on the Recognition of Qualifications concerning Higher Education in the European Region, CETS No. 165, explanatory report, <conventions.coe.int/Treaty/en/reports/html/165.htm>.

57 Art. VI.2 Lisbon Recognition Convention, CETS No. 165.

58 Schneider & Claessens 2005, p. 161-162.

which the profession of lawyer is in all Member States, the competent bodies governing those professions may ask for additional requirements.[59]

On the other hand, the European Court of Justice decided in the *Commission* v. *Austria* case[60] that when in conflict, European Union law clearly prevails over other international agreements such as the Lisbon Recognition Convention. In intra-EU situations therefore, the application of the Lisbon Recognition Convention shall always be subject to European law. Moreover, the CJEU decided in the same case that recognition of certain academic diplomas falls under access to the higher education. The non-discriminatory access to higher education is, however, subject to EU law. [61]

It seems, therefore, that the 1997 Lisbon Recognition Convention is of no major help for a prospective lawyer. As stated above the European Court of Justice has, however, in *Morgenbesser*[62] extrapolated its ruling in *Vlassopoulou*[63] so that it also applies to candidates from a regulated profession that cannot yet be considered as a *produit fini*, i.e. that they are not yet fully qualified in a regulated profession in another Member State. The ruling in *Vlassopoulou*, and in *Morgenbesser* for that matter, entails that the candidate is entitled to a fair assessment of his or her qualifications, taking into account all the relevant knowledge and experience obtained by that candidate (also by means of courses and other, practical, experience). After such a comparison has been conducted, the national authority will then take a decision on what the candidate still has to do in order to obtain recognition.[64]

Compared to the system of the Lisbon Recognition Convention, application of the *Morgenbesser* ruling seems to have more effect for the prospective lawyer, since it leads, or must lead, to a decision of a national authority that states what the

59 Convention on the Recognition of Qualifications concerning Higher Education in the European Region, CETS No. 165, explanatory report, <conventions.coe.int/Treaty/en/reports/html/165.htm>.

60 Case C-147/03, [2005] ECR I-5969.

61 See more recently the case C-73/08 *Bressol*, nyr.

62 Case C-313/01, *Christine Morgenbesser* v. *Consiglio dell'Ordine degli avvocati di Genova*, [2003] ECR I-13467.

63 Case C-340/89, *Vlassopoulou* v. *Ministerium für Justiz, Bundes- und Europaangelegenheiten Baden-Württemberg*, [1991] ECR 2357.

64 It must be noted at this point that application of the *Vlassopoulou*-formula in *Morgenbesser* like cases does not lead to academic recognition per se, or in the sense of the Lisbon Recognition Convention. The candidate will not receive a certificate of recognition, but the effect is similar. Ms. Morgenbesser wanted to be registered as a *practicanti* in Italy, but according to the rules in force in Italy one could only be admitted to that register if one had a diploma conferred (or recognised) by an Italian University. Application of the *Vlassopoulou*-formula in her case led to the same effect as a recognition of her French law degree, namely being accepted in the register of *practicanti*. That is also why it must be maintained that although the European Court of Justice has encroached upon academic recognition, because the effect in the *Morgenbesser* case is similar, it still does not exercise academic recognition as such. *Morgenbesser* had applied for recognition of her *maîtrise* but she was denied such recognition by an Italian University. The University concerned did inform her of what she needed to do in order to qualify for recognition, which basically added up to a full bachelor in Italian law.

candidate must do in order to achieve access to the profession of the lawyer, or to one of its preparatory stages. The Lisbon Recognition Convention on the other hand, states that recognition can be withheld in cases where substantial differences exist. This leads to the very unfortunate situation that the national authorities confused by this unclear and complicated legal framework might give prospective lawyer a negative answer based on the Lisbon Convention without considering even the application of the *Vlassopoulou* formula.

In addition, it must also be mentioned that the application of both recognition systems, at least in the case of prospective lawyers from EU Member States, is not necessarily contradictive. It might even be construed in such a fashion that the general rule of the Lisbon Convention Recognition, i.e. the incentive to recognise each others higher education qualifications unless substantial differences exist, can be further elaborated on by the EU obligations based on the case law of the Court of Justice, namely that all relevant qualifications, knowledge and experience must be taken into account when taking a decision on the equality of certain academic and professional qualifications.

In conclusion, it can be said that because the Lisbon Recognition Convention still leaves enormous discretionary powers for national recognition authorities, it also contains the possibility that a candidate requesting recognition is confronted with a negative decision on recognition without any further directions as to how to obtain recognition and also provides for additional criteria to be imposed by national authorities governing regulated professions.[65] This situation is very unsatisfactory.

5. How to Proceed?

In the paragraphs above it was made clear that the position of students trained in one Member State who seek to become a professional lawyer in a different Member State is not an easy one. They are certainly in a worse position in comparison to the fully professionally trained lawyers who can rely on three European Directives. There is little help to be expected from the Lisbon Recognition Convention and also until now quite little encouragement given by the case law of the European Court of Justice as one could notice in the *Peśla* judgment where the Court in our opinion has missed an opportunity to contribute to the further developing of academic mobility. How then should one proceed in order to make it easier for students to switch between Member States during their academic and professional training?

65 At this point it must be mentioned that the Council of Europe has also issued a recommendation on the freedom to exercise the profession of lawyer. This Recommendation (Rec(2000)21, via <www.coe.int>, last accessed 11 April 2011, entails nothing that concerns the cross border migration of lawyers but it does contain safeguards for the freedom to exercise the profession of lawyer within one Member State. Because of this fact the recommendation is of little use to the thesis put forward in this book.

The key solution lies, in our view, in the contents of the academic programmes in the different Member States.[66] Traditionally, a law study focuses very much on the national law of the state in which it is taught. Room for specialisation or international legal developments and mobility possibilities often only occurs in the final part of the study, which, in many cases, is now often part of the master programme due to the Bologna Process which has encouraged the introduction of a two-cycle system.[67] Generally, national Bar Associations, require a sound knowledge of national law before they admit candidates to the legal profession of that state. This means that in order to avoid aptitude tests and adaptation periods later on in life, students should actually try to obtain a bachelor degree in the Member State where they later wish to work. When students start their bachelor studies, however, they are often at an age when taking a decision to move abroad to study directly after having finished secondary school might still be a rather too big step to be taken even if they might consider a future professional career abroad already. It can, however, be noticed that recently an increasing number of students is willing to take this step. This is certainly a rather new phenomenon and perhaps a direct consequence of the Bologna Process. Educational institutions will have to adept to this new development.

In the light of later professional mobility it might, however, be better or at least worth serious consideration to offer the sound knowledge of the national law in the master-phase of the two-cycle degree system directly before entering the professional training.[68] The training of national law in conversion courses as offered in the UK might also be a solution in other Member States in the future. Questions

66 This is also the view of the European Law Faculties Association (ELFA) that has immediately after the adoption of the Bologna Declaration started the discussion of reform of legal education in Europe. See: ELFA, *For a European Space of Legal Education*, via: <www.elfa-afde.org>, last accessed 28 April 2011; ELFA, *ELFA Resolution on the London Communiqué and the general development of the Bologna Process*, via: <www.elfa-afde.org>, last accessed 28 April 2011; ELFA, *Strengthening the European Dimension of Legal Education*, via: <www.elfa-afde.org>, last accessed 28 April 2011; ELFA, *Tuning Legal Studies in Europe: Initial Findings*, via: <www.elfa-afde.org>, last accessed 28 April 2008; Pichonnaz & Hirte 2006, p. 79-81; Posch 2005; Reich 2002-2003, p. 21-38 and Steger 2007.

67 This is actually the system that ELFA proposes, see: ELFA, *For a European Space of Legal Education*, via: <www.elfa-afde.org>, last accessed 28 April 2011 and Reich 2002-2003, p. 21-38. Remarkably ELFA proposes direct access to the professional training of the legal profession after obtaining a masters degree in another jurisdiction (where the bachelor degree focuses on national law of the home member state and the masters degree on international (European) law) without having to resort to the 'cumbersome and lengthy process of Directives 89/48/EEC and 98/5/EC. In our opinion this is not a realistic option due to the value that Bar Associations give to the knowledge of national law, where this system would provide access to the legal profession without any knowledge of the national law of the host Member State.

68 Dubbed by ELFA as the 'upside-down system' see: ELFA, *For a European Space of Legal Education*, via: <www.elfa-afde.org>, last accessed 28 April 2011 and Reich 2002-2003, p. 21-38 where it is concluded that this system is 'premature on a general scale' mainly due to the absence of adequate teaching materials. Main advantage of this approach in my opinion is the fact that the knowledge of national law that the student obtains is in the field of the national law of the host member state where he seeks to enter the legal profession.

remain with regard to what needs to be studied during the bachelor phase if such a choice would be made. This is not an easy question to answer. In the past, when Roman law was studied at the different Universities in Europe people who had studied Roman law taught themselves, by means of books specially issued for that purpose, the law of the jurisdiction they chose to work in.[69] In that sense the reconceived Roman law was a true *Ius Commune Europeaum*. Nowadays there is no clear *Ius Commune* that is the basis for all the legal systems in Europe, but there are still ties that bind legal systems close together, often closer than what is assumed in those national jurisdictions.[70]

It may therefore provide a solution, if a bachelor programme in law was developed that would focus largely, or completely, on the common ground between two or more legal systems. Even with close ties in place, it would be overambitious to create a bachelor study that tries to capture every legal system in Europe, but it would be possible to create such a bachelor study on a regional level. Such a bachelor study would then be followed by a master concentrated more on the precise content of national legislation of that Member State in question. Such a system would give students the possibility to prepare during the Master studies for the professional training of the Member State in question independent whether the student has received already in this jurisdiction his bachelor degree.

Maastricht University in the Netherlands has tried to create exactly such a bachelor curriculum. Because of its geographical location, Maastricht is perhaps in comparison to the universities in the centre of the country less orientated towards the rest of the Netherlands and has developed more ties with the surrounding regions in Belgium and Germany. Legal problems in a border region become easily cross-border problems. A comparative approach to legal problems is in such a region quite evident. Maastricht University has a very good reputation in these countries and other faculties, which prepare for non-regulated professions, have always greatly benefited from considerable student influx from Belgium and Germany. Although the Law Faculty has a considerable number of Belgian and German students, these students are always faced with the extra hurdle of having to apply for recognition of their Dutch degree in their home countries. Close cooperation between Belgian and Dutch authorities[71] now ensures that this process is smooth. Differences between the Dutch and German legal systems, and educational systems for that matter, prove to be still too great to overcome for a long time. Traditionally, therefore very few German students enrolled in the Law Faculty in Maastricht. This situation, however, has changed in recent years considerably. In 1995, the Law Faculty created a new curriculum called the European Law School.[72] The purpose of this curriculum was to provide students with a sound foundation in Dutch law, good knowledge of the surrounding legal systems (i.e France, Germany and the United Kingdom) and the law of the

69 Lokin & Zwalve 1992, p. 110-120. See for a very detailed overview of the reception of Roman Law in Europe: Mather 2001-2002, p. 323-362.

70 Van Gerven 2001, p. 485-503.

71 See Bologna Stocktaking Report.

72 Heringa 2002, p. 3-15. See also De Groot 1992.

European Union in order to prepare students for a career in law (predominantly in law firms that operate internationally) yet without sacrificing the *civiel effect* which qualifies students with a law degree to enter the training stage of the Dutch Bar Association in order to qualify as a Dutch *advocaat*. This curriculum has proven to be attractive for both students and employers and is now a very well established part of the curricula offered by the Law Faculty.

More recently, the Law Faculty created a new version of this European Law School which leads to a bachelor degree that is also appealing for students who do not predominately seek to obtain a degree that gives them the opportunity to become an *advocaat* in the Netherlands.[73] This new bachelor curriculum includes two years of English-taught courses (focussed on comparative law and International and European law) and a third year that as one offered option puts much more focus on the national legal systems. In this last year students have an option to follow a track based on Dutch law, go abroad and study there the national system of another jurisdiction or choose for a more general programme.

The national track might prepare students for a masters degree (in the respective countries) that also focus on national law, which then, in turn, leads to access to the qualification track for the legal profession. When proven effective, the curriculum of the new European Law School which started in September 2006, can serve as an example throughout Europe as a method by which, at least the regional furthering of the free movement of lawyers in Europe can be achieved. In the line of this development a second initiative has also been taken. In the Bologna Stocktaking Report, it is mentioned that the Netherlands and Belgium share a Transnational University.[74] Maastricht University and Hasselt University are both partners in this Transnational University. Recently, a new bachelor law curriculum has been created between the Universities of Maastricht (Netherlands) and Hasselt (Belgium) in cooperation with the Catholic University of Leuven (Belgium) and started in 2008. The first bachelor diplomas have been handed out to the students in July 2011. This degree should have as originally planned qualified students to enter the professional qualification process to become a lawyer in both Belgium and the Netherlands after having obtained a Master degree in one of the two Member States. This has until now, unfortunately not be realized fully as the bachelor does not contain enough Dutch law to fulfil the requirements for the Dutch *civiel effect*. The bachelor programme does give students, however, a sound foundation in Belgian, Comparative, International and European law. It has to be seen whether a Master programme can be developed in order to qualify fully for both jurisdictions. Such a law degree could become specifically interesting not only for lawyers who want to work in large international law firms but also for lawyers who intend to establish themselves in small to medium sized law firms that operate in the Dutch-Belgian border area.

73 The *civiel effect* requires curricula by law to include specific subjects in Dutch law.

74 The Transnational University of Limburg, or TUL, is a cooperation between the University of Hasselt and Maastricht University.

It must be questioned whether such an approach, i.e. leaving national law as a starting point for legal education is at all viable.[75] In that sense a number of other initiatives will be looked at,[76] and a short excursion to the United States will be made. Although Maastricht University has been used as an example, it is not the only example of legal education that is more or less detached from one specific legal system. With regard to Europe, many efforts include participation of Dutch Universities. The University of Groningen participates with the University of Bremen and the Carl Ossietzky University in Oldenburg in the Hanse Law School.[77] This law school, which offers both a bachelor and a masters degree, focuses mainly on Dutch and German law, but also looks at the core of English Common law. Strategic choice of subjects allows students to qualify for the qualification track of the legal profession in either Germany or the Netherlands. Graduates from the Hanse Law School cannot become member of the judiciary in Germany if they do not pass the required state exams, however.[78] They might become members of the German Bar after having first fully qualified in the Netherlands due to the application of Directive 98/5/EC. The Radboud University in Nijmegen (Netherlands) has a cooperation structure with both the University of Leuven (Belgium)[79] and the University of Münster (Germany) in connection to a Masters degree programme in Belgian and German law, respectively.[80] In Europe also exists a number of co-operation initiatives between European Universities and Universities in the United States of America. The University of Paris I, The University of London and the University of Frankfurt all have developed joint degrees with Columbia University in New York that lead to double degrees i.e. an American and respectively French, English or German degree.[81] Additionally, the Bucerius Law School in Hamburg has a programme that is highly internationalised and considers in the required programme comparative law extensively but also requires the German State Exam.[82] Rather new is also the initiative of the Humboldt University to create a network of *'European Law Schools'*.[83]

Several European universities have started double degree programmes offering to their students to qualify in two jurisdictions. Such programmes have been specifically developed between French and British Universities.[84] Lastly, there are some initiatives that are worth mentioning in North America. McGill University

75 Apart from the absence of practical matters such as teaching materials as was indicated in ELFA, *For a European Space of Legal Education*, via: <www.elfa-afde.org>, last accessed 28 April 2011 and Reich 2002-2003, p. 21-38.

76 For a very good overview see Gordley 2000-2001, p. 1003-1014.

77 <www.hanse-law-school.de>, last accessed 30 January 2011.

78 *Ibidem.*

79 See also Vanistendael 1999-2000, p. 457-466.

80 <www.ru.nl>, last accessed 30 January 2011.

81 <www.law.columbia.edu/center_program/intl_progs/Double_degrees>, last accessed 31 January 2011.

82 <www.law-school.de>, last accessed 31 January 2011.

83 www.european-law-school.eu/pages/de/netzwerk/netzwerk-der-universitaeten.php, last assessed 28 April 2011.

84 E.g. King's College London and Paris.

in Canada[85] has specialised itself in trans-systemic degrees, i.e. degrees that combine both knowledge of common law and civil law.[86] By far the most ambitious effort in this field is conducted in the United States of America where New York University has created the 'Hauser Global Law School'.[87] This law school envisages teaching students law in a global context, i.e. by comparing the major legal systems of the world.[88]

Where a university chooses to depart from traditional legal education that is strongly rooted in national law and the national legal system, the question immediately arises as to how the content and programme of such a legal education should look. In the literature on this subject[89] there seems to be a consensus that at least some form of comparison between different legal systems, preferably including the home legal system, must be offered. As Gordley explains this comparison serves two goals. First, and most obviously, comparison leads to awareness of other legal solutions and the some knowledge concerning another legal system than one's own. Lawyers with a basic training in other legal systems than their own are more capable of entering an international market where they are confronted with those legal systems. Secondly, comparison offers another, less obvious, but more important advantage. When a student studies law in a comparative context i.e. studies legal problems and the different solutions to those problems in different legal systems, the student learns that the solution of his own legal system is a choice rather then an empirical truth. Comparative law encourages students to think about the ratio of a certain solution, and therefore leads to a deeper knowledge and understanding of the legal systems studied, including one's own. Comparative law therefore also leads to better national lawyers. The debate in the literature, as Gordley portrays it, centres on the question of what place the national legal system should take in this approach. There is an opinion voiced by Pound and Reimann[90] who state that such a comparison should be made while studying the national law, i.e. the national law should form the basis of the comparison that takes place in a later phase of the study.[91] On the other hand, Gordley presents a number of writers, Kötz, Flessner, Coing, Sacco and de Groot,[92] who state that legal studies should begin with a comparison of basic themes in law and that the main focus on the national law should only take place at a later stage. A similar approach is voiced by Jan Smits in his contribution to this volume.[93]

85 See also Valcke 2005, p. 483-505.

86 <www.mcgill.ca/law-admissions/undergraduates/programs/>, last accessed 31 January 2011.

87 <www.nyulawglobal.org/>, last accessed 31 January 2011.

88 See also Fine 2000, p. 567-610. See also, although not specific on the global law school Morris 2005, p. 53-82 and Tarr 2004-2005, p. 199-206.

89 See for an excellent overview Gordley 2000-2001, p. 1003-1014.

90 *Ibidem*, p. 1005.

91 Which is also the general view held by ELFA. See: ELFA, *For a European Space of Legal Education*, via: <www.elfa-afde.org>, last accessed 28 April 2011 and Reich 2002-2003, p. 21-38.

92 *Ibidem*.

93 Smits 2011.

With the two versions of the European Law School that Maastricht University offers, both variants are included. The 'traditional' European Law School that was started in 1995 begins with offering a solid foundation in Dutch law. After the first one and a half years that is basically shared with the ordinary Dutch law students who have chosen for the more traditional national approach (and which is taught in Dutch) the European Law School students change course and take an English-taught programme that focuses on comparative law and the law of the European Union. The 'new' European Law School called the European Law School-English track that started in 2006 follows the second method since it offers a programme where the first two years (completely taught in English) focus on comparative law and the law of the European Union. In the final year of the bachelor (and in ensuing masters degrees) students can take different routes (tracks) that focus on the Dutch legal system or take a more general track (that does not give *civiel effect* nor does it lead directly into the qualification track for the legal profession of other countries). Maastricht does therefore not take a definite stand in the discussion displayed above. From the perspective of the free movement of lawyers, the choice between the two models offered by Maastricht University is clear. Aside from the doctrinal issue, that takes centre-stage in the discussion described above, there is a practical issue that leads to the conclusion that the 'traditional' European Law School, or any other programme that is strongly based in a national legal system, are less beneficial for the furthering of the mobility of young people in Europe. These systems might be of a more limited interest to foreign students, particularly as they are offered in countries that have a language which is not a world language, such as Dutch. Such programmes will mainly attract 'home' students. Only the second variant, which is more detached from the legal system of the country in which it is taught, is also just as interesting for foreign students, and is capable of initiating a cross-border movement of law students.

When these general bachelor systems become more prevalent, where comparison between the major legal systems in Europe (France, Germany and the United Kingdom) and the law of the European Union serve as a true *Ius Commune Europaeum*,[94] education in national law and knowledge of national law can be reserved for master programmes, professional education, or similar to the United States, left to the workings of the free market. Having established that the adoption of a new approach to law studies, based on the general characteristics of the main legal systems in Europe and European Union law as a new *Ius Commune* could benefit the furtherance of the free movement of lawyers in Europe it must be ascertained who has the power to actually realise this feat.

In the absence of legislative initiatives of the European Union, the most likely candidates for achieving this feat are obviously the universities themselves. It has

94 Or as Flessner put it (translated by Gordley): 'Legal instruction which already treats the basics of law in Europe as a unified system in which national legal systems resonate like variations of a general theme'. See Gordley 2000-2001, p. 1003-1014, p. 1005; Flessner 1996. The French delegation to the CCBE was of the opinion back in the nineteen nineties that European law was integrated so much that it could serve as a *Ius Commune*. See Hagan 2003, p. 149-172.

been shown above that universities are already (and have been for a while) busy with creating such curricula. Universities are, in some ways, the best candidates since they obviously know best in determining what is feasible with regard to the creation of such curricula, and they would also be able to find, or hire, the necessary experts to create such a curriculum. The recent creation of the English language variant of the European Law School at the Faculty of Law at Maastricht University is but one example of the fact that such curricula can be created. However, it also shows the potential danger of leaving the initiative to universities. This danger lies in the fact that generally speaking, universities do not make the rules that determine which degrees are accepted for qualification tracks for the legal profession. These are often determined by respective Bar Associations, and are in quite some Member States laid down in national law. This leads to the situation where graduates of such a curriculum, could find themselves in a vacuum if Bar Associations refuse, or are forced to refuse, to accept such a degree as sufficient entry to the professional qualification track.

With regard to the ELS-ET of Maastricht University, agreements have been made between the University and the Dutch Bar Association to assure that the curriculum give *civiel effect* i.e. that it qualifies graduates for the professional training that leads to the profession of the *advocaat* as long students have chosen sufficient courses concerning Dutch law during their studies. Whether as a result of the faulty interpretation of the *Morgenbesser* judgment in paragraph 112a of the *Deutschen Richtergesetz* German ELS-ET students are forced to obtain Dutch *civiel effect* first in order to even be allowed an assessment of their knowledge in German law to enter the professional qualification track in Germany *(Referendariat)* will have to be seen in the future and might only be decided when a new case is brought be for the European Court of Justice. Although universities are technically the best candidates to create these new curricula, such expertise is useless if there is no acceptance of such degrees on the level of the authorities that decide whether such a degree may lead to entrance in the professional qualification track of the legal profession. This means that these authorities will have to be involved.

Luckily, European law provides the possibility for their involvement, and still guaranteeing the flexibility that was deemed necessary earlier in this paragraph. That flexibility can be found in Article 15 of Directive 2005/36/EC which provides a new form of governance which was unknown before in the realm of the free movement of professionals, and more specifically lawyers. This Article provides for the possibility for Member States or professional organisations to communicate common platforms to the Commission. These common platforms are defined as a set of criteria for professional qualifications suitable for compensating substantial differences (that must be identified by at least two thirds of the Member States including all those who regulate the profession) between the professional qualifications for the regulated profession (or the entry to the qualification track thereto) in the different Member States. If such a common platform is then presented to the Commission, it may adopt an implementing decision through the comitology procedure provided for in Article 58(2) of Directive 2005/36/EC. This new form of governance has considerable advantages over the long and very difficult path through harmonisation of legal education (if at all legally possible). First of all, the prime candidate for preparing such a common platform, the CCBE,[95] would be the most important player in this process not only be consulted as in case of harmonisation according to the classical procedure. Secondly, the stakes would be less high compared to the traditional method, since politics would only be involved at a later stage, when preparation of the common platform is already completed. On the other hand, an approved and implemented common platform would have the same legal consequences as harmonisation of legal education in the classic sense, namely the fact that recognition would be automatic and not dependent on compensatory measures that must be fulfilled by the candidate.

It must be bourn in mind that a common platform in this sense will be much broader than the legal education in the Member States alone, and would affect the legal profession as a whole as it would guarantee the entrance of the candidate into the legal profession of a Member State. It is rather unlikely, that a common platform will be adopted for the legal profession in the near future, and in all honesty it is even doubtful whether such a common platform will ever emerge. Developing a legal curriculum that would facilitate a candidate's mobility to another Member State professional qualification track under the direction of the CCBE would at least be the first step towards such a common platform.

6. Concluding Remarks

For EU students, who study law, these developments mean that in the future they might complete one part of their legal education in one Member States and the professional part in another Member State. The national education at the faculties of law and the practical legal training programmes will have to adapt to this new situation. Legal education at academic institutions such as the European Law School in Maastricht, the Hanse Law School in Oldenburg, Bremen and Groningen as well as for instance the academic programmes at the universities of Nijmegen and Münster, Paris and Cambridge, Bordeaux and Liverpool prove by their current success that the mobility of students in the course of legal training is inevitable. This new generation of lawyers will be certainly making a positive contribution to the international legal disputes in Europe in the coming decades. Member States should not try to hinder this development through new obstacles, but rather encourage this great success for the European integration process.

If student mobility is supposed to be a key element for the European Higher Education Area,[96] then it should be possible also for law students to benefit from this mobility without facing any challenging bureaucratic or legal difficulties. Time-consuming and difficult recognition procedures should be avoided as far as

95 Which is already brainstorming about this possibility as can be read from the materials of it annual conference that was held on 25-27 October 2007 and that was completely dedicated to legal training. See: <www.ccbe.org>, last accessed 8 December 2007.

96 As it was stated in the explanation of the Ministers of Higher Education on the Bologna Process in Leuven in April 2009.

possible. Mutual trust in the quality of the educational system in other Member States should generally govern the recognition proceedings. An application for admission to professional training in a Member State, other than in which the academic education was completed, should be generally met with a positive attitude by the competent authorities without ignoring the necessary knowledge of national law.

The applicants' prior education and experiences have to be fully taken into account. In doing so, past experiences, with respect to recognition procedures concerning qualified lawyers and the principle of proportionality, should be taken into consideration. Law faculties should continue to strengthen their international networks by developing joint programmes as well as conversion programmes which will facilitate the mobility of law students in order to make the best choices for their future professional careers. These programmes should be developed in close cooperation with the national Bar associations. It can be hoped that in a future case in Luxembourg the CJEU will have an open eye towards this development. On the long run this development might lead to the truly 'European lawyer', educated in one Member State, professionally trained in another and working in a third, aware of differences in the legal systems as well as conscious of their common legal heritage.

Bibliography

Baas 2003
Baas, A., 'Grensoverschrijdende advocaat-stagiaires', *Advocatenblad,* 2003, Vol. 83, No. 22, p. 973.

Claessens 2008
Claessens, S., *Free Movement of Lawyers in the European Union*, Nijmegen: Wolf Legal Publishers, 2008.

De Groot 1992
De Groot, G.R., 'European Education in the 21st Century', in De Witte, B. & Forder, C. (eds.), *The Common Law of Europe and the Future of Legal Education*, Deventer: Kluwer, 1992, p. 7-29.

Fine 2000
Fine, T.M., 'The Globalization of Legal Education in the United States', *European Journal of Law Reform*, 2000, Vol. 2, No. 4, p. 567-610.

Flessner 1996
Flessner, A., *Deutsche Juristenausbildung. Die Kleine Reform und die europäische Perspektive*, Antrittsvorlesung 16-11-1995, Humboldt-Universität zu Berlin, 1996.

Garben 2011
Garben, S., *The Bologna Process and Higher Education Law: Harmonisation by Stealth,* Deventer: Kluwer, 2011.

Garben & Schneider 2011
Garben, S. & Schneider, H., *Der Bologna-Prozess: Aus der Perspektive des Europäischen Rechts betrachtet,* in Odendahl, K. (ed.), *Europäische Bildungspolitik,* Berlin: Berliner Wissenschafts Verlag, 2011, p. 395-446.

Gordley 2000-2001
Gordley, J., 'Comparative Law and Legal Education', *Tulane Law Review*, 2000-2001, Vol. 75, p. 1003-1014.

Hagan 2003
Hagan, C., 'The Free Movement of Lawyers', *Irish Student Law Review*, 2003, Vol. 11, p. 149-172.

Heringa 2002
Heringa, A.W., 'Towards a European Law School! A Proposal for a Competitive, Diversified Model of Transnational Co-operation', in Faure, M. *et al.* (eds.), *Towards a European Ius Commune in Legal Education and Research,* Antwerp: Intersentia, 2002, p. 3-15.

Lokin & Zwalve 1992
Lokin, J.H.A. & Zwalve, W.J., *Hoofdstukken uit de Europese Codificatie-geschiedenis*, Groningen: Wolters-Noordhoff/Egbert Forsten, 2nd ed., 1992.

Lubina & Schneider 2011
Lubina, K. & Schneider, H., 'Freizügigkeit von Rechtsanwälten in der Europäischen Union: ein Beispiel für andere Berufsgruppen?', in Odendahl, K. (ed.), *Europäische Bildungspolitik*, Berlin: Berliner Wissenschafts Verlag, 2011, p. 305-346.

Mather 2001-2002
Mather, H., 'The Medieval Revival of Roman Law: Implication for Contemporary Legal Education', *Catholic Lawyer*, 2001-2002, Vol. 41, No. 4, p. 323-362.

Morris 2005
Morris, R.J., 'Globalizing & De-Hermeticizing Legal Education', *BYU Education and Law Journal*, 2005, p. 53-82.

Pichonnaz & Hirte 2006
Pichonnaz, P. & Hirte, H., 'Where is Law Thaught? Who Teaches Law? An Exchange of Experiences of the Institutions in which Law is being Taught and of the Persons who teach Law', *European Journal of Legal Education*, 2006, Vol. 3, No. 1, p. 79-81.

Posch 2005
Posch, W., *Die Zukunft der Rechtswissenschaften and den Universitäten*, 2005, via: <www.elfa-afde.org>, last accessed 28 April 2011.

Reich 2002-2003
Reich, N., 'Recent Trends in European Legal Education: the Place of the European Law Faculties Association', *Penn State International Law Review*, 2002-2003, Vol. 21, p. 21-38.

Schmidt-Räntsch & Schmidt-Räntsch 2009
Schmidt-Räntsch, G. & Schmidt-Räntsch, J., *Kommentar zum Deutschen Richtergesetz*, München: C.H. Beck, 2009.

Schneider 1995
Schneider, H., *Die Anerkennug von Diplomen in der Europäischen Gemeinschaft*, Antwerp, Maklu, 1995.

Schneider & Claessens 2005
Schneider, H. & Claessens, S., 'The Recognition of Diplomas and the Free Movement of Professionals in the European Union', in Schneider, H. (ed.), *Migration, Integration and Citizenship; A Challenge for Europe's Future*, Vol. I, Maastricht: Forum Maastricht, 2005, p. 123-166.

Smits 2011
Smits, J., 'European Legal Education, or: How to prepare Students for Global Citizenship?', in Heringa, A.W. & Akkermans, B. (eds.), *Educating European Lawyers*, Antwerp: Intersentia, 2011, p. 43-64.

Steger 2007
Steger, W., *Die Position der Europäischen Anwaltschaft zur Studienreform nach dem Bologna Modell Punktation*, 2007, via: <www.elfa-afde.org>, last accessed 28 April 2011.

Tarr 2004-2005
Tarr, A.A., 'Legal Education in a Global Context', *University of Toledo Law Review*, 2004-2005, Vol. 36, p. 199-206.

Terry 2006
Terry, L.S., 'Living with the Bologna Process: Recommendations to the German Legal Education Community from a U.S. Perspective', *German Law Journal*, 2006, p. 863-905.

Terry 2007
Terry, L.S., 'The Bologna Process and its Implications for U.S. Legal Education', *Journal of Legal Education*, 2007, p. 237-252.

Terry 2008
Terry, L.S., 'The Bologna Process and its Impact in Europe: It's So Much More than Degree Change', *Vanderbilt Journal of Transnational Law*, 2008, p. 107-228.

Timm & Kempter 2005
Timm, S. & Kempter, D., 'Diskriminierung beim Zugang zum Referendardienst in Deutschland - Schein oder Sein?', *Neue juristische Wochenschrift*, 2005, Vol. 59, No, 39, p. 2826-2828.

Valcke 2005
Valcke, C., 'Comparative Legal Education in Canada', *Revue Juridique Themis*, 2005, Vol. 39, p. 483-505.

Van Gerven 2001
Van Gerven, W., 'A Common Law for Europe: The Future Meeting the Past', *European Review of Private Law*, 2001, Vol. 4, p. 485-503.

Vanistendael 1999-2000
Vanistendael, F.J., 'Blitz Survey of the Challenges for Legal Education in Europe', *Dickinson Journal of International Law*, 1999-2000, Vol. 18, p. 457-466.

PART II

EDUCATING EUROPEAN LAWYERS IN MAASTRICHT

Bram Akkermans

THE DEVELOPMENT OF EUROPEAN PRIVATE LAW AND ITS CHALLENGES ON THE LAW SCHOOL CURRICULUM

1. Introduction

Private law takes an important place in any legal curriculum. The classical areas of private law, obligations (contracts and torts) and property law, offer law students basic essential knowledge and necessary skills to become lawyers. In many programs, private law courses are taught in the first year. In a traditional curriculum, these are also courses that create the 'national identity' of students. For example, this could be the importance of good faith in civil law systems, the concept of legal acts as the basis of private law and the concept of ownership as a unitary and absolute right. For common law systems this can be doctrines of privity of contract, consideration, tort of conversion and the concept of estates.

Times are changing and in the last two decades, like many other areas of law, private law has seen an increasing influence of European Union law causing fundamental changes to the traditional system. Some EU Member States have chosen to change their private law completely as a result of these developments.[1] However, national legal education has not changed substantially because of this.[2] Of course, national law that has changed as a result of Europeanisation and internationalisation is studied, but not the processes behind this. Therefore, students and with them also lawyers are often unaware that a certain rule of national law is actually a rule of European law. The danger of this might not seem obvious to the national lawyer, but to the European (private) lawyer it is obvious. The power of interpretation of these rules of national law is not for the national authority - legislature or judiciary - but for the European Court of Justice. Of course

1 For example the German *Schuldrechtsreform* and French *Avant-projet de réforme du droit des obligations* and the *réforme du droit de sûretés*. See Zimmermann 2002, p. 265-288; *Avant-projet de réforme du droit des obligations et du droit de la prescription*, Rapport à Monsieur Pascale Clément Garde des Sceaux, Ministre de la justice, 22 septembre 2005, Ordonnance No. 2006-346 du 23 mars 2006 relative aux sûretés, *JORF* 24 March 2006.

2 See Akkermans 2009, p. 803-814.

national courts will interpret and apply this legislation, but they will do so as courts of European law.[3]

For some time already, national private lawyers are not seeing or even denying the influence of European law.[4] Nonetheless, research shows a clear influence of European law.[5] Unfortunately, this is usually not reflected in the national curricula. Time has come to change national private law education and train private lawyers that can work in a European legal environment. They should become European private lawyers.

This contribution will deal with some of the major challenges faced in European private law, the translation of these challenges into the curriculum followed by law students and, finally, some perspectives for the future.

2. Challenges in European Private Law

The study of European private law is not new, for a half a century already comparative law has been subject of academic research.[6] For a long time, comparative private law was a rare area of research, which occupied a very small number of researchers. Moreover, results of comparative research were usually intended to supplement conclusions reached on the basis of national legal research. Comparative results, rather than comparison itself, therefore, suited to strengthen the conclusions drawn at a national level, often taken over doctrine or solutions from other legal systems.[7] Even a smaller number of researchers than those comparing for this purpose, compared for the sake of comparison. In that approach, the objective is finding underlying thought patterns and similar approaches to solutions. With the great danger of prejudice of foreign legal systems, as well as the over-functionalism in finding areas of law to compare with, this type of study gained popularity. Perhaps the most famous example is the standard work by Zweigert and Kötz on the *Einleitung in die Rechtsvergleichung*, later translated into English by Tony Weir.[8]

In the last decades, the study of comparative law, especially private law, has become much more complicated. However, with each complication the field becomes more and more interesting. As it turns out, finding functional equivalents is much more difficult than anyone ever imagined,[9] comparing results is science on its own,[10] and, moreover, the effects of 'borrowing' a doctrine from another legal system and implementing it in your own - a legal transplant - is much more

[3] See Claes 2005, p. 1-4.
[4] See Van Erp 2006, p. 3-5.
[5] See, *inter alia*, Van Erp 2006, p. 5-11; Akkermans 2008, p. 475 *et seq.*; Saarloos 2010; Kieninger 1996, p. 165 *et seq.*; Rutgers 1999, p. 93 *et seq.*; Israël 2005.
[6] David 1964; Dannemann 2006, p. 383.
[7] See, *inter alia*, Ioriatti & Van Erp 2007.
[8] Zweigert & Kötz 1996, translated into English by Weir 1998.
[9] Michaels 2006, p. 339-382; Jansen 2006, p. 305-338.
[10] Jansen 2006, p. 305-338.

complex than imagined at first.[11] Besides these complications, comparative law has become integrated with European law, law and economics, sociology and political science. The result is an immensely rich domain of study that remains underdeveloped in relation to the fields of science it is borrowing from. Furthermore, the result is a field that has become so vast that it has become impossible - with the exception of a few very experienced academics - for a single researcher to keep track of all developments.

Three main developments may be distinguished: more and more researchers seek cooperation to be able to take on large comparative projects, both comparing legal systems and European Union law and the law of the Member States; the influence of European Union law on private law is so extensive that more and more European Union specialists are turning to private law and vice versa; finally, multidisciplinary research offers opportunities to gain new and renewed insights in private law.

2.1. *Cooperation as the Key-solution to Move Forward*

Individual legal research often focuses on a very specific aspect of law. Even if a study has a larger scope, such as the principle of good faith in contract law or transfer of movables, this is still a very limited aspect of the system of private law.[12] When, in the 1980s ideas rose to create a European private law, be it in the form of a European Civil Code or otherwise, cooperation was needed to be able to deal with larger aspects of private law. Professor Ole Lando formed the Commission on European Contract Law that would draft the Principles of European Contract Law (PECL), a set of rules, accompanied by comments of the drafters and comparative notes, which could offer a basis for a common contract law of Europe based on comparative research.[13] This cooperation turned out to be very successful. Cooperation was soon entered into in the Trento Common Core Project, which does not draft principles (rules), but searches for a common core between European legal systems on the basis of questionnaires and country reports, the Ius Commune Casebook Project for the Common Law of Europe, which drafts casebooks on the basis of primary source materials and case-law to illustrate the commonalities between legal systems in Europe and, finally, the creation of the Study Group on a European Civil Code and the Research Group on EC private law, better known as the Acquis Group.[14] It are the latter two groups that have recently become widely known as the principal authors of the Draft Common Frame of Reference, a project initiated by the European Commission seeking to offer, based on a revision of the PECL, an analysis of primary aspects of the contract law *acquis* and additions based

11 Graziadei 2006, p. 441-476.

12 Zimmermann & Whittaker 2000, and Van Vliet 2000.

13 Lando & Beale 2000; Lando, Clive, Prüm & Zimmermann 2003.

14 The Common Core of European Private Law, see <www.common-core.org>; Ius Commune Casebooks for the Common Law of Europe, see <www.casebooks.eu>, and the Joined Network on European Private Law (coPECL), see <www.co-pecl.org>.

on comparative and economic research, model rules for private law in Europe.[15] The Draft Common Frame of Reference is intended to form the basis of a Common Frame of Reference (CFR) on Contract Law, to be adopted by the European Union. What specific form it will take, depends on a political process and may vary from a toolbox for the European and national legislatures to assist the drafting of new contract law legislation, an optional code of contract law that can exist as a 28th legal regime, and - although not very likely - a civil code of contract code for the European Union replacing existing national legislation.[16]

One of the most important aspects of the CFR, besides of course its content, is the fact that it was made in cooperation between academics, both junior and senior, from all Member States of the European Union. Moreover, during the process of drafting other parties were also included. First and foremost, this was the European Commission that funded a large part of the research, but also the inclusion of stakeholders, i.e. interested parties invited by the commission. These stakeholders include practicing lawyers, judges, interest groups and politicians.[17] Thus, new forms of cooperation were created.

Most recently of all, a group of academics is seeking the creation of a European Law Institute (ELI), created by analogy of the American Law Institute (ALI). The ALI has become a renowned institution which drafts restatements of law, based on a thorough analysis of case law and doctrine in the jurisdictions of the law at State level. The ELI would seek to draft restatements based on an analysis of doctrine and case law in the Member States of the European Union. Moreover, it would include, based on new ideas on the need for cooperation as the solution to move forward in the creation of European Union private law, also members from practice, government and interest groups.

2.2. *European Union Developments and Private Law*

As mentioned above, comparative private law is no longer restricted to horizontal comparisons. The influence of European and International instruments on national systems of private law is gaining, so much that some academics exclusively specialize in this vertical effect. When it comes to the European Union, this discipline has become known as European Union private law.

The interesting aspect of European private law is that it cannot be studied without thorough knowledge of European Union law, i.e. the primary and secondary sources as well as the case law and the effect of the case law of the European Court of Justice. Moreover, a European private lawyer can also not do without extensive knowledge of private international law. A few developments will illustrate this.

15 It is precisely this mixed content that has received some serious criticism; see Eidenmüller, Faust, Grigoleit, Jansen & Zimmermann 2008, p. 529-550.

16 See Von Bar *et al.* 2009, paras. 4 and 6-8. See also Green Paper on Policy Options for Progress towards a European Contract Law for Consumers and Businesses COM(2010) 348 final.

17 Report from the Commission. Second Progress Report on The Common Frame of Reference COM(2007) 447 final.

In the area of contract law there is a substantive body of secondary European Union legislation. Most of this legislation is concerned with consumer protection and therefore known as the EU consumer *acquis*. However, there is also other legislation, which focuses on business-to-business (B2B) transactions only.[18] Most of this legislation takes the form of Directives, which must be implemented into national law in order to take effect and create rights for individuals.[19] These Directives are not always implemented correctly in all Member States. When this is the case, national legislation will be interpreted in conformity with the text of the Directive whenever possible, with the limit of an interpretation *contra legem*.[20] When Directive-conform interpretation does not solve the problem, the Member State is liable for the incorrect implementation.[21] The knowledge of most lawyers will reach until this point. However, in the past decade there is a development in European Union law that fundamentally changes this rather simple system into a complicated constitutional relationship between the European Union and national level of legislation. This complication exists in the form of principles of European Union law.[22] These principles are so important to the European Union that their effect reached beyond the system of implementation described above. It is best illustrated with the decision of the European Court of Justice in the case of Mangold.[23] Mangold was a German case that was brought to the European Court of Justice under the preliminary question procedure of Article 267 TFEU. It concerned a German law dealing with labour contracts. A 56 year old Mr. Mangold concluded a temporary contract to work for mr. Helm citing a provision of German law justifying the temporary nature of the contract. Mr. Mangold challenged the contract based on age discrimination - Germany differentiated the acceptance of temporary contracts by age - contained in Directives 1999/70 and 2000/78. A successful challenge of the contract relied on the provisions in Directive 2000/78 that had been published but which implementation period had not expired yet. The European Court of Justice relied on the constitutional relevance of the Directive incorporating the principle of equal treatment into European Union law. The Court of Justice considered that the principle of equal treatment is so important to European Union law that it could apply, regardless of the non-expiry of the implementation period.[24]

The Mangold case shows how general aspects of European Union law can have a far reaching effect on systems of private law. Although this case and its effects are controversial, there are many other situations in which principles of

18 See, for instance, Directive 2002/47/EC of the European Parliament and of the Council of 6 June 2002 on Financial Collateral Arrangements.

19 On Directives and their workings see Craig & de Búrca 2008, p. 85, p. 279-303.

20 Craig & de Búrca 2008, p. 289-291.

21 Joined Cases 6/90 and 9/90 *Andrea Francovich and Danila Bonifaci* v. *Italy* [1991] ECR I-5357.

22 Before the entry into force of the Lisbon Treaty, which changed the European Community into the European Union, these were known as principles of Community law.

23 Case C-144/04 *Werner Mangold* v. *Rüdiger Helm* [2005] ECR I-9981.

24 Case C-144/04 *Werner Mangold* v. *Rüdiger Helm* [2005] ECR I-9981, para. 74. See Schiek 2006, p. 329 *et seq.*; Devroe 2007, p. 144-151.

European Union law have effect on national rules of private law.[25] This potentially includes the effect of the precautionary principle on general contracts, insurance contracts and labour contracts.[26]

The above shows how the European Court of Justice protects and enforces the application of European Union law. It does so, in other instances, irrelevant to private law at first sight. The case of Möllendorf concerns the application of Regulation 881/2002 on specific measures directed against persons and entities associated with Usama bin Laden, the Al-Qaida network and the Taliban.[27] This regulation was adopted under the European Union's anti-terrorism policy and is thus very far remote from private law. However, the parties in this case had concluded a contract to transfer ownership of a piece of land in Germany. In order to transfer ownership of a piece of land in German law, registration in the *Grundbuch*, the land registry, is a constitutive requirement.[28] Land registration in Germany is a complicated matter that takes the registry officials some time to complete. As a result there is a considerable period of time between the concluding of the contract of sale and the actual transfer of ownership of the land. It is precisely in this period that one of buyers was placed on the black-list created by Regulation 881/2002. The result was the freezing of all accounts the buyer and the voidness of all transactions entered into. However, the contract of sale was concluded before the buyer was placed on the list and the European Court of Justice was asked what the effect of the application of the Regulation was to the property aspects of this case. The European Court of Justice looked at the effectiveness of the Regulation and concluded that the transfer of ownership could not take place now that the buyer was on the list.[29]

Thirdly, a final example of the effects of European Union law on national law. In the case of Schulte the European Court of Justice was confronted with another German case. This case concerned a series of three linked contracts which had been 'sold' to consumers in a doorstep-selling situation. The contracts concerned a credit agreement (loan), a contract for the acquisition of ownership of an immovable and a contract creating a property security right on that immovable to secure the performance of the debtor under the credit agreement. The immovable was what became known as a junk-immovable (*Schrottimmobilie*). In a series of case law the European Court of Justice decided that these contracts were concluded in a doorstep selling situation. At first, German law did not recognise the factual situation as a doorstep-selling situation because parties were unaware that this was

25 See Devroe 2007, p. 133-189.

26 Devroe 2007, p. 171-180.

27 Council Regulation (EC) No. 881/2002 of 27 May 2002 imposing certain specific restrictive measures directed against certain persons and entities associated with Usama bin Laden, the Al-Qaida network and the Taliban, and repealing Council Regulation (EC) No. 467/2001 prohibiting the export of certain goods and services to Afghanistan, strengthening the flight ban and extending the freeze of funds and other financial resources in respect of the Taliban of Afghanistan (*OJ* 2002 L 139, p. 9), as amended by Council Regulation (EC) No. 561/2003 of 27 March 2003 (*OJ* 2003 L 82, p. 1) ('Regulation No. 881/2002').

28 See Akkermans 2008, p. 204.

29 Case C-117/06 *Gerda Möllendorf and Christiane Möllendorf-Niehuus* [2007] ECR I-8361.

the case. The ECJ disagreed.[30] As a result Directive 85/588/EEC on Contracts Concluded away from Business Premises, better known as the Doorstep Selling Directive, applied, offering the consumer a right of withdrawal for 7 days after the notification of that right of withdrawal by the seller to the consumer. However, Article 3(2)(a) of the Directive explicitly excludes contracts concerning immovables and security rights on immovables from the scope of the Directive. The case of Schulte concerned a situation where the consumer was not notified of the existence of his right of withdrawal. The European Court of Justice held that the consumer was therefore still allowed to withdraw from the credit agreement, the other agreements being excluded on the basis of Article 3(2)(a) of the Doorstep Selling Directive.[31] In previous cases, the European Court of Justice had reached a similar conclusion, deciding that national law must deal with the other contracts, but leaving a situation of uncertainly in regard to the excluded property contracts.[32] In Schulte the Court answered this problem in the following way:

> 69 Although it is thus for the Member States to legislate as regards the legal effects of cancellation, that power must be exercised in accordance with Community law and, in particular, the rules of the Directive interpreted in the light of its objective and in such a way as to ensure that it is fully effective. In fulfilling their obligations under a Directive the Member States are to take all the measures necessary to ensure that the directive is fully effective, in accordance with the objective it pursues (Case C-336/97 Commission v Italy [1999] ECR I-3771, paragraph 19, and Case C-324/01 Commission v Belgium [2002] ECR I-11197, paragraph 18).[33]

The doctrine of *effet utile* or effectiveness should therefore decide whether national law does justice to the Directive it has implemented. In doing so, not the national law, but the European rule sets the standard, not the national courts, but the European courts have authority and much more national law can be included than just the specific area a Member State chose to implement the Directive in. As the European Court of Justice makes clear in Schulte, it remains to be seen whether the Doorstep Selling Directive, which specifically excludes matters of immovable property law, can actually have effect on matters of immovable property law. Under German law – the cases on the Doorstep Selling Directive come from Germany – the *Trennungsprinzip* or principle of separation brings a strong separation between the law of contract and the law of property.[34] Under this system a transfer of ownership of land requires the conclusion of a contract after which property law provides its own rules and requirements to effect the transfer of ownership.[35] Following the principle of separation, the system of transfer is an abstract transfer system.[36] Under

30 Case C-481/99 *Heiniger* v. *Bayerische Hypo- und Vereinsbank AG* [2001] ECR I-9945.

31 Case C-350/03 *Schulte* v. *Deutsche Bausparkasse Badania AG* [2005] ECR I-9215.

32 Case 229/04 *Crailsheimer Volksbank Eg* v. *Kaus Conrads and others* [2005] ECR I-9273 and C-481/99 *Heiniger* v. *Bayerische Hypo- und Vereinsbank AG* [2001] ECR I-9945.

33 Case C-350/03 *Elisabeth and Wolfgang Schulte* v. *Deutsche Bausparkasse Badenia* [2005] ECR I-9215, para. 69.

34 See Akkermans 2008, p. 167-169.

35 See Motive 1888, p. 1-3.

36 See Van Vliet 2000, p. 31.

this abstract system, there is separation between the contract and the transfer of ownership. Invalidity of the contract under this system does not normally lead to the invalidity of the transfer.

This is the classical model of property law, created by the drafters of the German civil code.[37] Times are different, and we see the rise of a modern dynamic property law. The developments stimulating this happen partly at a European level. The doctrine of *effet utile* contributes to this and the examples mentioned above illustrate this.[38] Arguments that private law is outside the scope of European Union law, or that certain areas of private law do not fall under the scope of European Union law - such as the general exemption of property law under Article 345 TFEU that states that the treaties 'shall in no way prejudice the rule of property ownership in the Member States - do not hold ground.[39] It is long standing case law of the European Court of Justice that the form of national law is irrelevant when it comes to the effect of European Union law. Any type of national law can be subject to European Union law.[40]

2.3. *Multi-disciplinary Research*

A final development in European private law is the increasing multi-disciplinary research. This does not only include somewhat more traditional law and economic analysis of law, but also behavioural science and law, law and political science and law and sociology. The effect of the inclusion of these fields of science is an enrichment of the knowledge of private law. This enrichment does not only concern a better knowledge of existing private law, but also entails a broader perspective on European private law in general. In this respect, more and more attention is paid to the stages before legislation is drafted and adopted as well as more attention to the effect future legislation will have and the effect existing legislation has on society. A few examples will illustrate.

In European contract law, much attention is paid to the unequal situation between a consumer and a multi-national trader that conclude a contract.[41] In order to resolve some of this inequality, European law creates information duties for the trader so that the consumer can make a more informed decision.[42] This method of consumer protection seeks to attack the information asymmetry that exists between the parties.[43] However, law and behavioural law and economics studies have shown that there is a tipping point in the information processing power of an average

37 See Van Erp 2009a, p. 1517-1533.

38 See Case C-350/03 *Schulte* v. *Deutsche Bausparkasse Badania AG* [2005] ECR I-9215.

39 On this property law aspect see Akkermans & Ramaekers 2010, p. 292-314.

40 See Case 11/70 *Internationale Handelsgesselschaft mbH* v. *Einfuhr- und Vorratstelle für Getreide und Futtermittel* [1970] ECR 1125, para. 3. See also Craig & de Búrca 2008, p. 346.

41 Study Group on Social Justice in European Contract Law 2004, p. 653-674.

42 See, for example, Art. 5 E-Commerce Directive (2000/31); Art. 4 Distance Selling (97/7); Art. 6 Consumer Credit Directive (2008/48).

43 See Micklitz, Stuyck, Terryn & Droshout 2010, p. 5-6.

consumer. At a certain moment there is so much information given to a consumer that he or she cannot make a well-informed decision anymore.[44]

Furthermore, in European private law, there are new developments. These include green papers and white papers on new upcoming legislative initiatives, but also the interpretation of impact assessments - the predictions of effectiveness of future legislation made for the European Commission - and the creation of expert groups advising the European Commission on the way forward.[45] For lawyers, these developments occur before the actual legislative process is started. However, the process before the legislative track is equally interesting. In fact, in European contract law, this is where the debate has centered on for the last ten years. In 2001 the European Commission published a communication on European contract law, starting a lengthy process that would, for now, lead to the Draft Common Frame of Reference of contract law.[46] After an action plan in 2003, in 2007 only a green paper was launched.[47] In October 2008 a draft Directive on Consumer Rights was proposed, which remains under debate in 2010.[48] Finally, in 2010 a new Green Paper was published in which the European Commission presented its policy options for a future European Contract Law.[49] This Green Paper now forms the centre of the European contract law debate.

As a result of this lengthy process, initially only a small selection of legal scholars took interest in the process. Only after the publication of the Draft Common Frame of Reference (DCFR), a set of model rules accompanied by comments and comparative notes of the drafters, the scope has become much wider. Although the drafters themselves seem to want to avoid any political decision making, the process is certainly one of European politics.[50] Only a few researchers seem to have realised this.[51] Regardless of this realisation, European private law as a field of study has become almost political science. Cross-fertilisation has taken place and most recently European private law scholars venture into aspects of political science.[52]

Finally, there is an increase in studies following a law and sociology methodology. These studies especially concern the measuring of the effectiveness of

44 Shleifer 2000, p. 216 and Thaler 2005, p. 712.

45 See, for example, the Expert Group on a Common Frame of Reference in the Area of Contract Law, created by Commission Decision of 26 April 2010 (2010/233/EU), *OJ* 27 April 2010 L 105/109.

46 Communication from the Commission to the Council and the European Parliament of 11 July 2001 on European Contract Law, COM(2001) 398 final; Von Bar *et al.* 2009.

47 Communication from the Commission to the Council and the European Parliament of 12 February 2003, A More Coherent European Contract Law, an Action Plan, COM(2003) 68 final, Green Paper on the Review of the Consumer Acquis of 8 February 2007, COM(2006) 744 final.

48 Proposal for a Directive of the European Parliament and of the Council on Consumer Rights of 8 October 2008, COM(2008) 614 final.

49 Green Paper on Policy Options for Progress towards a European Contract Law for Consumers and Businesses COM(2010) 348 final.

50 Von Bar *et al.* 2009, p. 3-5.

51 See Hesselink 2004, p. 675 *et seq.*; Van Erp 2008, p. 249 *et seq.*; Van Erp 2009b, p. 105 *et seq.*

52 See, *inter alia*, Sparkes 2007; Van Erp & Akkermans, forthcoming.

legislation. Sociology provides researchers with the tools to measure whether a certain aspect of law is actually effective. This includes the over-informed consumer mentioned above, but also the effectiveness of rules regulating notaries or criminal offenses.[53]

This type of research therefore provides further insights into the workings of law; it increases awareness of the limits of legislation and, most importantly, creates a deeper understanding of the field of study. Researchers often propose new and better type of legislation or even resolve the problems they have discovered.

3. Translating the Challenges into Teaching

A brief overview of some of the most relevant developments in European private law research shows many challenges. Of course these challenges must and will be resolved by researchers themselves, but as teaching and research activities tend to go hand in hand in most universities, these challenges should be reflected in the private law curriculum. As mentioned already above, not many law school curricula pay close attention to the development of European private law. Moreover, even if this is so, it is usually taught in a traditional sense, focussing on comparative law. Depending on the interest of the researcher/teacher, a course will focus on very specific aspects or take a more general (comparative) point of view.

Private law has traditionally been a central subject in any law school curriculum. It is considered useful to teach students how to reason, used to create a strong connection to courses in legal history, especially those dealing with Roman law, and to create a sense of national doctrinal identity for future lawyers. In classical, i.e. traditional, law school curricula private law plays a central role. However, the developments described above call for a new approach in teaching private law.

European private law requires a whole different approach. First and foremost, a student needs a thorough basis in European law, especially the law of the European Union. Secondly, a student also requires essential basic knowledge of private law, preferably comparative law. In Maastricht we teach a curriculum in which students are not required to study one legal system first, but in which comparative courses are offered immediately. Such an approach has the danger of not introducing a student properly into one legal system, but the advantage of not immediately creating a prejudice for only one legal tradition. Students following this comparative courses tend to have a more open mind, aimed at problem solving and able to look beyond the mere rule of law, rather than thinking already in an existing framework of possibilities. Moreover, a student with a serious basis in European Union law is used to think in terms of effectiveness and possibilities, rather than in private law doctrine and obstacles to create solutions.[54] Courses in

53 See, *inter alia*, Laclé & Ter Voert 2006; Diephuis, Eshuis & de Heer-de Lange 2008; Kalidien & Eggen 2009.

54 Students in the Maastricht European Law School curriculum take a full course in European Union Institutional law, focussing on the institutions and the law around these, and one full →

European private law are therefore best placed at the end of the basic curriculum or offered at a master level.

The combination of a student with thorough knowledge of European Union law and basic knowledge of private law create a very suitable starting point for a course on European private law. Teaching European private law requires a revolutionary change in thinking. Traditionally, private law is taught from a national perspective. Comparative perspectives are added, but one legal system will usually be more central than the others under discussion. European private law requires changing focus from the national to the European perspective. But such a change has far-reaching consequences.

3.1. *Changing Focus*

These consequences create a shift of emphasis from national private law to a European perspective looking at the private law of the Member States. By changing focus to a European level, it becomes possible to teach without an in-depth analysis of a single legal system, creating a true European perspective to a course. Two examples can illustrate this. In the area of contract law there is a large body of European Union *acquis*, i.e. existing legislation and case law of the European Court of Justice as well as case law of national courts applying European Union law in their capacity as courts of the European Union law. In fact, the body of *acquis* is so extensive, that an entire course can be easily devoted to it. It includes Directives dealing with doorstep selling, distance selling, e-commerce, consumer credit, but also financial collateral arrangements, prospectuses for financial services and vertical restraints.[55] As was already dealt with above, there are decisions by the European Court of Justice on the interpretation of these acts of European Union law and their relationship to national law. The case of Schulte, dealing with the Doorstep Selling Directive, changed German private law. There are many more examples of such case law. For example, recently a decision of the European Court of Justice concerning the interpretation of the Unfair Commercial Practices Directive showed the potential scope of application of the Directive. The case concerned a sales promotion used by the supermarket Plus. Through the collection of points the customers of Plus could receive a lottery ticket. German law prohibits such a promotion if permission is not obtained, as this is, at least in the eyes of the German government, leading to the participation in a game of chance. Hence, the German authorities banned the promotion. However, the European Court of Justice, asked to consider whether this was an unfair commercial practice, considered that the Unfair Commercial Practices Directive is a full harmonisation device. As a result it sets the standard, from which Member States may not deviate. The Directive contains a list in the Annex of what practices constitute unfair commercial practices

course in European Union substantive law, focussing on the four freedoms and competition law.

55 Directive 85/577 (Doorstep Selling); 97/7 (Distance Contracts); 2000/31 (E-Commerce); 2008/48 (Consumer Credit); 2002/47 (Financial Collateral Arrangements); 2003/71 (Prospectus) and Regulation 330/10 on Vertical Agreements.

and are prohibited under the Directive. However, because the Plus-promotion was not mentioned in the list, it could not be an unfair commercial practice *per se* and therefore not be prohibited.[56]

This case decision offers a good starting point for discussion with students as the three most fundamental aspects of a course of European private law are contained in this case. First, the Unfair Commercial Practices Directive is part of the European Union's Consumer *acquis*. This does not automatically imply that the Directive itself is also a private law Directive. In fact, the Unfair Commercial Practices Directive offers an administrative procedure to combat unfair commercial practices. However, although the Directive does not directly affect contract law, in fact the Directive states explicitly it is without prejudice to the validity of the contract, the Directive is held to create information duties for traders which, if not fulfilled can lead to a misleading and therefore unfair commercial practice. In some Member States, notably France and Belgium, this can lead to avoidance of the contract.[57] The case therefore offers an example of European private law in the form of a Directive.

Secondly, the case also offers a good opportunity to discuss the form European contract law takes. There is no comprehensive system of European contract law, but rather a set of specific legislation dealing with certain aspects of contract law. The Unfair Commercial Practices Directive is one of the first Directives in the field with a larger scope. Moreover, it is a full harmonisation Directive, setting the maximum standard for Member States from which they may not, unless the Directive specifically allows them, deviate. The effects of such a type of Directive are more far reaching on national law than the more traditional minimum harmonisation Directives.

Thirdly, the case offers a possibility to discuss the relationship between European Union law and national (private) law. With the growth in euro-scepticism this debate is increasingly becoming more relevant. Full harmonisation as a topic will lead to this debate, but especially the effects of the Plus case and the interpretation of the European Court of Justice on what the effect of full harmonisation can be, offers perfect food for discussion.[58]

A second example can offered in property law. Property law usually perceived as being outside the scope of European Union law.[59] Although there is not an extensive body of *acquis* in this area, there is an increasing body of rules that deals with or affects property law. This includes the creation of a European Union mortgage market, financial collateral arrangements creating security ownership and property security rights, but also rules on cross-border insolvency, succession and

56 Case C-304/08 *Zentrale zur Bekämpfung unlauteren Wettbewerbs eV* v. *Plus Warenhandelsgesellshaft mbH* [2010] of 14 January 2010, not yet reported.

57 Because of *dol par* reticence. See Whittaker 2007, n. 160.

58 Also the Schulte case mentioned above (Case C-350/03) offers such a possibility as the ECJ suggests that the law of the Member States should hold linked immovable property contracts void when a right of withdrawal (named cancellation under the Directive) under the Doorstep Selling Directive is used.

59 Akkermans & Ramaekers 2010, p. 292.

matrimonial property law. Besides this, there is a body of case law that is of particular interest to European property lawyers. These cases concern the free movement of goods and free movement of capital and lead to two questions. First, whether a property right validly created in one Member State must be recognised as such in another Member State. Classical or traditional systems of property law resist such a recognition in their private international law rules because of the principle of *numerus clausus*.[60] In the case of Krantz the European Court of Justice hinted at the possibility that a property right on a good, in this case a machine, that is transferred to another Member State resulting in a chance of property right on that good because of the application of, in this case Dutch, private international law, was contrary to the free movement of goods.[61] In other case law the European Court of Justice has considered the application of the free movement of capital to property law. In the cases of Konle and Reisch Austrian local authorities required a declaration made before a court or authorisation of a court in order to acquire ownership of a piece of land. This requirement was introduced to prevent the creation of tourist-colonies, but was held to be against European Union law.[62]

These cases offer an excellent starting point for a discussion on European property law. Like European contract law, a discussion is possible on the content of existing legislation, its interpretation and the effect on, and therefore the relationship with, the law of the Member States, but these cases offer another element to the discussion: the influence of internal market law. The cases show that even sensitive issues such as ownership and the way in which ownership is acquired are not automatically excluded from the scope of European Union law. That is not to state that these national rules are automatically in violation of European Union Law. In fact, whether this is the case remains to be seen. After the application of internal market law is established, a court will look whether the national measure can be justified and whether this justification is proportional to the aim pursued.[63] The discussion on justification and proportionality offers a very good possibility to discuss matters of property law doctrine.

For example, when the non recognition of a property right validly created in another Member State leads to a violation of Article 34 TFEU (free movement of goods), the Member State will offer grounds for justification. These can be - for example - the national closed system of property rights, the *numerus clausus*. The *numerus clausus* in this context seeks to protect the national balance of property rights and, in case of security rights, the instances of priority over other creditors.[64] In this way the threat of another property right allows a debate on classical property

60 On the principle of *numerus clausus* see Akkermans 2008, p. 390-396.

61 This concerns the application of the *lex rei sitae* rule in combination with substantive property law. Case 69/88 *H. Krantz GmbH & Co* v. *Ontvanger der Directe Belastingen en de Staat der Nederlanden* [1990] ECR I-583; see further Akkermans & Ramaekers 2011, forthcoming.

62 Case 302/97 *Klaus Konle* v. *Republik Österreich* [1999] ECR I-3099 and Joined Cases C-15/99, C-519/99 to C-524/99 and C-526/99 to C-540/99, *Hans Reisch and others* v. *Bürgermeister der Landeshauptstadt Salzburg and Grundverkehrsbeauftragter des Landes Salzburg* [2002] ECR I-2157.

63 Barnard 2007, p. 65 *et seq.*

64 See Akkermans 2008, p. 415 *et seq.*

law doctrine. Moreover, when proportionality is discussed, the sense and non-sense of the principle of *numerus clausus* can also be addressed: it is at least questionable if an outright refusal to recognise a foreign property right can be a proportionate reaction. Registration might be able to solve many objections while accommodating the foreign property right in the host legal system.[65]

Courses of European private law that operate on the basis of a different focus, i.e. on European Union law rather than on national law, do not neglect national law, but consider it in a different perspective. The result is dealing with the real European private law.[66]

3.2. *Teaching Materials*

Teaching the real European private law requires sources that students can use that also have changed focus to a European perspective. These type of sources are rare and often difficult to find. Moreover, because these sources are rarely available in any country, they are not always available in English. In European private law often materials exist in French, German and Italian. More recently the body of literature is steadily increasing. This includes articles on specific subjects, but also sourcebooks such as the Ius Commune Casebooks for the Common Law of Europe, which are made under general editorship of former Advocate-General Prof. Walter van Gerven.[67] Although the first wave of these casebooks concerned comparative materials, the two most recent casebooks - dealing with non-discrimination and consumer law - are written from a European perspective.

Sometimes, primary source materials are available in English, translated by academics specifically for the use of students.[68] However, when no translation is available, students must still deal with the original source material in another language, restricting their research to the languages they are able to understand. The European Union, especially the European Commission, has also come to realise this is a problem, not only for students, but for any citizen dealing with the law and new initiatives are developed to remedy this. This includes the N-Lex database that contains national law implementing European Union Directives, but also a new forum that will contain information on the law of the Member States, both legislation and (important) case law, available in all languages of the European Union.[69]

There is, in other words, a growing need to develop teaching materials in European private law. Also here, the statements made above on cooperation as the

65 See Akkermans 2008, p. 515.

66 Or, in other words, the new European private law, see Akkermans 2009, p. 803.

67 On the Ius Commune casebook series, a joined initiative of the Catholic University of Leuven (Belgium) and Maastricht University (the Netherlands) see <www.casebooks.eu>.

68 See, for example, Kiiver & Kornet 2008.

69 Commissioner Designate Vivianne Reding for Justice, Freedom and Security during the hearing of the Committee on Civil Liberties, Justice and Home Affairs (LIBE), Legal Affairs (JURI) and Women's Rights and Gender Equality (FEMM) of the European Parliament, 12 January 2010 , *de auditu*.

key to move forward apply.[70] The Ius Commune casebook series offers a very good example of the success cooperation can have. The books are considered prestigious results of academic research and are therefore included in the research review of many universities in many countries. Academics are therefore more easily found willing to contribute.

4. Perspectives for the Future

Research in European private law will only increase with the developments taken at a European Union level. As a result, more and more researchers will devote their time to the field. Many universities have already realised that this research should be translated into teaching and are now offering courses in European private law. However, as I have tried to illustrate above, the field has become so vast that a single course can hardly be sufficient to deal with all interesting matters. For many universities, therefore, European private law remains European contract law.

However, other fields of private law, most notably, property, tort and unjust enrichment are slowly gaining strength, only complicating matters further. The Draft Common Frame of Reference, the academic result of the joined efforts of the Study Group on a European Civil Code and the Acquis Group, deals with all of these areas and therefore stimulates the enlargement of the field of European private law. More research is needed in order to enable researchers to develop course materials and to teach courses in these areas.

The result is likely to be master programs specifically devoted to European Private Law. Cooperation with other master programs is necessary, potentially leading to interesting multi-location programs enabling students to study at various places in Europe. The experiences of the Maastricht Faculty of Law, where we teach European Contract Law, European Property Law and European Tort Law for over ten years already, may offer an example. We are, in any case, more than willing to assist those who want to, in setting up new courses and other types of cooperation.

70 See above paragraph 2.

Bibliography

Akkermans 2008
Akkermans, B., *The Principle of Numerus Clausus in European Property Law*, Antwerp: Intersentia, 2008.

Akkermans 2009
Akkermans, B., 'Challenges in Legal Education and the Development of a New European Private Law', *German Law Journal*, 2009, Vol. 10, No. 5, p. 803-814.

Akkermans & Ramaekers 2010
Akkermans, B. & Ramaekers, E., 'Article 345 TFEU (ex. 295 EC). Its Meaning and Interpretations', *European Law Journal*, 2010, Vol. 16, No. 3, p. 292-314.

Akkermans & Ramaekers 2011
Akkermans, B. & Ramaekers, E., 'Free Movement of Goods and Property Law', *European Law Journal*, 2011, forthcoming.

Barnard 2007
Barnard, C., *The Substantive Law of the EU. The Four Freedoms*, 2nd ed., Oxford, Oxford University Press, 2007.

Claes 2005
Claes, M., *The National Courts' Mandate in the European Constitution*, Oxford: Hart Publishing, 2005.

Craig & de Búrca 2008
Craig, P. & de Búrca, G., *EU Law. Text, cases and materials*, Oxford: Oxford University Press, 4th ed., 2008.

Dannemann 2006
Dannemann, G., 'Comparative Law: Study of Similarities or Differences?', in Reimann, M. & Zimmermann, R. (eds.), *The Oxford Handbook of Comparative Law*, Oxford: Oxford University Press, 2006, p. 383-419.

David 1964
David, R., *Les grands systèmes de droit comtemporains*, Paris : Dalloz, 1964.

Devroe 2007
Devroe, W., 'Impact van door het Europees hof van justitie ontwikkelde algemene beginselen op privaatrechtelijke verhoudingen', in Hartkamp, A.S., Sieburgh, C.H., Keus, L.A.D. (eds.), *De invloed van het Europese recht op het Nederlandse privaatrecht*, I, Deventer: Kluwer, 2007, p. 133-189.

Diephuis, Eshuis & de Heer-de Lange 2008
Diephuis, B.J., Eshuis, R.J.J. & de Heer-de Lange, N.E. (eds.), *Rechtspleging Civiel en Bestuur*, Den Haag: Boom Juridische uitgevers, 2008.

Eidenmüller, Faust, Grigoleit, Jansen & Zimmermann 2008
Eidenmüller, H., Faust, F., Grigoleit, H.C., Jansen, N. & Zimmermann, R., 'Der Gemeinsame Referenzrahmen für das europäische Privatrecht - Wertungsfragen und Kodifikationsprobleme', *Juristenzeitung*, 2008, p. 529-550.

Graziadei 2006
Graziadei, M., 'Comparative Law and the Study of Transplants and Receptions', in Reimann, M. & Zimmermann, R. (eds.), *The Oxford Handbook of Comparative Law*, Oxford: Oxford University Press, 2006, p. 441-476.

Hesselink 2004
Hesselink, M.W., 'The Politics of a European Civil Code', *European Law Journal*, 2004, Vol. 10, p. 675-697.

Ioriatti & Van Erp 2007
Ioriatti, E. & Van Erp, S., 'La tutela della proprietà nel codice civile dei Paesi Bassi (Nieuw Burgerlijk Wetboek)', *Rivista di Diritto Romano*, 2007, p. 1-24.

Israël 2005
Israël, J., *European Cross-Border Insolvency Regulation*, Antwerp/Oxford: Intersentia, 2005.

Jansen 2006
Jansen, N., 'Comparative Law and Comparative Knowledge', in Reimann, M. & Zimmermann, R. (eds.), *The Oxford Handbook of Comparative Law*, Oxford: Oxford University Press, 2006, p. 305-338.

Kalidien & Eggen 2009
Kalidien, S.N. & Eggen, A.Th.J. (eds.), *Criminaliteit en Rechtshandhaving 2008*, Den Haag: Boom Juridische uitgevers, 2009.

Kieninger 1996
Kieninger, E.-M., *Mobiliarsicherheiten im Europäischen Binnenmarkt. Zum Einfluß der Warenverkehrsfreiheit auf das nationale und internationale Sachenrecht der Mitgliedstaaten*, Baden-Baden: Nomos Verlagsgesellschaft, 1996.

Kiiver & Kornet 2008
Kiiver, Ph. & Kornet, N. (eds.), *Selected National, European and International Provisions from Public and Private Law: The Maastricht Collection*, Groningen: Europa Law Publishing, 2008.

Laclé & ter Voert 2006
Laclé, Z.D. & ter Voert, M.J., *Trendrapportage Notariaat 2006. Toegankelijkheid, continuïteit en kwaliteit van de dienstverlening*, Den Haag: Boom Juridische uitgevers, 2006.

Lando & Beale 2000
Lando, O. & Beale, H. (eds.), *Principles of European Contract Law*, Parts I and II, The Hague: Kluwer Law International, 2000.

Lando, Clive, Prüm & Zimmermann 2003
Lando, O., Clive, E., Prüm, A. & Zimmermann, R. (eds.), *Principles of European Contract Law*, Part III, The Hague: Kluwer Law International, 2003.

Michaels 2006
Michaels, R., 'The Functional Method of Comparative Law', in Reimann, M. & Zimmermann, R. (eds.), *The Oxford Handbook of Comparative Law*, Oxford: Oxford University Press, 2006, p. 339-382.

Micklitz, Stuyck, Terryn & Droshout 2010
Micklitz, H., Stuyck, J., Terryn, E. & Droshout, D. (eds.), *Ius Commune Casebooks for the Common Law of Europe, Cases, Materials and Text on Consumer Law*, Oxford: Hart Publishing, 2010.

Motive 1888
Motive zu dem Entwurfe eines Bürgerlichen Gesetzbuches für das Deutsche Reich – Sachenrecht, III, Berlin: Verlag von J. Guttentag, 1888.

Rutgers 1999
Rutgers, J., *International Reservation of Title Clauses. A study of Dutch, French and German Private International Law in the Light of European Law*, Dissertation, The Hague: T.M.C. Asser Press, 1999.

Saarloos 2010
Saarloos, K., *European Private International Law on Legal Parentage. Thoughts on a European Instrument Implementing the Principle of Mutual Recognition in Legal Parentage*, Maastricht: Maastricht University Press, 2010.

Schiek 2006
Schiek, D., 'The ECJ Decision in Mangold: A Further Twist on Effects of Directives and Constitutional Relevance of Community Equality Legislation', *Industrial Law Journal*, 2006, Vol. 35, No. 3, p. 329-341.

Shleifer 2000
Shleifer, A., *Inefficient Markets – An Introduction to Behavioral Finance*, Oxford: Oxford University Press, 2000.

Sparkes 2007
Sparkes, P., *European Land Law*, Oxford: Hart Publishing, 2007.

Study Group on Social Justice in European Contract Law 2004
Study Group on Social Justice in European Contract Law, 'Social Justice in European Contract Law: a Manifesto', *European Law Journal*, 2004, Vol. 10, No. 6, p. 653-674.

Thaler 2005
Thaler, R. (ed.), *Advances in Behavioral Finance*, Vol. II, New York: Russell Sage Foundation, 2005.

Van Erp 2006
Van Erp, S., *European and National Property Law. Osmosis or Growing Antagonism*, Groningen: Europa Law Publishing, 2006.

Van Erp 2008
Van Erp, S., 'DCFR and Property Law: the Need for Consistency and Coherence', in Schulze, R. (ed.), *Common Frame of Reference and Existing EC Contract Law*, Munich: Sellier European Law Publishers, 2008, p. 249-261.

Van Erp 2009a
Van Erp, S., 'From "classical" to modern European property law', in, *Essays in Honour of Konstantinos D. Kerameus/Festschrift für Konstantinos D. Kerameus*, Vol. I, Athens/Brussels: Ant. A. Sakkoulas/Bruylant, 2009, p. 1517-1533.

Van Erp 2009b
Van Erp, S., 'Deconstruction and Reconstruction of European Property Law: A Research Agenda', in Ritaine-Cashin, E. (ed.), *Legal Engineering and Comparative Law/L'ingénierie juridique et le droit comparé. Rapports du colloque du 25e anniversaire de l'Institut Suisse de Droit Comparé du 29 août 2008 à Lausanne*, Zurich/Basel : Schultess, 2009, p. 105-121.

Van Erp & Akkermans forthcoming
Van Erp, S. & Akkermans, B., 'Harmonisation of the EU Mortgage Markets', *ZEuP*, forthcoming.

Van Vliet 2000
Van Vliet, L., *Transfer of Movables in German, French, English and Dutch Law*, Nijmegen: Ars Aequi Libri, 2000.

Von Bar *et al.* 2009
Von Bar, Chr. *et al.* (eds.), *Principles, Definitions and Model Rules of European Private Law. Draft Common Frame of Reference (DCFR)*, Outline Edition, Munich: Sellier European Law Publishers, 2009.

Weir, Zweigert & Kötz 1998
Weir, T., Zweigert, K. & Kötz, H., *An Introduction to Comparative Private Law*, Oxford: Oxford University Press, 3rd ed., 1998.

Whittaker 2007
Whittaker, S., 'The Relationship of the Unfair Commercial Practices Directive to European and National Contract Law', in Weatherhill, S. & Bernitz, U. (eds.), *The Regulation of Unfair Commercial Practices under EC Directive 2005/29*, Oxford: Hart Publishing, 2007, p. 139-158.

Zimmermann 2002
Zimmermann, R., 'Modernising the German Law of Obligations', in Birks, P. & Pretto, A. (eds.), *Themes in Comparative Law – In honour of Bernard Rudden*, Oxford: Oxford University Press, 2002, p. 265-288.

Zimmermann & Whittaker 2000
Zimmermann, R. & Whittaker, S. (eds.), *Good Faith in European Contract Law*, Cambridge: Cambridge University Press, 2000.

Zweigert & Kötz 1996
Zweigert, K. & Kötz, H., *Einführung in die Rechtsvergleichung auf dem Gebiete des Privatrechts*, Tübingen: J.C.B. Mohr (Paul Siebeck), 3rd ed., 1996.

Mieke Olaerts

TEACHING EUROPEAN AND COMPARATIVE COMPANY LAW

1. Introduction

In a globalizing world companies have become one of, if not the, most powerful players in an economic and social setting. Companies are at the heart of society; which makes company law a very interesting and vivid area to teach. Newspapers report daily on topics which are related to company law and which can be used to trigger students' attention and raise their interests. Not only is it important to raise the interest of our students but also to create awareness. After all, today's law students might grow into the business leaders of tomorrow, or play an important role in advising those leaders. In the age of globalization companies have acquired such an important role in society that their operations have a potential impact on the interests of a multitude of stakeholders. This group of stakeholders is no longer restricted to the shareholders of the company. The operations of multinationals also have an important direct effect on for example the position of their employees, creditors and the environment in general. In their cross border operations companies are faced with multiple cultural differences which they have to take into account if they want to turn their business into a success. More than ever have we been confronted with the fact that economic failures and the potential legislative failures, with which they are entangled, are not merely a regional problem. The financial crisis has shown that the consequences of those failures transcendent national boundaries. In their role as future business leaders, in-house lawyers or external legal advisors our law students will be faced with questions that transcendent their own national legal environment. They might have to advise and assist multinationals to overcome the legal hurdles those companies are faced with in the international business environment in which they operate. Furthermore, even outside the scope of company law our students are bound to be confronted with cross border transactions. The teaching of company and business law can therefore no longer be restricted to a national context.

Approaching legal issues from a comparative perspective has several advantages. It prepares students for future encounters with foreign legal systems and enables them to raise critical question with regard to their own national law.

The Maastricht Law Faculty places a strong emphasis on comparative law throughout its *curriculum*. This approach is also used in the introductory course European Company Law taught at bachelor level and the master course Comparative Company Law. In designing these courses we are faced with several challenges. Even though these courses have been taught for several years now and we have gained valuable experience in this field, the work is never done. It is an ongoing quest to find the optimal didactical approach to further improve our teaching methods. Our experience with comparative company law teaching will be dealt with in this contribution. The necessity of comparative company law teaching cannot be discussed without elaborating first on the nature and evolution of company law from a European perspective. The next section is therefore dedicated to the developments and characteristics of EU company law. In the third section the focus will be on the reason for and the necessity of a comparative approach in company law teaching. Subsequently the different approaches to company law teaching will be discussed in the fourth section. Section five sets out the challenges we face in using such a comparative approach in company law teaching. The main conclusions are reflected in section six.

2. Developments and Characteristics of EU Company Law: Its Hybrid Nature

Company law is constantly evolving, it is subjected to an ongoing process of modernization which is mainly market driven. Just like the organisms in Darwin's evolution theory, companies will constantly have to monitor their own position and implement changes and modernizations in order to survive. Company law will have to keep up with these systemic changes. Company law in Europe has developed, and is still developing, on two different levels which mutually influence each other. The first level concerns top-down harmonization of national company law of the various Member States of the European Union by the European legislature. The second level concerns bottom-up harmonization initiated by the national legislature of those Member States. In the early years the emphasis was more on the first level of harmonization. During the eighties and nineties the European legislature focused on harmonization of company law by making use of Directives, which touched upon core issues and had to be implemented in national law. Not all harmonization attempts were an unqualified success and some of these initiatives stranded due to too many cultural and social differences amongst Member States.[1] Nowadays, the focus has shifted from the first to the second level. This shift has materialized as a consequence of the landmark decisions of the European Court of Justice (ECJ) in cases such as *Centros, Uberseering, Inspire Art* and *Sevic systems*.[2] As a result of these cases Member States are forced to recognize

1 In this respect the attempt for a fifth directive on the internal structure and the failed attempt for a ninth directive on the company groups can be mentioned.

2 ECJ [C-212/97] *Centros;* ECJ [C-208/00] *Überseering;* ECJ [C-167/01] *Inspire Art Ltd.;* ECJ [C411-03] *SEVIC Systems.*

companies incorporated in a different Member State and allow them to do business on their territory while making use of a foreign business form. The judgments of the ECJ have given entrepreneurs more freedom to choose the company law of a Member State that is most appealing to them regardless of where their actual business is located. This has made entrepreneurs more demanding with regard to national company law. In order to satisfy these demands, Member States have adjusted the rules applicable to their limited liability companies making it easier to incorporate limited liability companies and making their rules more flexible.[3] The legal competition initiated by the judgments of the ECJ has forced Member States to approach company law from a comparative perspective. In order to keep up with the regulatory competition, they are forced to take developments in other countries into consideration. To that effect the regulatory competition can lead to a, be it slow, convergence between the laws of different Member States.

The two levels, on which company law in Europe is developing, influence each other. On the one hand, a consequence of the prior harmonization program of the European Union is that the laws of the Member States are more comparable. This harmonization with regard to specific areas of company law leaves less room for Member States to develop their own legal system in such a way that it becomes the most appealing system to entrepreneurs. On the other hand, as was already pointed out, regulatory competition in itself leads to a slow convergence between the laws of the different Member States, which in the long run makes it easier to reach political compromises on a European level and to bridge cultural differences in areas where this has proven to be impossible in the past. The question can be raised whether reaching such a political compromise is still necessary at that stage. Indeed, it can be argued that due to bottom-up harmonization, top-down harmonization will in the future no longer be relevant in certain areas. However, it should be noted that this process can take a long time and does not necessarily lead to full harmonization. There might be areas in which it is attractive for Member States to highlight and preserve the differences between various national systems. However, the efforts of the European legislature are still very much needed where it concerns issues enabling companies to cross borders, to cooperate at a cross border level, or to make use of a business form which transcends national boundaries and is similar in every Member State. Over the years the European legislature has developed multiple initiatives enhancing cross border activities, some of which have been successful, others are still under construction. In this respect one can think of the Directive on cross border mergers,[4] the Regulation for a Statute for the European Company[5] (*Societas Europaea* or SE) and the proposed Regulation for a

3 Germany has for example introduced the *Unternehmergesellschaft* and in the Netherlands there is currently a bill pending before parliament which strives to adjust the Dutch rules on private limited liability companies *Kamerstukken I* 2009-2010, 31058, No. A.

4 Directive 2005/56/EC of the European Parliament and of the Council of 26 October 2005 on cross-border mergers of limited liability companies.

5 Council Regulation (EC) 2157/2001 of 8 October 2001 on the Statute for a European company (SE).

Statute for the European Private Company[6] (EPC or *Societas Privata Europaea* or SPE).

It is important to note that, just like companies themselves, also European company law and the Directives and Regulations developed in this field do not operate in isolation. Companies form part of society and will have to work with several stakeholders. Therefore students should be made aware of the existence of other types of legislation that might also have an important impact on the functioning of companies across borders such as for example the European Works Council Directive,[7] the Directive on collective redundancies[8] and the European rules on the operation of financial markets. Next to that, the emergence of different types of regulation has to be taken into account. Company law is such a rapidly changing area that legislation often lags behind. Market developments require an instant reaction which the cumbersome legislative procedure in a democratic system is often unable to provide for. It often takes too long to wait for a reaction of the legislature which is why sometimes different sorts of regulation are used. This is especially the case in the area of Corporate Governance where (semi-voluntary) codes are used to regulate the internal governance of mostly listed companies. Even though these codes are soft law and do not constitute mandatory regulation, they play an important role in the functioning of companies on a daily basis.

3. Why a Comparative Approach?

The necessity to look beyond national borders when dealing with company law was already touched upon in the introduction. There are several reasons why developments in other countries and in the international setting have such a large influence on national company law and on the operation of companies in practice. Several motivations can underlie the use of a comparative approach to company law. These motivations can be divided into positive motivations on the one hand side and negative motivations on the other hand. The term negative motivations can be used to denote the incentives to engage in legal comparison which result from a fear for negative consequences if such an approach is not taken. A positive motivation on the other hand emphasizes the goals that can be achieved by making use of a comparative approach.

The first reason for a comparative approach to company law was already discussed above and can be found in the European ambition to create one European internal market. It has been pointed out already that this leads to two levels of harmonization that mutually influence each other: top down and bottom up harmonization. The desire to create one European market, to enable companies to

6 Proposal for a Council Regulation on the Statute for a European private company COM(2008) 396/3.

7 Council Directive 94/45/EC of 22 September 1994 on the establishment of a European Works Council or a procedure in Community-scale undertakings and Community-scale groups of undertakings for the purposes of informing and consulting employees.

8 Council Directive 98/59/EC of 20 July 1998 on the approximation of the laws of the Member States relating to collective redundancies.

operate across borders and the top down harmonization in which this desire has materialized can be seen as a positive motivation. Regulatory competition initiated by the decisions of the ECJ, however, can to a certain extent be seen as a negative motivator. It stems from the fear of losing this competition and ending up as a country of which the legal system is no longer appealing to business society. Member States fear losing their position as an attractive country for incorporation, ultimately resulting in national business types becoming extinct.

A second negative motivation can be found in the markets ability to penalize inefficiencies or conservative and protectionist approaches. Company law is pre-eminently an area in which the legislature as well as the subjects of their regulation, the companies themselves, are forced to look at developments in other countries. If they do not on a voluntarily basis take foreign developments into account, they will practically be forced by the market to do so. For example an American investor in the Netherlands might be used to different rules and might see his own role within the internal structure of a company differently due to the company law rules applicable in his country of origin. Such an investor might therefore have certain (different) expectations when investing in a Dutch company. He might try to force his ideas on the company in which he invests by making use of the membership rights granted to him by the national law applicable to that (Dutch) company. The distinction between company laws which use a stakeholder approach and those which use a shareholder approach can serve as an example in this respect. The stakeholder model is generally used on the European continent. In these countries, such as the Netherlands, for example, the corporate interest is defined as not solely reflecting the interest of the shareholders but rather those of a larger group of stakeholders such as, for example, the employees. The Anglo-America shareholder model on the other hand entails that priority should be given to the interests of the shareholders.[9] A shareholder or investor coming from a country that uses a shareholder approach will have different expectations when he invests in a company which is incorporated in a so called stakeholder model. The applicable corporate model inevitably influences the definition of the 'interests of the company' which in its turn affects corporate decision making by the management body as well as their potential liability in case of a breach of their duties owed to the company. A shareholder coming from a shareholder model might expect the board of directors to give priority to his shareholder interests whereas directors of a company embedded in the stakeholder model will have to take into account not only the interests of the shareholders but also those of other stakeholders when

9 Within Europe this model is used in England. However, this model has to a certain extent been modified by the Companies Act of 2006 with the introduction of the so-called enlightened shareholder approach in section 172. This new approach states that, although a director should promote the success of the company for the benefit of its members as a whole, he should also take other interests into account such as those of the employees, the community and the environment as well as the consequences of his decisions in the long term. This new approach leads to a certain extent to convergence between the two models used in the European Member States. Nevertheless, important differences between both models remain.

determining the course of the company. This distinction has lead to frictions in the past. In the case of Stork for example Hedge funds made an attempt to impose their strategy upon the directors of a Dutch company Stork and tried to persuade them to split up the company because this would, in their view, create more shareholder value.[10] Even though directors of a Dutch company are supposed to adhere to Dutch company law and will have to respect the duties and responsibilities imposed upon them by Dutch legislation, they will inevitable want to satisfy their investors and also take their wishes into account. The market itself will therefore to a certain extent be able to 'claim' changes. If these requested changes are not made or the expectations are not lived up to, the consequence will be an immediate punishment by the market. This can for example entail that it renders the country less attractive as country for incorporation and/or foreign investment. Therefore, companies as well as national legislatures are 'forced' by the market to keep an eye on developments in company law across the borders. This doesn't mean that they have to implement all changes which are made to company law abroad on an equal footing. However, they will have to keep up with these developments in order to remain in the race.

Company mobility can be mentioned as a third negative motivator. First of all companies increasingly engage into cross border transactions which will confront them with foreign legal systems. This encounter will not be restricted to the area of company law but can also encompass for example foreign rules on contract law. Secondly, the mobility of investors can be mentioned in this respect as was already referred to above. However, not only investors have become more mobile. Not only do shareholders invest their money in companies which are situated all over the world. Companies themselves also increasingly make use of the possibility to make a worldwide public appeal to savings by listing their companies at foreign stock exchanges. Therefore, in the third place there is an increase of company mobility as an investment vehicle. Such a listing at a foreign stock exchange is of course not free of obligations. It subjects the company to a new set of listing rules which can also have an influence on its functioning on a daily basis. Some of these listing rules can therefore have extra territorial effect. As a consequence of this mobility it is possible that, for example, a Dutch company becomes subjected to American rules in case it is listed at the New York stock exchange. The American Sarbanes Oxley Act can lead to liability of directors of foreign companies if these companies are listed at an American Stock Exchange. This type of rules also forces companies to look beyond the boundaries of the national company law system from which they originate. It has to be noted that the so called 'negative' motivators indicated above do not entail that the development of which they form part is disadvantageous, they are merely 'negative' motivators (stemming from a fear to lose out on certain things) for a development which can overly be seen as a positive process.

Comparative company law is not only initiated by a fear of losing out, there are also positive motivations. These positive motivations are not the result of a fear to miss out on an opportunity but instead reflect the desire to reach a certain goal

10 Gerechtshof Amsterdam (OK) 17-01-2007, *JOR* 2007/42, *LJN* AZ6440.

which is attainable by making use of a comparative approach. One positive motivation to look beyond the boundaries of one's own national system has already been mentioned above namely, harmonization. Harmonization can be achieved by taking into account national company laws in order to find a common denominator and create a level playing field with comparable rules on a European level. A second positive motivation can be found in the desire to evaluate one's own legal system. Comparative law enhances critical analysis of one's own national legal system. By looking beyond the boundaries of national law it might be discovered that certain issues which have lead to a lot of discussion in national law, do not pose such a problem in other systems. It might reveal that certain choices which have been made in the past are actually not that logic or efficient as they seemed at that time. Thirdly, comparative law can serve as a source of inspiration. In that case the goal of comparative law is to find solutions to problems encountered in national law. Some might contend this to be an exponent of 'lazy layering'. Instead of coming up with a solution to a national problem, one looks beyond the borders to see if such a solution can be borrowed. However, there might be good reasons to choose for such an approach. It provides the possibility to see how certain solutions operate because of the experiences previously gained in other legal systems. That legal system can serve as a test case. It shows the potential pitfalls of a certain legal remedy. This of course does not mean that solutions which have proven to be effective in one national system are also the best option for other legal systems. All peculiarities of that national system and the differences between the system from which one wants to take a solution on the one hand and the country which wants to adopt that solution on the other have to be taken into account.

4. The Role of Comparative Company Law in Teaching

The necessity of using a comparative approach to company law has been demonstrated above. It has been shown that sometimes looking beyond the borders of the national system is a necessity. In other situations it can be a useful tool to reach certain goals. The question is now how all of the above can be translated into company law teaching in practice and in what way this line of teaching can be optimized. Comparative company law teaching can take place at different levels depending on its positioning in the *curriculum* and the desired standard of comparison. Designing a course in a comparative manner requires certain choices to be made: which countries should be selected as material for comparison and which topics are most suitable and interesting for such a comparison? These choices amount to two possible approaches: a comparison on a country-by-country basis and/or a thematic comparison on a subject by subject basis.[11] The country-by-country approach means that a selection of jurisdictions is covered one by one. The comparison is made on the basis of certain themes which are discussed for each system. In a thematic approach on the other hand carefully selected subject-areas

11 See with respect to these two approaches and their advantages and disadvantages the contribution of Kiiver & Eliantonio 2011.

are used as point of departure (e.g. the internal structure of the company, director liability, the position of employees etc.). Each selected area is covered in a number of jurisdictions. The different levels of comparative and European company law teaching will be discussed below. A distinction will be made between comparative company law integrated in a course on domestic law and comparative and European company law as a separate subject at bachelor and at master level. Some of the challenges related to the positioning of these subjects in the *curriculum* will be mentioned here. Other, more general challenges intrinsic to comparative company law teaching as such will be discussed in the next section.

4.1. *Comparative Company Law as Part of Domestic Law*

One way in which comparative company law can be introduced into the *curriculum* is by integrating it in a course on domestic company law.[12] A course on Dutch company law can for example devote some attention to the position of directors and shareholders in other countries. This approach helps students to better understand their own system, to see its merits but also its deficiencies. It creates awareness of choices made in the domestic legal system and it stimulates them to raise critical questions with regard to that legal system. It also shows them that there is more beyond the horizon. This at least enables them to discover the magnitude of that horizon later on in their study or in corporate practice. From a didactical point of view the comparison can best take place on a subject-by-subject basis and not country by country. After all, the emphasis is on the domestic legal system which is used as a point of departure for an exploratory journey across the borders. The most obvious approach is not to focus on similarities but on the differences between several legal systems by choosing those subjects for which different solutions are used. The fact that not all legal systems are given equal attention during the course and that for example for certain subjects German law is used while for certain other subjects English law is chosen as material for comparison, is not problematic. After all, the course should not have the pretension to provide students with a full overview of company law from a comparative point of view. The integration of certain comparative elements merely serves to broaden their horizon.

4.2. *Comparative and European Company Law as a Separate Subject at Bachelor and Master Level*

4.2.1. Introduction to European Company Law at Bachelor Level

The introduction of comparative elements in a course on domestic law is relatively straight forward. More cumbersome is the introduction of a course entirely devoted to comparative company law which posses more difficult methodological and didactical questions. The goal of such a course is different. Its aim is not to educate students on domestic company law but to teach undergraduate students

12 See with regard to this approach also the contribution by Kiiver & Eliantonio 2011.

comparative company law as part of a broader *curriculum*. The course is also different in that it is oriented at a different student population. A course on domestic law might be easy accessible to national students of the home faculty or for exchange students who already have acquired some prior knowledge on company law at their home university.[13] The bachelor students in our comparative law courses by contrast start with a clean slate. This is essentially their first encounter with company law as such.

One of the first questions that have to be answered is that of demarcation: which subjects should be studied and/or which legal systems deserve to be compared? It can be difficult to use a thematic approach at bachelor level. After all, different from the situation in which comparative elements are introduced in a course on domestic company law, students in this case do not have prior knowledge of one legal system with which foreign concepts can be compared. This means that students first have to have an idea of what a company is, how it is established and how it operates before a proper subject-by-subject comparison can be made. A country-by-country approach therefore seems to be a more suitable way to approach comparative company law at bachelor level. However, such an approach also deserves a clear demarcation. Unfortunately time is restricted, not all legal systems can be discussed and compared. Moreover, a too elaborate comparison can confuse students. A consequence could be that students acquire a very diffuse picture of several legal systems without really acquiring knowledge of the most important focal points within each system. Another disadvantage of a country-by-country approach is that students might be able to answer comparative questions on a country-by country basis but that they might not see the links between the various systems. In a short time frame they might not have the ability to combine everything they learned and point out the similarities and distinctions between the various systems which ultimately is the goal of a comparative law course. Even though a county-by-country approach is more suitable for bachelor students than a thematic approach due to a lack of prior knowledge, it is not be best method for this subject. Another disadvantage of a country-by-country approach is that it can be rather tedious and technical. Moreover, students might have difficulties in keeping the different national systems apart.

At the Maastricht University's Faculty of Law we have chosen for an introductory course on European Company Law at bachelor level. The course focuses on the existing European framework with regard to company law and at the same time provides students with insights into national company law of a selected number of European Member States. One of the methodological challenges involved in this method is how to approach the hybrid nature of European company law. This hybrid nature is a result of its development. As already discussed in section two above, certain issues of company law have been harmonized by the European legislature. Certain other topics such as for example the internal structure of companies and the position of employees within that internal structure were left outside of the harmonization program due to the

13 See the contribution by Kiiver & Eliantonio 2011.

absence of political consent on these topics. Moreover, there is more harmonization with regard to public limited liability companies than with regard to private limited liability companies. This hybrid nature of European company law does not only pose challenges, it also creates opportunities. I prefer a more hybrid approach to a topic which is largely hybrid in nature. This approach consists of a country-by-country comparison along the life cycle of the company starting with the most important characteristics of limited liability companies, their incorporation and moving on to their functioning by introducing the various corporate decision makers, their role, powers and potential liabilities. This approach enables students without prior knowledge of company law to grasp the basic internal structure and functioning of a company. The European harmonization program can be used in order to give students an idea of the state of the art of European company law. It enables us to show a European framework with regard to certain topics and allows us to dive into national provisions with regard to others. The harmonized European framework is complemented with a country-by-country comparison. From a didactical point of view the hybrid nature of European company law provides the possibility to start off with the European perspective by focusing on those issues which have been harmonized throughout the European Union and from there on move to the national level to see the existing differences which still remain in national company law despite the harmonization efforts of the European legislature. This approach gives students a full and comparative overview of the state of the art of European company law on the one hand and company laws in Europe on the other. This also means that given the hybrid nature of European company law a country-by country comparison is not the most suitable format.

4.2.2. European and Comparative Company Law at Master Level

The design of a master course on Comparative company law gives the course planners some more latitude. Students at master level often have already encountered company law at some point during their studies and therefore have some prior knowledge, which allows for a thematic approach. An advantage of such a thematic approach is that it creates an opportunity for more in dept discussions.[14] Students do not first need to acquire a systemic overview of the functioning of a company before they can concentrate on the selected topics and study these from a comparative point of view. A master course should stimulate students to debate and critically analyze general principles of company law. They should be made aware of the ethical and social questions with which the functioning of companies is surrounded and in what way these issues are dealt with in different legal systems. Subjects which can be covered in this respect are for example the involvement of employees, creditor protection, the role of companies in society in general, the independence of non-executives, remuneration of board members etc. Students can be stimulated and triggered by linking the selected

14 See with regard to the advantages and disadvantages of this approach also the contribution of Kiiver & Eliantonio 2011.

themes to topical subjects in the media.[15] The connections between the different legal systems, which might still be lacking in a bachelor course, can be made at master level. Students should be made aware of the differences in culture and the social differences between Member States of the European Union but also outside of the European territory. After all, these differences can have major impacts on the company law design in different countries. From a didactical point of view it is no longer necessary to restrict the territorial scope of the course to European law and the domestic law of the Member States of the European Union. A thematic approach is most suitable in this respect because it does not call for an intrinsic comparison of for example 'American' or Chinese law all along the line. The most interesting themes can be selected and their positioning in several jurisdictions can be discussed in depth. The Statute for a European Company (SE) and the proposed Statute for a European private company (SPE) can serve as interesting test cases to check the knowledge acquired by students and to enable them to understand commonalities and differences across systems. With the SE Regulation the European legislature aimed to introduce a company type which could be used across borders and would be the same no matter in which Member State of the European Union it is incorporated. A comparable approach was taken with the introduction of a proposed Statute for a European Private Company difference being that the latter is more targeted towards small and medium sized enterprises whilst the European Company can be used for cross border activities by larger (mostly public) companies. The SE statute and the (proposed) statute for the SPE contain several provisions which reflect important company law themes. The internal structure, creditor protection, the position of employees and the applicable board structure are just a few themes that can be mentioned in this respect. Unfortunately, not all areas are covered by one uniform regulation and the regulation itself often refers to the applicability of national law. After having studied certain selected themes from a comparative perspective, it can be interesting for students to discover which choices have been made in this respect with regard to the SE and the SPE. It provides student with a good overview of the European harmonization program as it now stands with its accomplishments but also its flaws. By analyzing these two statutes students can discover for themselves which questions are left unanswered at the European level. Those gaps in the puzzle can be filled with national law.

One of the challenges we face when introducing a thematic comparative approach at master level is that the student population is not always homogeneous. Due to the bachelor/master structure students can have rather diverse backgrounds. Not all students who participated in our bachelor course stay for the master. They might opt for a different university while students from other universities enter our master courses. Furthermore, not all master students necessarily have a background in legal studies. This is not only a challenge for the course designers but also for the students themselves. Part of the challenge can be surmounted by equipping students with all modern facilities enabling them to

15 This of course does not mean that whatever is 'hot' in the media at a certain point should be guiding in the design of the course.

familiarize themselves with the basic concepts of company law. This challenge has more to do with the system in general and is not inherently connected with comparative company law as such. Company law even has a competitive advantage in this respect. The anatomic structure of companies in various jurisdictions is largely the same, which makes it easier for students to grasp the basic concepts of company law.[16]

5. Challenges

Several challenges of creating a comparative company law course have already been mentioned. A disadvantage of a country-by-country approach is that it can become rather tedious and confusing for students to keep the different systems apart. Moreover, it might take them some time before they acquire the ability to compare and see the similarities and differences of company law across borders. Within a country-by-country approach a disproportion in treatment of certain legal systems with regard to specific issues is sometimes inevitable. After all, in some countries a certain topic has lead to elaborate discussion and deserves a lot of attention while in others it is hardly touched upon and therefore provides far less ground for discussion. Some issues in the national law of one country cannot be found or at least not to the same extent in other legal systems. The influence of a conflict of interest of directors of a company on their power to represent that company can serve as an example in this respect. In the Netherlands the existence of a conflict of interest restricts the representational power of the director who engages on behalf of the company in a transaction. The problem of conflicting interests is however dealt with differently in various legal systems. In the Netherlands such a conflict of interest can have consequences for third parties who transacted with the company. In other countries this problem is purely an internal matter requiring that for example a director, who engages into such a transaction, acquires prior authorization of the general meeting or another organ of the company. A hybrid approach based on a country-by-country comparison along the life cycle of a company might be successful to surmount some of the challenges connected to a country-by-country approach. A thematic approach on the contrary allows for more in dept discussions and is therefore a more suitable approach for comparative company law teaching at the master level. However, the diversity in student population can be challenging.

Next to these challenges that are closely related to the position of the comparative company law course in the *curriculum*, there are some other challenges that are of a general nature and common to both approaches. In the first place it is important to realize that companies do not operate in isolation. They form part of a (national and international) society. This means that not only rules of company law are of importance. Other types of regulations also have to be taken into account as they play a role in a company's daily operations. In this respect one can think of soft law such as corporate governance codes but also mandatory rules which the

16 Kraakman *et al.* 2009.

company will have to adhere to such as labour law, insolvency law, and rules on collective redundancies. Consideration has to be given to the fact that in some legal systems the position of for example creditors and employees is to a certain extent safeguarded by rules of company law while in other countries the protection of these stakeholders is embedded in other types of legislation. For example, in some countries there is less attention for the position of creditors in company law. However, this deficit is compensated by strict rules on insolvency. The employees for example can find protection in regulations on works councils. Unfortunately, not all of these issues can be dealt with in a comparative company law course. However, it is important to draw students' attention to the existence of these rules so that they can choose to look into these matters more thoroughly during the rest of their studies or so that they at least know where to look when faced with such a problem later on in corporate practice. A second challenge is finding the right literature. The quality and coherence of a course often depends on the quality of the literature that is prescribed. Students often prefer a handbook over a literature reader compiled of selected journal articles and selections out of various handbooks. Handbooks give them a better overview and clearly demark the areas they have to study. Most journal articles are written by and for academics which makes them rather difficult for students to comprehend. This is especially the case for bachelor students who lack prior knowledge of company law. For these students a handbook might be the best option.[17] Finding balanced literature is a difficult task. The prescribed literature has to be comprehensible yet detailed enough. Books written by experts in their own legal system tend to go too much into detail with regard to certain issues which are of less importance in other legal systems. There is the risk that the authors do not transcendent their own national system, turning the book more into a county report lacking a proper comparison between the different legal systems. Such 'country reports' of course also have their merits. They can be used by students in class to base their own comparative conclusions on and they can be a useful tool to start discussions. However, this might not yet be attainable at bachelor level. It is important that the prescribed literature gives students a good overview. A course book can help them to put the pieces of the puzzle together by providing them an elaborate comparative overview. The national approaches can subsequently be derived from the literature. A third challenge is related to the academic staff. Comparative teaching requires lecturers to dive into different legal systems. Therefore, it requires an investment in lifelong learning for staff member so that they have the possibility to acquaint themselves with other legal systems. This is not only a challenge but also an opportunity. It can provide valuable insight which can be used for future research.

17 There are some handbooks in the area of European and comparative company law. In this respect Dorresteijn *et al.* 2009 and Andenas & Wooldridge 2009 can be mentioned. Both of these handbooks are divided into themes followed by a country-by-country treatment.

6. Conclusion

To conclude, the necessity and added value of a comparative approach to company law teaching has been demonstrated above. Companies are at the heart of society. In a globalizing world their operations increasingly influence the lives of others and of society as a whole. Companies and their operations are no longer restricted to one jurisdiction. Entrepreneurs have become more demanding with regard to company law rules. In their future careers, our students are bound to encounter questions which transcendent one national legal system. In order to prepare them for the future, a comparative approach to company law teaching is vital. In this contribution several positive as well as negative motivations for comparative company law have been discussed. Regardless of the fact that these motivations might stem from a fear of being left out, they emphasize the necessity of approaching company law from a comparative perspective. At Maastricht University's Law Faculty we have introduced an introductory course on European company law at bachelor level and a course on comparative company law for master students. Both courses have their own challenges depending on their placement in the *curriculum*. However, some common challenges to comparative company law in general can be mentioned such as finding the appropriate literature and the realization that companies, and therefore also company law, do not operate in isolation. Other sources of law can also have an important impact on the operations of companies on a daily basis. Comparative company law constitutes an ongoing quest to find the optimal didactical approach in order to further improve existing teaching methods. A clear demarcation with regard to the subject matters that have to be discussed as well as with regard to the legal systems under comparison is key.

Bibliography

Andenas & Wooldridge 2009
Andenas, M. & Wooldridge, F., *European Comparative Company Law*, Cambridge: Cambridge University Press, 2009.

Dorresteijn *et al.* 2009
Dorresteijn, A.F. *et al.*, *European Corporate Law*, Alphen aan den Rijn: Kluwer Law International, 2009.

Kiiver & Eliantonio 2011
Kiiver, Ph. & Eliantonio, M., 'Teaching European and Comparative Constitutional Law', in Heringa, A.W. & Akkermans, B. (eds.), *Educating European Lawyers*, Antwerp: Intersentia, 2011, p. 209-217.

Kraakman *et al.* 2009
Kraakman, R. *et al.*, *The Anatomy of Corporate Law. A Comparative and Functional Approach*, New York: Oxford University Press, 2009.

Remme Verkerk
Remco van Rhee

TEACHING COMPARATIVE CIVIL PROCEDURE

1. Introduction

An experienced Dutch lawyer once remarked - in private - that 'teaching the rules of procedure at a university is like explaining the rules of poker without having a deck of cards at hand.' This view well summarizes the general approach to teaching civil procedure in the Netherlands: procedural law is regarded to be a technical and practical discipline only which, according to some, barely deserves a place in a university *curriculum*. After all, it is argued that one will learn the procedural rules quickly once started working at a law firm. One of the aims of this contribution is to show civil procedure can also be taught in an academic manner and, consequently, is a valuable course for law students. The paper will pay attention to a comparative course on civil procedure entitled 'Civil Litigation in Europe', introduced eleven year ago as an elective course for master students at the Maastricht University European Law School.[1] Each year, between 30 and 40 students enrol for this course. From 2011, the course will become compulsory, albeit within the context of the European Law School bachelor's programme. The paper provides a short overview of the topics that are of central importance to it. However, before doing this, the topic 'civil procedure' needs a definition that can be used in a comparative legal context.

2. What is Civil Procedure?

A French lawyer knows perfectly well what is to be understood by *procédure civile*. To the German lawyer, the notion *Zivilprozessrecht* is self-evident. His English colleague will have little difficulties to explain what civil procedure is all about. Once the three meet, issues may however get complicated. It is much like ordering coffee in a foreign country: one is served obviously with coffee, but it always tastes slightly different than what one is used to.

1 The authors have both actively taught the course.

Let us first consider a case in which a young girl, that has been ran over by a cart belonging to a tobacco manufacturer, claims personal injury damages. In the classic 'Blanco' case (1873), the French *Conseil d'État* decided that the matter had to be tried by the administrative court as the manufacturer was government owned.[2] A German lawyer would be surprised to hear that an administrative court rather than a civil court would be competent to hear such a case. The English lawyer would frown and wonder why one would need administrative courts at all.

A second example concerns the law of evidence. A German lawyer may contend that evidence law is obviously part of civil procedure. Most relevant German provisions on evidence are neatly codified in a separate section of the *Zivilprozessordnung*. The French lawyer will probably disagree, arguing that certain elements of the law of evidence are not really procedural in nature but belong to the realm of substantive private law. He will cite a number of provisions in the French *Code civil* devoted to evidence. The English lawyer will argue that Evidence really is a separate branch of the law altogether. It cannot be classified as a part of procedural or substantive private law. He might argue that common law codifications of evidence law, such as the U.S. Federal Rules of Evidence, apply to both civil and criminal cases.

Definitions and categories matter. Whether or not a case is classified as a civil case has important implications for the procedure and the substantive rights of the parties involved. It is also relevant to know whether specific rules can be qualified as (civil) procedural rules. Courts are, for example, generally willing to apply foreign substantive law but are prohibited from applying foreign procedural law (*lex fori* rule).

Definitions and categories also matter if one teaches civil procedure. A working definition of civil procedure is needed to clarify terminology and to set boundaries to the course. The definition by J.A. Jolowicz is suitable for this purpose: Professor Jolowicz defines civil procedure as 'a process before a court of law, voluntarily initiated by a plaintiff acting in what he sees as his own interest and opposed by a defendant who refuses, in what he, in his turn, sees as his interest, to meet the plaintiff's claim against him.'[3]

3. Teaching Civil Procedure

Teaching a course on comparative civil procedure at master's level is a balancing act due to the different legal backgrounds of the students. Some have very little knowledge of civil procedural law, whereas others have in depth knowledge of a particular procedural system (Dutch, German, French, etc.). This diversity is both challenging and enriching.

By its very nature, a course on comparative law must be reflective, and concentrate on the underlying principles of the systems on which it focuses. A

2 Conseil d'État, 8 February 1873, D. 1873.3.17. By now, the case would be decided differently in France.

3 Jolowicz 2000, Chapter 2, p. 22.

comparative course on civil litigation should therefore not concentrate on minute rules and regulations. It should not aim to teach students to draft all sorts of procedural documents in accordance with the requirements and practice in various jurisdictions. On the other hand, if one confines oneself to general principles and an abstract conceptual analysis, students may not be able to reflect on the system in depth. After all, procedural law, by its very nature, is also law in action. The course 'Civil Litigation in Europe' emphasizes the general principles and features of the legal systems under scrutiny. It also strives to offer a perspective on of what civil litigation is like in everyday practice. One method used to provide this view is studying legal materials on specific areas of a national legal system, supplementing this with information on the law in action, for example by visiting court hearings or using video of such hearings and interviews with practitioners and other key figures,[4] followed by a discussion on what has been observed from a comparative perspective (taking the student's own national perspective as a starting point). In addition to a study of national procedure from a comparative perspective, a detailed and practical discussion of transnational legal sources is necessary in order to relate international developments to national law. Students are required to study and apply a selection of EU regulations dealing with cross border litigation as well as some of the Hague conventions.

Another challenge lies in the fact that the time available for the course is limited and the number of potentially relevant jurisdictions large. This results in tough choices. In general, the course puts a greater emphasis on the procedural systems of England, France and Germany than on other systems. Nevertheless, other systems are discussed whenever they provide an original approach to a particular procedural issue which is absent in the main jurisdictions under scrutiny. An example is procedural flexibility as regards the handling of cases in some of the Nordic countries.[5] Lectures are the obvious place to address these matters.[6]

A similar problem is that not all relevant procedural topics can be dealt with. One would like to address a variety of topics, such as pre-action procedures, the serving of documents, jurisdiction, venue, standing, pleading, preparatory hearings, settlement procedures, alternative dispute resolution (ADR), cost regimes, evidence, interim measures, judgments, execution of judgments, and recognition of judgments. Obviously, it is not possible to deal with all of these issues in depth. Therefore, a general and broad overview of litigation in the jurisdictions mentioned is accompanied by a selection of topics that are discussed in greater depth. The topics are chosen on the basis of the interests of the students and the relevance for the aims of the course, i.e. reflecting on the underlying values of procedural systems. The main themes that are addressed are presented below. In the footnotes references to the most important literature are provided.

4 In the 2010 course, for example, an interview with Lord Woolf, the English law reformer, was shown to the students.

5 Ervo 2009, p. 26.

6 To provide one example of such lectures, in 2010, Prof. Alan Uzelac, from Zagreb University in Croatia, gave guest lectures on 'the survival of the third legal tradition', discussing civil litigation in post socialist jurisdictions. Cf. Uzelac 2009.

4. Comparative Civil Litigation: History and Categories

The basic dichotomy in modern civil procedure between the systems derived from the Romano-canonical procedure and those rooted in the English common law system remains a useful starting point. Many differences in the modern systems of procedure can, to a large extent, be explained on the basis of this historical division. A comparative course on civil procedure in Europe or on a global scale must therefore include a discussion of the historical precursors of modern procedural law.[7]

At the start, students study the spread of the common law tradition as a result of the expansion of the British Empire. This expansion has left a lasting impression on the legal systems of, for example, the United States of America, Canada, Australia, India and South Africa. Originally, common law and equity knew different courts and different procedural rules.[8] The ordinary procedure at common law generally consisted of a pleading phase and a trial stage during which evidence was orally presented in open court to a civil jury. The rules of procedure governing the various cases were not uniform, however, since the precise procedural rules depended on the particular writ that had been issued. In equity, a procedure more akin to the learned procedure of the European Continent was used. Procedure in equity was largely in writing, witnesses were not heard in open court and cases were tried by a professional judge. From the nineteenth century, however, this system changed considerably. Procedural legislation, such as the 1848 Code of Procedure for the State of New York, the 1859 Code of Civil Procedure for British India, the English Judicature Acts (1873-1875) and the U.S. Federal Rules of Civil Procedure (1938) produced a uniform procedure that was applicable in all cases in the various common law jurisdictions.

During the recent decades, it seems that common law jurisdictions have adopted diverging approaches to civil procedure.[9] In the United States, for example, the civil jury and the adversarial system remain prominent features in the civil procedural system. In most other common law countries, however, the civil jury (if existing at all) has virtually disappeared, a development that started in the nineteenth century. In England, the procedural system has been radically overhauled in 1998 with the introduction of the new Civil Procedure Rules (Woolf Reforms). These reforms did, *inter alia*, curb adversarialism, introduced pre-action protocols, and promoted the use of single joint experts. Generally speaking, these new rules have been received well. Nevertheless, it is currently doubted whether the Woolf Reforms achieved their aim of making civil litigation in England quicker, more affordable and less complex.[10]

7 Van Caenegem 1973, p. 3-7, p. 11-32, p. 54-55, p. 87-89 and p. 109-111, and Van Rhee 2005a.

8 It should, however, be noted that these different types of courts were not exported to all colonies; South Africa, for example, has never known separate courts for law and equity.

9 See e.g. Jolowicz, who argues that U.S. and English civil procedure have considerably grown apart: Jolowicz 2000, Chapter 2, p. 23-58.

10 Zuckerman 2008, p. 435-467.

On the European Continent, learned scholars developed the Romano-canonical procedural model, based on both Roman and canonical legal sources (twelfth and thirteenth centuries). Originally, this model was primarily influential within the ecclesiastical sphere. Soon however, it served as a model for the procedural rules at the secular courts. Superior courts like the *Reichskammergericht* for the German States, the French *Parlement de Paris*, as well as the *Grand Conseil de Malines* in the Low Countries were thoroughly inspired by the learned Romano-canonical model. It was this model that, with national adaptations, was transferred to the civil procedural codes that were introduced in the various European jurisdictions during the so-called codification period. Prominent features of the Romano-canonical model were retained, such as the passive role of the judge, the doctrine of formal proof, the use of professional judges and the extensive reliance on documentation. If one compares the codifications that were in force throughout the European Continent in the eighteenth and the nineteenth centuries, one finds many similarities.[11]

Throughout the twentieth century, various important features of the Romano-canonical model were abandoned. The 1895 Austrian Code of Civil Procedure provides an early and influential example of 'modern' legislation. This codification strengthened the role of the judge, emphasized the pursuit of the substantive truth as opposed to the truth fabricated by the parties, favoured oral proceedings and adhered to the principle of the free evaluation of evidence. In many other jurisdictions, such as Germany and France, similar changes were adopted during the twentieth century.

As stated, we have chosen the divide between common law and civil law as the dominant starting point of categorization.[12] It is doubtful, however, whether the use of the rather crude 'civil law' and 'common law' categories is always meaningful. Many differences and local peculiarities can be observed in present day Europe. Cost regimes, for example, differ greatly.[13] Similarly, the rules of evidence in, for example, France and Germany are far from similar, even though these jurisdictions are both classified as civil law jurisdictions. With regards to the enforcement of judgments, there seems to be no common ground either.[14] In addition, it may well be argued that the English and the Continental European systems have converged since the second half of the nineteenth century.

5. Comparative Civil Litigation: the Ordinary Course of a Lawsuit and Court Structures

Traditionally, the ordinary course of a lawsuit was very different in common law and in continental jurisdictions.[15] In England, all evidence was traditionally

11 Van Rhee 2005b.

12 Zekoll 2006, Chapter 41. See also Van Rhee & Verkerk 2006, p. 120-134.

13 Zuckerman 2008, p. 435-467.

14 Hess 2005, p. 25-46.

15 American Law Institute & UNIDROIT 2006, Principle 9. Chase, Herschkoff, Silberman, Taniguchi & Varano 2007, Chapter 1.

presented to the jury at one uninterrupted oral hearing, i.e. trial. Although the civil jury is all but extinct these days, vestiges of the old system remain. In England, 'trial' continues to exist and evidence is generally still presented to the trier of fact during one uninterrupted oral hearing. Nevertheless, the 1998 Woolf Reforms slightly abandoned the old system. It is now often possible to replace (parts of) the oral testimony at trial by written expert reports or written witness depositions.

On the continent, procedures were traditionally in writing and evidence was often presented at several hearings scheduled several weeks or months apart. Throughout the twentieth century, many countries reduced the number of written pleadings and emphasized the use of oral preparatory hearings. In many of these countries, it is encouraged that evidence is presented during one main hearing. The changes brought about in the German system in 1976 provide a telling example.[16]

In most jurisdictions, it is now generally accepted that the course of litigation should be adjusted to meet the needs of the individual case. In France, for example, a distinction is made between a short, middle and a long track (*circuit court, circuit moyen* and *circuit long*).[17] The *président* of the court will assign relatively simple and unimportant cases to the short track, whereas more important and complex cases will be allocated to the middle or long track. Similarly, in England, the Woolf Reforms introduced a system with multiple tracks. The philosophy behind the English system is that the resources invested in each case should be proportional to the importance, complexity and the value of the case. This implies that a full range of procedural devices will be used in complex cases (multi track or fast track). Less complex and low value cases are allotted to the small claims track. This track provides for a more rigid and simple procedure: there is no disclosure and the use of expert evidence is restricted.[18]

The typical court structure in most European states is that of a pyramid with a Supreme Court at the apex. The details of the various systems differ greatly. Most jurisdictions provide for separate courts of first instance that hear low value cases, such as the English County Courts, the German *Amtsgericht* and the French *Tribunal d'instance*. In these courts, the procedures are generally more informal and often litigants are not assisted by a lawyer. In Continental jurisdictions, there are usually also numerous courts of general jurisdiction that handle mostly high value cases. Examples include the French *Tribunal de grande instance* and the German *Landsgericht*. In England, there is only one superior court of general jurisdiction that hears cases at first instance in civil matters: the High Court. In essence, the High Court is the successor of the old royal courts. The separate divisions of the High Court (such as the Chancery Division) are remnants of the medieval court structures.[19]

Apart from first instance courts, most jurisdictions provide for appellate courts and courts of last resort. Traditionally, the possibilities to challenge a decision of a court of first instance were very limited in common law countries. In continental

16 Murray & Stürner 2004, p. 3-21 and p. 37-65.
17 Ferrand 2005, p. 9-29.
18 Zuckerman 2006, Chapter 11, p. 482-500.
19 Glendon *et al.* 2007, p. 372-404.

jurisdictions, on the contrary, appeal is widely available. In some continental jurisdictions, the right to appellate review is even enshrined in the constitution. Appellate procedures on the European continent can often be seen as a continuation of the first instance procedure. Appellate courts are more willing to try the case again rather than to judge whether the court at first instance has rightly decided the case. In many continental jurisdictions, litigants can also lodge an appeal with the court of last instance as a matter of right. Only recently there seems to be a trend in which the scope of appeals to the appellate courts is being reduced. In order to limit the case load of the Federal Court (BGH) and the Courts of Appeal (OLG), German law was changed in 2001. The Reform Act (*Zivilprozess-Reformgesetz*) that entered into force on 1 January 2002 basically no longer required the Court of Appeal to try each case anew, but held that this court should in principle be bound by the factual findings of the first instance court. A review of the factual findings of the first instance court was only admissible if there were reasonable doubts with regard to the correctness and completeness of these findings.[20] At the same time, the Reform Act revised access to the court of last resort, i.e. the Federal Court (BGH). In essence, a system has been put in place that requires leave before a case can be heard by the Federal Court.[21]

6. Comparative Civil Litigation: Trends and Challenges

European jurisdictions are presently facing common challenges. Often they opt for similar solutions. One example is the rise of e-justice. Increasingly, advanced technological methods are used to facilitate the speedy and efficient administration of justice. The Austrian system designed to facilitate the order for payment procedure provides an interesting example.[22]

Throughout Europe, there seems to be a greater interest for group litigation and class actions. Cases, such as the 'Deutsche Telekom Cases' in Germany,[23] illustrate that there is a need for procedures that facilitate the swift resolution of large numbers of similar cases. In the United States, class actions have long been available. In Europe, however, the traditional model did not provide for procedural mechanisms similar to those provided in US class actions.[24] In many European systems, there are no real mechanisms other than the traditional joinder of parties to resolve large numbers of similar cases.[25] In some countries, tentative steps have been taken to provide for mechanisms to efficiently address situations in which large numbers of people have a similar claim. In England, the Woolf Reforms broadened the possibilities for group litigation.[26] Italy has recently empowered

20 Oberhammer & Domej 2005, p. 103-128.
21 Trocker & Varano 2005, p. 265.
22 Rechberger & Simotta 2009, p. 349-359.
23 See for a description: Stürner 2007, p. 250-278.
24 Sherman 2002-2003, p. 401-419 and Taruffo 2001, p. 405-421.
25 Baumgartner 2006-2007, p. 301-349.
26 Sorabji 2009, p. 498-514.

consumer associations to initiate litigation on behalf of consumers.[27] In the Netherlands, a Class Settlement Act was passed that enables the Court of Appeal in Amsterdam, upon a request by a claimant, to declare a negotiated settlement between some (representatives of) claimants applicable to all individuals that suffered a similar harm, except for those that explicitly opted out.[28] In Germany, recently a mechanism was introduced that allows a more efficient resolution of pending cases related to capital markets. It makes it possible to use the (factual) findings of a 'model case procedure' in related cases, thereby potentially reducing the need to address the same issues over and over again.[29] The European Union in its turn promotes effective methods of group litigation in consumer cases and in cases in which antitrust rules are violated.[30]

Another trend in most European systems is the greater emphasis on alternative dispute resolution (ADR). In many national systems, authorities promote the use of arbitration and mediation. Jurisdictions such as Austria, Belgium, Finland and Norway have recently enacted legislation on mediation. Recently, a European Union directive was enacted that regulates and promotes the use of mediation in cross border cases.[31]

7. Civil Litigation in Europe, the greater Europe and beyond

The study of civil litigation in Europe should emphasize the sources of law common to all or many European jurisdictions. In this regard, it is important to discuss the legislation of the European Union as well as the influence of the European Charter of Human Rights. In addition, wider international attempts to harmonize civil procedural rules and to resolve problems that arise in transnational civil litigation ought to be studied. These are the subjects of the final part of the course.

Before the 1990s, the Brussels Convention (1968) was the main achievement of judicial co-operation in civil matters within the framework of the European Union. This Convention contained rules on international jurisdiction as well as the recognition and enforcement of judgments, authentic instruments and settlements.[32] The Lugano Convention (1988) extended the application of these rules to the Member States of the European Free Trade Area.[33]

27 Art. 140 *bis* of the Italian Consumer Code ('azione collettiva risarcitoria').

28 Van Hooijdonk & Eijsvoogel 2009, p. 84-87.

29 Stürner 2007, p. 250-278.

30 See e.g. Directive 98/27 and the White Paper on Damages Actions for Breach of the EC Antitrust Rules COM/2008/0165.

31 The Directive on Certain Aspects of Mediation in Civil and Commercial Matters (ADR Directive, No. 52/2008). Also see the Green Paper COM/2002/0196 on Alternative Dispute Resolution in Civil and Commercial Law.

32 This Convention has been replaced by the Regulation on Jurisdiction and the Recognition and Enforcement of Judgments in Civil and Commercial Matters (Brussels I Regulation, No. 44/2001).

33 A renewed version of the Lugano Convention was signed in 2007 and entered into force on 1 January 2010.

Since the Treaty of Maastricht (1992), judicial cooperation in civil matters is more explicitly put on the European Union agenda. The Treaty of Amsterdam (1999) transferred matters of judicial co-operation from the third - intergovernmental - pillar to the first - supranational pillar. The Treaty of Nice (2003) specified that judicial co-operation in civil matters - with the exception of family law - would be dealt with according to the co-decision procedure of Article 251 of the European Community Treaty. Currently, Article 81 of the Treaty on the Functioning of the European Union provides the Treaty basis for legislation on judicial co-operation in civil matters.[34]

Since 1999, there has been an ever growing number of regulations and directives that affect the rules of procedure. All these rules apply to cross-border cases only. As the overwhelming majority of cases handled by the national courts are domestic ones, the significance of EU legislation should not be overestimated. EU legislation now includes, amongst other things, rules on the service of documents abroad,[35] the taking of evidence abroad,[36] legal aid,[37] and the enforcement of uncontested claims.[38] In addition, a small claims procedure and a new order for payment procedure have been created to facilitate the efficient resolution of cross-border cases.[39] At present, there is a wide range of rules available to make transnational litigation in Europe more expedient.

Within Europe, Article 6 of the European Convention of Human Rights has had a harmonising effect on the systems of civil procedure of the Member States of the Council of Europe (47 Member States). Only the first paragraph of Article 6 ECHR is applicable to civil litigation. It lays down that '[i]n the determination of his civil rights and obligations or of any criminal charge against him, everyone is entitled to a fair and public hearing within a reasonable time by an independent and impartial tribunal established by law.' Although it was only sporadically used after the coming into force of the European Convention on 3 September 1953, Article 6 now figures prominently in the case-law of the European Court of Human Rights. On the basis of it, the European Court has worked out a detailed scheme of fundamental principles that must be observed by the courts of the Members States

34 See in general Ervo *et al.* 2009, Chapter 1 ('European procedural law as a part of international procedural law'), p. 3-20; Storskrubb 2009.

35 The Regulation on the Service in the Member States of the European Union of Judicial and Extrajudicial Documents in Civil or Commercial Matters (Service Regulation, No. 1348/2000, replaced by No. 1393/2007).

36 The Regulation on the Cooperation between the Courts of the Member States in the taking of Evidence in Civil or Commercial Matters (Evidence Regulation, 1206/2001).

37 Directive to improve Access to Justice in Cross-border Disputes by establishing Minimum Common Rules relating to Legal Aid for Such Disputes (Legal Aid Directive, No. 8/2003).

38 The Regulation creating a European Enforcement Order for Uncontested Claims (EEO Regulation, No. 805/2004).

39 The Regulation establishing a European Small Claims Procedure (Small Claims Regulation, 861/2007), and the Regulation creating a European Order for Payment Procedure (Payment Order Regulation, No. 1896/2006).

of the Council of Europe.[40] Thereby, the Court has created a set of minimum procedural requirements that applies equally to all Member States.

Other projects aimed at the harmonization of procedural law include the proposals of a working group chaired by Professor Marcel Storme from Ghent. In their report, published in 1994, the working group presented a series of articles with explanations aiming at the harmonisation of civil procedural law in the European Union. The project failed to have any direct influence.[41]

More recently, another project was completed in the field of the harmonisation of civil procedural law: The Principles Transnational Civil Procedure. The Principles were drafted within the framework of the American Law Institute and UNIDROIT. They aim at providing broad and general principles that a legislator or a judge might adopt for the adjudication of disputes arising from international transactions that find their way into the ordinary courts of justice.[42] The Principles of Transnational Procedure are clearly the result of comparative legal scholarship.

8. Concluding Remarks

The comparative course on civil procedure taught at the Maastricht University European Law School differs greatly from ordinary courses that discuss only a single procedural system. It is by its very nature more reflective. It emphasizes the broader context of procedural rules. The historical and comparative approach enables students to look beyond the fixed boundaries of the legal system they are most familiar with. The course focuses on the basic principles underlying the different systems of procedural law. Studying the principles of civil procedure ultimately requires students to reflect on the relationship between procedural law and substantive law, and the goals of the civil process in general. Another distinctive feature of the course is that it puts considerable emphasis on transnational litigation.

A comparative course on civil procedure requires a skilled teaching staff. They need to be familiar with a variety of legal systems, preferably at first hand. The course has to be organized in such a manner that the tutorials, aiming at a deeper understanding and discussion of the materials that are focused on, are supplemented by guest lectures of experts from the various jurisdictions under scrutiny. These lectures may, amongst other things, be used to explore the relationship between black letter law and legal practice in the relevant jurisdictions. In this manner, the course will offer a rewarding experience for both the students and the teaching staff.

40 Ovey & White 2006, p. 158-159, p. 169-191.

41 Storme 1994.

42 ALI/UNIDROIT 2006. See also Stürner 2005, p. 201-216.

Bibliography

ALI/UNIDROIT 2006
ALI/UNIDROIT, *ALI/UNIDROIT Principles of Transnational Civil Procedure: as adopted and promulgated by the American Law Institute at Washington, D.C., U.S.A., May 2004 and by UNIDROIT at Rome, Italy, April 2004*, New York: Cambridge University Press, 2006.

American Law Institute & UNIDROIT 2006
American Law Institute & UNIDROIT, *Principles of Transnational Civil Procedure*, Cambridge: Cambridge University Press, 2006.

Baumgartner 2006-2007
Baumgartner, S., 'Class Actions and Group Litigation in Switzerland', *Northwestern Journal of International Law & Business*, 2006-2007, Vol. 27, p. 301-349.

Chase, Herschkoff, Silverman, Taniguchi & Varano 2007
Chase, O.G., Herschkoff, H., Silberman, L., Taniguchi, Y. & Varano, V., *Civil Litigation in Comparative Context*, Thomson West: St. Paul, 2007.

Ervo 2009
Ervo, L., 'Party Autonomy and Access to Justice', in Ervo, L. *et al.* (eds.), *Europeanization of Procedural Law and the New Challenges to Fair Trial*, Groningen: Europa Law Publishing, 2009, p. 21-41.

Ervo *et al.* 2009
Ervo, L. *et al.* (eds.), *Europeanization of Procedural Law and the New Challenges to Fair Trial*, Groningen: Europa Law Publishing, 2009.

Ferrand 2005
Ferrand, F., 'The Respective Role of the Judge and the Parties in the Preparation of the Case in France', in Trocker, N. & Varano, V. (eds.), *The Reforms of Civil Procedure in Comparative Perspective*, Torino: G. Giappichelli, 2005, p. 9-29.

Glendon *et al.* 2007
Glendon, M.A. *et al.*, *Comparative Legal Traditions*, Thomson West: West Publishing Company, 3rd edition, 2007.

Hess 2005
Hess, B., 'Comparative Analysis of the National Reports', in Adenas, M., Hess, B. & Oberhammer, P. (eds.), *Enforcement Agency Practice in Europe*, London: British Institute of International and Comparative Law, 2005, p. 25-46.

Jolowicz 2000
Jolowicz, J.A., *On Civil Procedure*, Cambridge: Cambridge University Press, 2000.

Murray & Stürner 2004
Murray, P.L. & Stürner, R., *German Civil Justice*, Durham, NC: Carolina Academic Press, 2004.

Oberhammer & Domej 2005
Oberhammer, P. & Domej, T., 'Germany, Switzerland and Austria (ca. 1800-2005)', in Van Rhee, C.H. (ed.), *European Traditions in Civil Procedure*, Antwerp: Intersentia, 2005, p. 103-128.

Ovey & White 2006
Ovey, C. & White, R., *The European Convention on Human Rights*, Oxford: Oxford University Press, 4th ed., 2006.

Rechberger & Simotta 2009
Rechberger, W.H. & Simotta, D.A., *Zivilprozessrecht: Erkenntnisverfahren*, Vienna: Manz, 2009.

Sherman 2002-2003
Sherman, E.F., 'Group Litigation under Foreign Legal Systems', *DePaul Law Review*, 2002-2003, Vol. 52, p. 401-419.

Sorabji 2009
Sorabji, J., 'The Hidden Class Action in English Civil Procedure', *Civil Justice Quarterly*, 2009, Vol. 28, p. 498-514.

Storme 1994
Storme, M. (ed.), *Rapprochement du Droit Judiciaire de l'Union Européenne*, Dordrecht: Kluwer, 1994.

Storskrubb 2009
Storskrubb, E., 'What Changes will European Procedural Harmonization bring?', in *Conference Proceedings of the International Association of Procedural Law*, Toronto, 2009, available at: <http://www.iapl2009org/documents/5EvaStorskrubb.pdf> (last consulted in October 2010).

Stürner 2005
Stürner, R., 'The Principles of Transnational Civil Procedure: An Introduction to Their Basic Conceptions', *Rabels Zeitschrift*, 2005, p. 201-216.

Stürner 2007
Stürner, R., 'Model Case Proceedings in the Capital Markets - Tentative Steps Towards Group Litigation in Germany', *Civil Justice Quarterly*, 2007, Vol. 26, p. 250-278.

Taruffo 2001
Taruffo, M., 'Some Remarks on Group Litigation in Comparative Perspective', *Duke Journal of Comparative & International Law*, 2001, Vol. 11, p. 405-421, available at: <http://www.heinonline.org/HOL/Page?handle=hein.journals/djcil11&div=25&collection=journals&set_as_cursor=5&men_tab=srchresults>.

Trocker & Varano 2005
Trocker, N. & Varano, V., 'Concluding Remarks', in Trocker, N. & Varano, V. (eds.), *The Reforms of Civil Procedure in Comparative Perspective*, Torino: G. Giappichelli, 2005, p. 243-267.

Uzelac 2009
Uzelac, A., 'Survival of the Third Legal Tradition', in *Conference Proceedings of the International Association of Procedural Law*, Toronto, 2009.

Van Caenegem 1973
Van Caenegem, R.C., 'History of European Civil Procedure', in Cappelletti, M. (ed.), *International Encyclopedia of Comparative Law*, Volume XVI (Civil Procedure), Tübingen [etc.]: J.C.B. Mohr, 1973, p. 3-7, 11-32, 54-55, 87-89 and 109-111.

Van Hooijdonk & Eijsvoogel 2009
Van Hooijdonk, M. & Eijsvoogel, P., *Litigation in the Netherlands*, The Hague: Wolters Kluwer, 2009.

Van Rhee 2005a
Van Rhee, C.H., 'General Introduction', in Van Rhee, C.H. (ed.), *European Traditions in Civil Procedure*, Antwerp: Intersentia, 2005, p. 3-24.

Van Rhee 2005b
Van Rhee, C.H. (ed.), *European Traditions in Civil Procedure*, Antwerp: Intersentia, 2005.

Van Rhee & Verkerk 2006
Van Rhee, C.H. & Verkerk, R., 'Civil Procedure', in Smits, J.M. (ed.), *Elgar Encyclopedia of Comparative Law*, Cheltenham: Edward Elgar, 2006, p. 120-134.

Zekoll 2006
Zekoll, J., 'Comparative Civil Procedure', in Reimann, M. & Zimmermann, R. (eds.), *The Oxford Handbook of Comparative Law*, Oxford: Oxford University Press, 2006, p. 1327-1363.

Zuckerman 2006
Zuckerman, A.A.S., *Zuckerman on Civil Procedure. Principles of Practice*, London: Thomson, Sweet & Maxwell, 2nd ed., 2006.

Zuckerman 2008
Zuckerman, A.A.S., 'Court adjudication of civil disputes: a public service to be delivered with proportionate resources, within a reasonable time and at reasonable cost', in Van Rhee, C.H., Heirbaut, D. & Storme, M. (eds.), *The French Code of Civil Procedure (1806) after 200 Years*, Mechelen: Kluwer, 2008, p. 435-467.

Philipp Kiiver
Mariolina
Eliantonio

TEACHING EUROPEAN AND COMPARATIVE CONSTITUTIONAL LAW

1. Introduction

In many respects, the study of constitutional law is much like the study of any other classical area of law such as criminal or private law. It contains a system of rules, with different sources, hierarchies, and means of interpretation. True, some aspects of constitutional law are more relevant to everyday (private) practice than others. For instance, the formulation of arguments from fundamental rights law, a branch of constitutional law, is part of everyday practice in dealings with, mainly, public authorities; institutional law governing the legislative process or cabinet formation, on the other hand, is sometimes barely law at all. Yet, even where constitutional law is not of immediate importance to the local law firm or municipal authority, subject-matters like institutional law remain crucial as foundational content in a legal *curriculum*: these are issues that every lawyer must have dealt with at least once in his or her lifetime in order to acquire methodological knowledge and a holistic understanding of the legal system, and of the rule of law. And some of those issues do remain acutely important to legal business. After all, matters like rules on procedure and competence allocation may affect the validity of the set of regulations to be applied. They are also indispensible for regulatory consultancy. And even apart from the actual substance of human rights law, i.e. the scope of various fundamental rights, knowledge and understanding of institutional and procedural rules regarding hierarchies and remedies between and within different court jurisdictions are crucial for any lawyer who wishes to be able to make a strong case in a multijurisdictional environment such as Europe. Indeed, much like other areas of law, constitutional law has been undergoing its very own kind of Europeanization process. And also the study of constitutional law in a comparative perspective has gained increasing relevance - sometimes with actual commercial value, yet always with a foundational educational value for lawyers who are expected to work and think across borders.

2. Constitutional Comparison and Europeanization

There are several reasons why it is worthwhile to engage in comparative constitutional law.[1] One is undoubtedly sheer academic curiosity. Yet, there is more: international comparison allows us to better understand our own system. The consideration of foreign law may reveal that our own constitutional text is verbose on a subject that in other systems is left unregulated in their written constitutions, while those other constitutions deal extensively with a matter that in our own constitution is treated implicitly at best.[2] In each case, comparison reveals that none of our own constitutional solutions is self-evident, 'natural', or otherwise unchallengeable. For a legal upbringing in a (hopefully) post-nationalistic world, such awareness and, in some sense, relativism is not only healthy but vital.

There are instances where comparative constitutional law actually becomes an applied science, a hands-on craft. That is when nation-building or a constitutional overhaul calls for blueprints and at least for experiences to be provided from other systems.[3] Comparative constitutional law has had such a heyday in the early 1990s when a relatively great number of former Socialist countries, in Central and Eastern Europe and the former Soviet Union, (re-)gained independence and in either case were in need of a structural reform of their constitutional system.[4] These days, reforms take place rather incidentally but they still happen. Note, for example, France's constitutional reform of 2008 that saw, *inter alia,* the introduction of a parliament-triggered referendum, the office of a national ombudsman, and a procedure for constitutional review of statutes not just before, but also after their entry into force.

Examples of comparative constitutional law that take place more frequently, but with less media attention, meanwhile, lie in the practice of constitutional interpretation by judges. In that context, courts would interpret provisions of domestic constitutional law in the light of law from other jurisdictions. Here even a harmless field like constitutional law may actually become controversial: notably in the US, literalist scholars are very much opposed to stealthily importing what they see as foreign law into the US legal system. This stands in marked contrast with the South African constitution which actually invites judges to consider foreign law in constitutional interpretation.[5] It also stands in marked contrast with what we may call a European tradition. Here we see that European courts, chiefly the European Union's Court of Justice and the Strasbourg-based European Court of Human Rights routinely rely on the constitutional solutions, or traditions, of their respective

1 See Claes 2006a; Jackson & Tushnet 2002.

2 A practical example is, in the context of the legislative process, the right for a legislative chamber to propose amendments to bills. The Dutch (Art. 84) and, even more so, the French Constitution (Arts. 40 and 44) deal with this explicitly, while the US Constitution (Art. I(7)) mentions this only in passing and the German Basic Law (Arts. 76 and 77) does not make it explicit at all.

3 See, specifically on the development of post-war constitutionalism in Japan: Takahashi 2002.

4 See Epstein & Knight 2003.

5 Art. 35(1)(c) of the South African Constitution.

Member States. Thus, the ECJ has been deriving general principles of Community law from constitutional traditions of the Member States long before this practice was codified in the Maastricht Treaty. And the European Court of Human Rights (ECtHR) surveys the law of the contracting states as a matter of course in order to identify common ground and to determine whether certain human rights interpretations and policy priorities have been evolving across the continent, which would in turn narrow the states' margin of appreciation.[6]

Due to the nature of the European constitutional space, such use of comparative constitutional law is not actually a one-way street, it rather resembles the water cycle. Applicants may invoke EU law in the course of domestic proceedings, from where sometimes a reference is made to the European Court of Justice (ECJ); at the end of domestic proceedings, which may or may not have involved an EU aspect, applicants may file an action against their state before the ECtHR. The ECJ may use general principles of EU law to resolve a dispute or provide guidance to the domestic tribunal; those principles in turn are generated from Member State traditions and the ECHR, which in turn is interpreted by taking into account common ground between the contracting states. The adoption of the EU Charter of Fundamental Rights[7] and the envisaged accession of the EU to the ECHR[8] merely strengthens this link between EU law and Strasbourg case-law. The EU Charter in fact not only builds upon the ECHR for EU purposes; the ECtHR in Strasbourg also uses the Charter as the most recent authoritative expression of common ground at least between those contracting states that are also EU members.

Apart from this highly intriguing set of interrelations, the Europeanization of constitutional law or the study thereof may point to at least two more sub-areas. One is the study of the effect of EU membership on national constitutional arrangements. This concerns the hierarchy of norms and the scope of court jurisdictions, including the question of how to reconcile the supremacy of European law with the supremacy of the national constitution in domestic (constitutional) jurisprudence.[9] It also concerns government-parliament relations, as legislative authority passes from national parliaments to the EU, where the governments are key actors but where parliamentary oversight over those governments is notoriously difficult to maintain.[10] Either way, a course of domestic constitutional law that omits the relevant country's EU membership is simply incomplete at best, and misleading at worst. The second sub-area, which is perhaps chiefly something for academics rather than for practitioners, concerns the tentative application of notions from domestic constitutional law to the institutional arrangements of the European Union.[11] In an organization that resembles a state, and that fulfils some of

6 See, for example, the Court's comparative consideration of domestic law and practice regarding the disenfranchisement of prisoners for parliamentary elections in *Hirst* v. *UK* (Grand Chamber, 6 October 2005, No. 74025/01).

7 Art. 6(1) EU (post-Lisbon).

8 Art. 6(2) EU.

9 See Claes 2006b.

10 See Kiiver 2006; the comparative chapter is available at <http://ssrn.com/abstract=1426078>.

11 See e.g. Von Bogdandy & Bast 2005.

the functions of a state, the drawing of lessons from the state in identifying shortcomings or devise solutions has led to a rich supply of literature. Obviously, differences are as important to point out as similarities, in order to avoid disappointment if the EU is held to standards, for example democracy and accountability, that only nation-states can fulfil and that, sometimes, even nation-states cannot possibly fulfil.[12] This is where one should think twice before applying national standards to the EU.

3. The Teaching of Comparative Constitutional Law

On the premise that constitutional law studies require attention to transnational aspects in order to capture the full picture, and to make students aware of cross-country variation, it is a relatively straightforward exercise to include comparative elements in studies of the constitutional law of a law faculty's home system. Thus, where a course on US constitutional law at an American university devotes attention to the legislative process in the US, it may devote attention to the legislative process of other countries as well. As a matter of didactics, the logical consequence in this setting is that comparison takes place subject-by-subject, not country-by-country. After all, one starts out with one's own constitutional law and takes a look across the border for each area discussed, usually to look at systems which feature different solutions.[13]

3.1. *Comparative Constitutional Law as a Separate Subject*

A deeper methodological challenge arises when comparative constitutional law is introduced as a subject on its own. The subject is then to a large extent divorced from the domestic background. Practically, this means that for example exchange students may easily participate in the course along with nationals of the faculty's home country, and gain knowledge and insights that are of universal value. In addition, comparative constitutional law as a separate subject can be used to teach undergraduate students, irrespective of their nationality, in a broader *curriculum*. Maastricht University's European Law School programme, for instance, teaches European, international and comparative law in English from the very first day, already at bachelor level. It thereby seeks to satisfy the labour market's increasing need for lawyers who are used to think and work in an international, cross-border setting. However, the format also requires course planners to make a fundamental choice. Essentially, and notwithstanding hybrid solutions, the choice is between a thematic and a country-by-country approach. In a country-by-country approach, selected jurisdictions are covered one by one, and the same range of themes is discussed for each of them. Gradually, and with each new system discussed,

12 See e.g. on the German Lisbon ruling: Kiiver 2010.

13 A fine example of such an approach is Jackson & Tushnet 2006, a US-centred volume where American law is contrasted with texts and materials from countries most relevant to the respective subject-area.

students learn to distil differences and similarities from the sequence of systems. A thematic approach, meanwhile, takes subject-areas as a starting point (e.g., lawmaking, government-parliament relations, human rights) and considers each selected area in a number of selected jurisdictions.

The greatest advantage of a thematic approach is that it allows for a discussion of aspects of constitutional law in greater depth. Since the object of comparison is defined and delimited from the outset, students can concentrate on the relevant part of foreign law only. The drawback, or rather the precondition, however, is that students must have a basic understanding of foreign constitutional systems to begin with. If they do not have such an overview, they risk considering aspects of law in isolation from their immediate context and thus fail to fully understand the relevant aspects themselves. To return to the above example of the legislative process, the possibility for the National Assembly to override the Senate in France cannot be understood without being aware of the historical foundations and institutional design of the French Constitution: national or popular sovereignty; the history of French unicameralism, bicameralism and, in the late eighteenth century, a brief period of tricameralism in France; the election process and rationale of the Senate; the government's dominant role in lawmaking, etc. This means that a thematic approach to comparative constitutional law as a separate subject is by definition more advanced, because it presupposes at least basic familiarity with the individual systems discussed.

A country-by-country comparison, meanwhile, can be introduced much more easily. A student will be able to follow such a course and learn about various systems in due course. The drawback here is that, depending on the time available, comparative insights emerge only gradually and there might not be enough time to actually weave the systems together at the end. During exams, students might then answer comparative questions in a country-by-country manner, which of course misses the point of comparative law. After all, the main aim is not to become an expert on individual foreign systems, but to understand commonalities and differences across systems.

3.2. *Choice of Literature*

The quality of available literature greatly affects the quality of a course. Typically, textbooks on (comparative) constitutional law reflect the didactical divide between thematic and country-by-country approaches. Tim Koopmans' *Courts and Political Institutions*[14] is an ideal example of a thematic textbook. It discusses the role of the judiciary as opposed to the government and the legislature in different constitutional systems. The style is erudite and, one might say, essayistic: it has a coherent narrative and takes the reader to a journey across diverse systems. It is ideal for a course which takes a thematic approach. Yet again, it has the same drawback as the course for which it is suited: it presupposes prior knowledge and is therefore appropriate for a relatively advanced level. It could be prescribed at the

14 Koopmans 2003.

end of a country-by-country course, or in a course which lists a country-by-country course as a prerequisite. The same holds true for other thematic publications on specific areas of constitutional law: in the case of federalism, for example, Michael Burgess' *Comparative Federalism*[15] is a volume comprising chapters on issues rather than individual countries.

At the opposite end of the scale we may find edited volumes, such as *Constitutional Law of 15 EU Member States* edited by Lucas Prakke and Constantijn Kortmann[16] or, again on the area of comparative federalism, *A Global Dialogue on Federalism* edited by John Kincaid and Alan Tarr.[17] Such volumes typically contain country chapters, each chapter devoted to one jurisdiction. The advantage of this format is that the individual chapters can be prescribed one by one in a country-by-country course. The drawback is that the value for comparative studies proper depends on the extent to which the editors have been able to weave the individual chapters together. Some edited volumes contain solid introductory and concluding chapters by the editors themselves, and succeed in committing the authors to a common style, chapter structure and choice of topics; other volumes are rather loose collections of essays.

A hybrid model has been adopted by Aalt Willem Heringa and Philipp Kiiver in their volume *Constitutions Compared – An Introduction to Comparative Constitutional Law*.[18] Here each chapter is devoted to a particular aspect of constitutional law (federalism and decentralization, election systems, the legislative process, government-parliament relations, the role of judges). Each chapter starts out with an elaborate comparative overview, but is then followed by more detailed country chapters on that specific aspect. Country chapters cover the US, Germany, the UK, France and the Netherlands, which in their diversity help illustrate broader concepts of constitutional law. The book's format is most user-friendly for thematic approaches, because it allows students to consider the details of individual systems as an illustration of the comparative overviews. But also the country chapters, since they consistently cover the same five jurisdictions, can be prescribed individually.

4. Conclusion

Just as constitutional law is indispensible in a legal *curriculum*, its comparative and transnational elements must be included in courses in order to give an accurate picture of the field. Some of the insight generated in such courses will be vital for practicing lawyers as they need to be aware that strong cases may be made not only based on purely domestic law but also on various overlapping European bodies of law, and that cases might actually have to be argued before transnational tribunals. Much of comparative constitutional law is crucial for policy-makers and consultants involved in policy-making as regulation increasingly takes place across different

15 Burgess 2006.

16 Prakke & Kortmann 2004.

17 Kincaid & Tarr 2005.

18 Heringa & Kiiver 2009; a free sample chapter is available at: <http://ssrn.com/abstract=1461411>.

levels of government and across national borders. Some of it may be mainly of interest to (future) academics, whether they will teach the subject or write about it, or both. Yet all of it is important for European lawyers as legal generalists: a study of constitutional law heightens their sensitivity of the fact that regulation is not just a given but is made under certain rules; the comparative perspective reminds them that none of those rules are self-evident but the result of choices; and the European perspective keeps them aware of the fact that Europe has an impact on constitutional law, that some constitutional law has an impact on Europe, and that constitutional law does not stop at national borders. So how to bring the message across in a legal *curriculum*? A country-by-country approach to comparative law, including comparative constitutional law, is most accessible as an introduction to the field for heterogeneous student populations. Thematic approaches to various *areas* of law, rather than to different systems, fits with the ultimate aim of cross-border comparison but requires more prior knowledge on the part of the students. As regards prescribed literature, country-based courses are initially best supported by edited volumes containing country chapters. An ideal hybrid might be a format whereby areas of constitutional law are discussed first in a comparative perspective, which is then illustrated with country chapters on that particular area. *Constitutions Compared* by Heringa and Kiiver[19] follows such an approach. Further cross-border exchange of ideas about didactics and prescribed literature will surely help us all to meet the challenges of teaching comparative law, and to keep improving the quality of our *curriculum* to the benefit of students and teachers alike.

19 Heringa & Kiiver 2009; a free sample chapter is available at: <http://ssrn.com/abstract=1461411>.

Bibliography

Burgess 2006
Burgess, M., *Comparative Federalism: Theory and Practice*, London: Routledge, 2006.

Claes 2006a
Claes, M., 'Constitutional Law', in Smits, J. (ed.), *Elgar Encyclopedia of Comparative Law*, Cheltenham: Edward Elgar, 2006, p. 187-199.

Claes 2006b
Claes, M., *The National Courts' Mandate in the European Constitution*, Oxford: Hart Publishing, 2006.

Epstein & Knight 2003
Epstein, L. & Knight, J., 'Constitutional borrowing and nonborrowing', *International Journal of Constitutional Law*, 2003, Vol. 1, p. 196-223.

Heringa & Kiiver 2009
Heringa, A.W. & Kiiver, Ph., *Constitutions Compared – An Introduction to Comparative Constitutional Law*, Antwerp/Oxford/Portland: Intersentia, 2nd ed., 2009.

Jackson & Tushnet 2002
Jackson, V. & Tushnet, M. (eds.), *Defining the Field of Comparative Constitutional Law*, Westport: Praeger, 2002.

Jackson & Tushnet 2006
Jackson, V. & Tushnet, M. (eds.), *Comparative Constitutional Law*, New York: Foundation Press, 2nd ed., 2006.

Kiiver 2006
Kiiver, Ph., *The National Parliaments in the European Union – A Critical View on EU Constitution-Building*, The Hague/London/New York: Kluwer Law International, 2006.

Kiiver 2010
Kiiver, Ph., 'The Lisbon Judgment of the German Constitutional Court: A Court-Ordered Strengthening of the National Legislature in the European Union', *European Law Journal*, 2010, Vol. 16, p. 578-588.

Kincaid & Tarr 2005
Kincaid, J. & Tarr, G.A. (eds.), *Constitutional Origins, Structure, and Change in Federal Countries*, Montreal: McGill-Queen's University Press, 2005.

Koopmans 2003
Koopmans, T., *Courts and Political Institutions: A Comparative View*, Cambridge: Cambridge University Press, 2003.

Prakke & Kortmann 2004
Prakke, L. & Kortmann, C. (eds.), *Constitutional Law of 15 EU Member States*, Deventer: Kluwer, 2004.

Takahashi 2002
Takahashi, K., 'Why do we study constitutional laws of foreign countries, and how?', in Jackson, V. & Tushnet, M. (eds.), *Defining the Field of Comparative Constitutional Law*, Westport: Praeger, 2002, p. 35-59.

Von Bogdandy & Bast 2005
Von Bogdandy, A. & Bast, J. (eds.), *Principles of European Constitutional Law*, Oxford: Hart Publishing, 2005.

André Klip

TEACHING CRIMINAL LAW IN ENGLISH

Whether we like it or not, law faculties across the Netherlands are increasingly teaching in English. Maastricht was the first university in Continental Europe to introduce entire English-language programmes, where students are required to function fully in English from day 1 until the day they graduate. Indeed, *Universiteit Maastricht* is no longer known as such, but rather as *Maastricht University*.

In this paper I discuss the problems and opportunities offered by English-language education. What experiences have we had? What challenges have we faced, and how have we attempted to deal with these? Does the fact that our focus is on criminal law and criminal procedure present an added problem? Where relevant, I also mention briefly the publication of research results in Dutch or in English.

1. Why English?

So why do we do all this teaching in English? In my opinion, the reasons are obvious. Society and law are globalising; where it was previously only natural that our graduates would find work in the Dutch setting, they are now looking elsewhere in Europe or even beyond. Law is globalising as well – the influence of European Union law can now be felt in all areas of law. And international law, too, helps to shape the law applied in domestic criminal cases.

Given all these developments, a student market for English-language education has also emerged. It is no longer self-evident that students will study in their own country, and universities are facing declining numbers of potential domestic students. Birth rates have been dropping for years and students are living at home longer. This explains why a faculty located in a somewhat remote corner of the country has been among the first to feel the effects of this progressive decline in Dutch students. Yet this geographical disadvantage for Maastricht within the Netherlands is at the same time an advantage in Europe as a whole. Maastricht's far-flung position makes the university attractive to German students in the region – and these students are voting with their feet. At home, the German student is faced with a university system that was last radically reformed and modernised in the

1960s, a good 50 years ago. Moreover, education in Germany is still in German and is based on a fixed curriculum, as the states (not the Federal government) determine what should be covered if the degree is to be recognised. And while university education was previously free of charge, more and more universities are now requiring tuition fees. The German student with initiative, therefore, need only look across the border to find an attractive alternative in English, where the programmes are also much shorter.

Students from other countries, too, partly make their choice of university by comparing the Dutch offer with what they can find in their own country. The mechanisms of free movement are decisive here: what is the relationship between the costs, the time and the quality? Many British students can no longer afford the exorbitant tuition fees that they face at home. A similar problem exists in Italy, which has also seen years of massive cuts in university funding. Finally, the prospect of free movement further increases the opportunities when students become graduates. With the mutual recognition of their high school diplomas and university degrees, there are no more barriers for students and graduates. The student market, therefore, has become indisputably international. It is the task of universities to respond to this. Incidentally, this also means that we in the Netherlands should not automatically assume that Dutch students will remain here; if they look around and see a better situation elsewhere, they, too, will take flight.

There are various consequences of the mixed nationalities in the student population. First, we can no longer assume that students know the law of their own countries. In traditional exchange programmes, it was precisely this element that was always useful when it came to comparative law. Yet because students have not studied their own legal system, this is often no longer the case. Asking students where they come from and how a particular aspect of law works in their home country does not necessarily yield an answer that can be usefully applied in comparative law. They simply do not know their own law. Sometimes, however, differences in legal systems appear to be culturally determined. In my experience, a student's gut feeling about his or her national system (i.e. intuition unhindered by legal knowledge) is in fact often fairly accurate.

Another striking aspect is the quality of the Dutch and international students. Students from abroad tend to perform better! They are more committed, and less susceptible to what is known in the Netherlands as the *zesjescultuur* – that is, where Dutch students tend to settle for a pass, i.e. a mark of 6, foreign students will frequently ask the tutor 'I got a 7, what can I do to get an 8?' I would suggest that students who take the initiative to study in a different country and in a foreign language are more daring, more talented, and more open to unfamiliar worlds. The range of quality among students seems to differ between the Dutch and Flemish on the one hand and the international students on the other. In the Dutch students we have the entire spectrum, from brilliant to mediocre. In the case of foreign students, those who would fall into latter category do not (or at least, rarely) cross the border; the range is thus smaller, as it is the better students who go abroad. This is another reason why universities should carefully position and profile themselves on the European and international student market.

2. No National Legal System and no Suitable Teaching Material

In most cases, teaching in English means that both the tutor and the student are using a foreign language. This places high demands on both participants. The tutor in particular needs to be able to function comfortably in English, though a certain level of proficiency is also expected of the student.

One of the main problems in implementing English-language education is that there is no national criminal justice system in which the specific subject is located. Given that the goal is not simply to teach the student about Dutch positive criminal law or that of another legal system, there is scarce suitable literature. The English-language literature focuses on a certain legal system and the literature on Dutch law is, naturally, predominantly in Dutch. New materials must therefore be developed.

3. Three Development Phases of English-language Education

Looking back, three development phases can be distinguished. The first courses introduced in English did not have purely national content, but instead naturally related to international and European law. We can identify different phases in the developments in educational exchanges and the introduction of English-language education.

The first phase, in the 1980s, saw the beginning of systematic European exchanges. Students could certainly opt to study abroad prior to this time, but there were no fixed arrangements in place and the individual would have to conform fully to the new environment. In the 1980s, however, the European Community began promoting such exchanges (Erasmus and Socrates Programmes). Students were able to cross borders and take part in education in the language of the particular country. Supplementary language courses in the national language were organised, but the legal education itself remained unchanged.

In the second phase (late 1980s/early 1990s), some courses began to be offered in English as well. There were several reasons for this. Having to learn Dutch first was certainly no draw card when it came to promoting exchanges. Foreign students were not arriving in droves, and those who did come found themselves bogged down in language education without gaining any real legal insight. The idea was thus to offer some courses in English. Initially, this primarily meant converting the Dutch-language course into English, which was a tricky business.[1] For courses focusing purely on European or international law, however, it was a relatively simple matter. The law covered in these courses is of a supranational nature and is generally applied in the same way in different countries. This also guaranteed the usefulness of the courses that students followed while on exchange. If European institutional law is the subject matter, whether you study it in Italy or in the Netherlands will not matter. International law and European institutional law allow relatively little scope for differences between countries. Certainly the effects of

1 And this was done initially only for foreign students; Dutch students were to avoid the English-language courses for a few more years.

international law can differ somewhat depending on the monistic or dualistic character. But the idea of using English for courses with a predominantly national origin, such as criminal law and criminal procedure, was not considered at all.

In the areas of criminal law and criminal procedure, courses such as human rights and criminal law, international criminal law and European criminal law were easier to deal with than economic criminal law, penitentiary law or evidence. If there was no strong international or European legal dimension, there was no cause even to consider teaching the course in English. Such was the case with, for example, international criminal law. The first version of this course was fully along Dutch lines. But this presented an important problem: there was not a single book or article to be found in the whole of the Netherlands. Case law was only very rarely available in English,[2] and legislation not at all.

In Utrecht, were I worked at the time, we thus wrote a book in English ourselves (*International Criminal Law in the Netherlands*)[3] in which we described all aspects of Dutch law on international cooperation in criminal matters and jurisdiction in English. We spent an enormous amount of time translating Dutch legislation[4] and also documented in English all conventions relating to criminal law applicable to the Netherlands. The aim was to present Dutch law to the outside world. Knowing what we now do, we may question how useful all this was when it came to teaching. Personally, I see this phase as having been a necessary step in the evolution towards fully English-language legal education. In terms of teaching we would do things differently now, but now we also have different goals. And the fact remains that the book still has value from a research perspective. It is indispensible in comparative law and is frequently referred to in discussions in the foreign literature on the international criminal law of the Netherlands.

My second experience of writing a book for teaching purposes was with *European Criminal Law. An Integrative Approach*. Once again, the need for the book arose from the fact that no suitable book yet existed. There were works on European law and on criminal law, on international cooperation in criminal matters and human rights in Europe, but nothing that combined all of this from the perspective of a newly developing legal field. In the course on European Criminal Law, we took legislation and case law in the EU as our starting points. Given our aim to cover certain aspects regardless of the peculiarities of different national legal systems, the effects in a national context were only discussed *in abstracto*. What we did discuss, for example, were the demands placed by EU law on a national criminal court if the court decides that a national penal provision cannot be applied. But we did not examine per Member State which criminal procedure decision should then follow.

2 The *Netherlands International Law Review* indeed translated some but not all Dutch case law.

3 Swart & Klip 1997. This is the bestselling book from the series *Ius Crim of the Freiburg Max Planck Institute*, and was used in education until 2006.

4 For the legislation, a great deal of use was made of translations by the Ministry of Foreign Affairs for the purpose of negotiating agreements on criminal matters in which the Netherlands was a party. However, these translations were of varying quality and often inconsistent; the translators rarely knew how others before them had translated the same legal term.

The decision to draw the boundary there was based on practical and substantive grounds: practical because it is impossible to do this for all Member States without knowing all the EU languages; and substantive because we then enter the territory of specifically national law.[5]

With respect to the background material (European legislation and European case law), a course on European Criminal Law was easy to covert from Dutch into English. All legislation and case law exists in all authentic languages, even with the same reference. Substantively, however, there were consequences in the sense that Dutch case law was no longer addressed with respect to European criminal law themes. Different universities are at different stages in this process: Utrecht had parallel Dutch- and English-language courses, while in Maastricht we used English only from the outset.

Concerning the experiences with a subject like European criminal law, it is interesting to see a constant in the difficulty that students encounter with this course. For years, the student population has consisted of two groups from different backgrounds. One group has a strong grounding in European and international law; these students have followed most of their education in English and generally have little knowledge of a national system of criminal justice. They are well versed in the abstract application of European law, familiar with the principles of free movement, and focused on the obligations of Member States. With regard to the latter, they recognise the obligation to transpose directives into national law, but have trouble with the enforcement obligation. Their weaknesses lie in addressing European regulations in national legal systems and in recognising the autonomous position of the accused. The second group consists of students of Dutch law, who generally specialise in criminal law. These students are good at analysing the position of the accused, and deal well with the interaction between criminal procedure and the ECHR. Their difficulty lies in recognising free movement cases from the facts and circumstances of a case. They also have trouble recognising what the enforcement obligation means from the perspective of criminal law. Some have a clear aversion to the complicating influence of the EU, or to the use of English as the language of this field.[6] Both groups tend to think in extremes when it comes to their preferences for national or European law: either European law takes precedence, or national law does. The reality, of course, often lies somewhere in between. All students have difficulties in understanding that, despite the clear non-compliance of a Member State's national criminal law with its obligations under Union law, this does not mean that a provision that should have been implemented

5 I was informed by numerous practitioners in the Netherlands that it was regrettable that in such an important legal field as European criminal law there was no good book dealing with problems relevant to the specific needs of the legal practice in the Netherlands.

6 This continues to have a negative influence on the evaluations given by students. For instance, in the last evaluation of European Criminal Law one student felt that an English-language course was of absolutely no use: '[it is] totally inappropriate for students of Dutch law.'

can be hold against an accused. General principles in favour of the accused prevail over enforcement obligation for Member States.[7]

We still have not found a good method to bring this interplay to the fore. This has to do with the fact that in order to do so there needs to be insight into a specific national system of criminal justice. Which system this is does not matter - but there has to be one. For a bachelor's course like European Criminal Justice Area, the fact that students have not mastered the ins and outs of such a system is a complicating factor. In a master's course like European Criminal Law, some students do have such prior knowledge (the students of Dutch law and the exchange students), but given the language issue it cannot be used. And in any event, the rest of the students are lacking such knowledge. For the courses in which positive law largely consists of supranational law, many students tend to see the issues in terms of absolutes. And though national law still plays an undiminished role, courses now pay no or little attention to it - after all, there is enough to deal with in terms of treaties, directives and decisions of the Court of Justice. In addition, in the anticipated linear process of European integration national law will reduce in importance as the area of freedom, security and justice develops further. Moreover, students are expected to become acquainted with national practice after obtaining their university degree, in legal practice.

We are presently in the third phase. The education in this phase is no longer modelled on that in the national law and language. Currently, two handbooks on criminal law and criminal procedure are being written in English. These are structured thematically, with topics addressed successively from a comparative law perspective. What choices have the different legal systems made? How does this fit in the context of a given system? By way of carefully selected case studies, students learn that comparing small aspects of law can reveal big differences, but the explanation for these often lies in the system. In this setup, too, positive law naturally plays a less central role.

4. Consequences of English-language Education for Course Content

So what consequences does teaching in English at a Dutch university have when it comes to content? First, the chosen topics are more thematic in nature and are elaborated from a comparative law perspective similar to US law schools. Courses revolve around themes such as legality, fair trial, defences and excuses. The comparative perspective is useful in that it helps to get the concepts across better; different legal systems have different solutions to the same problems, and these are very useful for highlighting the inherent logic behind each individual legal system. When trying to outline how the principle of legality relates to judicial interpretation, it becomes clear that a system like the common law system, which by nature is not a codification of criminal law, allows for much greater freedom of interpretation than a system that aims to codify everything. Does this mean that only the court can

7 3 May 2005, Cases C-387/02, C-391/02 and C-403/02, *criminal proceedings against Silvio Berlusconi and others* [2005] ECR I-3565.

initiate a change in the interpretation of a crime? This is not strictly necessary. Something that I have found particularly instructive is how a common law country deals with changes in common law offences. In South Africa, legislators have changed the status of rape from a common law offence to statutory offence.[8] Presently, all common law countries are proceeding to codify penal provisions. The number of remaining offences exclusively based on case law differs from state to state. In South Africa, the list of common law offences is now closed,[9] meaning that the courts cannot create any more common law offences.

In my view, the third phase of English-language education in the Netherlands represents an attempt to overcome the drawbacks of the second. However, the approach in this third phase is in fact based on a model of the national criminal justice system, where the international and European elements are emphasised much less. Looking ahead, the question arises whether we will ever reach a fourth phase, in which criminal law and criminal procedure become genuinely European? Only time will tell. But this has already happened in the area of international crimes, for example, where a fully supranational criminal justice system has been developed. Substantive and procedural legislation already exists, as does enforcement and adjudication. It is regrettable, however, that in education we no longer address the fact that a national element still exists parallel to the international legal system. In criminal law in the Netherlands we have an International Crimes Act, we cooperate with the criminal tribunals - but our education system no longer deals specifically with the legal questions that arise from this. Yet these are not unimportant questions. How should a Dutch court interpret the crimes in the International Crimes Act? In interpreting genocide or war crimes, does the court look to the views of international criminal tribunals, or take only Dutch law into consideration and interpret this in and of itself? Who decides this? And if we choose to give precedence to the interpretations of international criminal courts, does this then also apply to the general part of criminal law, which the legislation applicable to these courts does not address? Does co-perpetration in the Netherlands have to be shaped by the forms of 'joint criminal enterprise' of the tribunal case law?

How bad would it be, anyway, if there were no more Dutch-language legal education? Is education in one's own language necessary? How bad is it that Dutch law is not being taught? Looking at the situation in the United States, we see that students there are also not taught positive law per state. They have opted for a thematic approach instead, in which case law is also an important factor. However, the US has an advantage that we are lacking; both their federal and state law are in English.

Although I support the trend towards more English-language education, the drawbacks must also be acknowledged. One of these drawbacks is that it makes Dutch (as well as any other) legal practice seem increasingly remote. More and more often, I find myself being approached by courts looking for courses in European criminal law. It is also notable that legal practice is not (yet) ready for a

8 See Snyman 2008, p. 355–357, and Burchell 2010, p. 699-727.
9 Burchell 2010, p. 96-97.

great deal of literature in a language other than Dutch. In other words, as our academic publication culture becomes increasingly dominated by English, it drifts away from practice. The result is that practitioners then no longer gain new insights from the dynamic developments in legal studies. I doubt that this is purely a generational problem that will pass once today's students, who are being educated in English, start to occupy the relevant positions.

The rise of English offers major advantages with respect to interaction in research. Research, too, will come to be set up in terms of comparative law, much more than is presently the case. Individual researchers will see an increase in the interchangeability of their work, and their participation in the European and international debate is guaranteed. On this note, it is always disappointing when excellent books or articles are neglected because they are 'only' in Dutch. And by focusing expressly on English publications in their recognition and promotion policies, universities across the Netherlands do little to rectify this.[10]

5. Personal Experiences in South Africa

What I noticed in South Africa is that a common law system is far less strict about taking sources from other legal cultures than continental European countries tend to be. For several years I have been teaching annual courses at the universities of KwaZulu-Natal and Stellenbosch. Initially I thought I would need to learn a great deal about South African criminal law in order to communicate concepts of criminal law to practitioners. This did not turn out to be the case.

Preparing to teach in English was in itself extremely instructive, if only in the sense of comparing the structure of handbooks for common law and civil law. A common law handbook for criminal law is structured on the basis of principles and foundations of the non-codified, general part in order to then elaborate at length on particular offences.[11] A civil law handbook, on the other hand, pays ample attention to codified general part, and little or no attention to specific offences.[12] And the use of sources, too, is altogether different. On the Continent, we are used to attaching great weight to the history of how legislation has come about, the explanatory memorandum and the parliamentary discussions; yet not to common law. Once a common law legal text is included in the statute book, it becomes the plaything of the judiciary, which is heavily influenced by the literature. With respect to the influence of doctrine, our unwritten rule is that judges do not refer to the literature they have used or are following,[13] the only exception being the conclusions of the

10 As a quality indicator, the choice of language says little. And the same can be said for the peer-reviewed journals in which we are expected to publish. I see these as mechanisms that make it easy from a management perspective to distinguish between the quality of researchers without the assessor actually having to read the papers.

11 Ashworth 1999.

12 De Hullu 2009.

13 For a Dutch example of a verdict in quite an 'international' form, see the verdict of the 's-Gravenhage District Court in the Van Anraat case, 23 December 2005, AV6353.

Attorneys-General at the Dutch Supreme Court. Judges in common law countries take no issue with this.

Another aspect that struck me is that the two handbooks on substantive criminal law used in South Africa both make far greater use of foreign sources than Dutch handbooks do. This even includes sources like the ECHR and jurisprudence from the United States Supreme Court; that is, sources for which it is doubtful whether they should in fact influence African law. However, the use of sources between these books also differs somewhat: Snyman makes use of many German and Dutch examples,[14] for instance, and Burchell focuses more on the Anglo-Saxon world.[15] In general, though, they are highly receptive to input from beyond the strictly national legal circle. This refers not to the origin of a concept or idea, but the concept or idea itself. It may be that in common law, the traditional practice - where courts themselves had to seek out sources on which to base their decisions - still echoes; there was no definitive text for each law, but rather all sorts of writings by different lawyers.

Finally, we can also learn something from the US Model Penal Code, perhaps more so because of its method than its content.[16] Where the US legislators were unable to design a coherent criminal justice system, this was done instead by academics. Does this approach depend on certain circumstances,[17] or could we apply it to the EU? Just as in the US of the 1950s and 1960s, the European and Dutch criminal legislator is becoming less and less able to watch over the system and its dogma. Incident legislation and legislation on non-existent problems give rise both to legislative problems and to difficulties when it comes to education. One answer may be the formulation of a European Model Penal Code. Given the practice of Europol and Eurojust that in a rather general manner were declared to have jurisdiction over certain offences, without any definition of the crimes or reference to a specific criminal justice system, a model restatement of the law does not seem to be too far away from practice.

6. Conclusion

English, it appears, is set to be the primary language of criminal law education and research. In this sense it is gradually taking the place that was once occupied by Latin. This promotes the exchange of students as well as lecturers and researchers, but naturally also of ideas. In research, it is essential that a broad discourse emerges, and that the same problems are not discussed in different languages unbeknownst to those involved in the discourse in a different language area. Perhaps we have to conclude from this that law will also come to manifest more elements of common law. I do see a great deal of truth in the statement that writing and teaching in

14 Snyman 2008.
15 Burchell 2010.
16 Dubber 2011.
17 Stapert 2002, p. 109-114.

English promotes a common law approach.[18] So is there still a need or space for Dutch? Naturally there is, but only for specific, local aspects of law.

18 Klip 2009, p. 10.

Bibliography

Ashworth 1999
Ashworth, A., *Principles of Criminal Law*, Oxford: Oxford University Press, 3rd ed., 1999.

Burchell 2010
Burchell, J., *Principles of Criminal Law*, Pietermaritzburg: Juta, 2010.

Dubber 2011
Dubber, M.D., 'The American Law Institute's Model Penal Code and European Criminal Law', in Klip, A. (ed.), *Substantive Criminal Law of the European Union*, Antwerp: Maklu, 2011, forthcoming.

Hullu de 2009
Hullu, J. de, *Materieel strafrecht* [*Substantive Criminal Law*], Deventer: Kluwer, 4th ed., 2009.

Klip 2009
Klip, A., *European Criminal Law. An Integrative Approach*, Antwerp: Intersentia, 2009.

Snyman 2008
Snyman, C.R., *Criminal Law*, Durban: LexisNexis, 5th ed., 2008.

Stapert 2002
Stapert, B., 'American Approach to Harmonization an Example for Europe?', in Klip, A. & Van der Wilt, H. (eds.), *Harmonisation and Harmonising Measures in Criminal Law,* Amsterdam: Royal Netherlands Academy of Arts and Sciences, 2002, VLN 186, p. 109–114.

Swart & Klip 1997
Swart, B. & Klip, A. (eds.), *International Criminal Law in the Netherlands,* Contributions and Materials from the Max Planck Institute for Foreign and International Criminal Law, Band S 66, Freiburg im Breisgau, 1997.

Ellen Vos

EU LAW AFTER LISBON: SOME CHALLENGES AHEAD

1. Introduction

On 25 March 1957 the European Economic Treaty was signed in Rome by its six founding members. Today, 54 years later, we have an EU with 27 Member States and 495 million inhabitants, covering more than 4 million km^2. Within the time-scale of history, we can say that within a rather short time period of a bit more than 50 years, the European integration process has made an enormous progress.[1] The EU has provided an economic and legal setting in which the occurrence of yet another war has become unthinkable; which was one of the main aims of European integration in the 1950s. The creation of a common market with various institutions that could adopt laws, implement them and settle disputes, thus appeared to have been very successful. At the same time, the inexorable stream of EU activities in ever more areas and the accompanying surrender of competence to the EU as well as the continuous enlarging of the EU also led to much criticism and led to negative connotations as regards the EU especially in the context of the discussions on the ratification of the Constitutional Treaty in 2004. In the 'post-constitution' era that took off after the French and the Dutch 'no', the EU faced a crisis of credibility and confidence. How to restore and regain credibility and confidence is still subject of discussion in the Post-Lisbon era. In addition, the EU is today faced with a number of important challenges to be addressed, such as the economic and financial crisis, climate change, energy, migration, border control, enlargement and foreign policy. The discussion of these issues could easily fill all pages of this book. For the purpose of this contribution we will therefore limit ourselves to discussing selected issues of three general challenges of European Union law and integration: its level, its legitimacy and its global setting. Having discussed these, this contribution will analyse their impact on the teaching of EU law at universities.

1 Piris 2006.

2. The Level of European Integration

Probably the most important question that the EU today still faces is the one on the state and the very purpose of European integration: *Quo vadis Europa*? This issue was addressed by the commemorable Humboldt lecture of Joschka Fischer, then German minister of foreign affairs, in May 2000. With his vision of a European Federation which would be fully sovereign but still based on self-assured nation states and his plea for a European Constitution, Fischer kicked off a lively and far-reaching debate about the future of Europe.[2] Whilst unsurprisingly the finality of the European Union was not agreed upon by the political leaders, the idea of a European Constitution was soon picked up and set on the political agenda. At the Nice Summit of December 2000 and the Laeken Summit of December 2001 it was agreed that wide-ranging institutional reform was needed and to this end a European Convention was set up that was to consider key issues for the EU's future development and possible solutions. Already soon, the project of a Constitutional Treaty was brought to prominence by the chair of the Convention, Giscard d'Estaing. Whilst the Convention would probably have fallen apart, if it had attempted to answer the 'Quo vadis' questions of European integration,[3] it did address one fundamental question of European integration, namely the delineation of powers between the EU and its Member States, thus the division of powers between the EU and the Member States and the legitimate scope and limits of powers of the EU as well as the relationship between these powers and those of the Member States.[4] This issue was brought to prominence by the constitutional agenda set by the European Council at Nice.[5]

Although under the principle of attributed or conferred powers[6] the EU could only act to the extent to which the Members States have conferred powers upon it, this had never prevented the EU from substantially expanding its activities. On the one hand, this was due to the formal introduction of a series of 'new' competences by the Single European act, the Maastricht Treaty and the Amsterdam Treaty, although this was to some extent softened by the introduction of the subsidiarity principle that required that the EU would exercise these competences only if and in so far as the objectives of the proposed action cannot be sufficiently addressed by the Member States.[7] On the other hand, this was due to the case law of the ECJ and its broad interpretation of the EU's legislative competence, both through the recognition of the implied powers doctrine and the broad use of the former residual competence Article 308 EC (now 17 TEU), thus leading to a nearly unlimited EU

2 Joerges, Mény & Weiler 2000.

3 Mayer 2004, p. 40.

4 See in general, de Búrca 2011.

5 Declaration of the Future of the Union (No. 23) (Nice declaration), 26-2-2001, attached to the Nice Treaty. It expressly raised the question of 'how to establish and monitor a more precise delimitation of powers between the European Union and the Member States, reflecting the principle of subsidiarity.'

6 Now Art. 5 TEU.

7 See among the long list, *inter alia*, Toth 1994, p. 37-48; Estella 2002.

competence.[8] Whilst difficult to legally enforce,[9] the introduction of the subsidiarity principle by the Maastricht Treaty was nevertheless a clear signal that the post-Maastricht era was characterized by a political environment that was less conducive to continuing centralisation of authority.[10]

This signal was reinforced by the German *Länder*, who feared that the continually expansion of EU competences would harm the competences of the Member States (and particularly the regions).[11] They made the question of how to contain and delimit these competences, to become one of the compelling issues in the debate on the Future of Europe. The 'creeping' internal competences of the EU[12] thus also appeared prominently on the political agenda of the European Convention, addressing the fundamental question of the division of powers between the EU and the Member States and the legitimate scope and limits of powers of the EU as well as the relationship between these powers and those of the Member States.[13] Yet, the idea put forward by the German *Länder* of establishing a precise and rigid catalogue of competences, a *Kompetenzkatalog*,[14] was only shortly discussed in the Convention.[15] It was quickly abandoned, as it would be too difficult to establish, inappropriate and undesirable in view of the EU multi-level characteristics and the need for flexibility especially in relation to the internal market.[16] The Convention nevertheless recognized the need for clarification and the need to balance between precise delimitation of competences and a degree of flexibility.[17] The Constitutional Treaty addressed this need by introducing a competence taxonomy whilst also recognising a general resort provision: a flexibility competence clause. This was largely taken over by the Lisbon Treaty.

Today, post-Lisbon we find an explicit reference to the principle of attributed powers. Article 5 TEU thus states that 'the limits of Union competences are governed by the principle of conferral'. This principle, Article 5 TEU explains, means that 'the Union shall act only within the limits of the competences conferred upon it by the Member States in the Treaties to attain the objectives set out therein. Competences not conferred upon the Union in the Treaties remain with the Member States'.[18] Importantly, the Treaties provide for a list of three general categories of Union competences: exclusive, shared and supporting competences.[19] In that

8 See e.g. Usher 1988, p. 32-33.
9 See e.g. de Búrca 2003, p. 51 *et seq*.
10 Pollack 2000, p. 537.
11 Piris 2006, p. 79.
12 That have been a recurring issue of European constitutional law in academic literature, see e.g. Constantinesco 1974; Usher 1985, p. 121; Dashwood 1996, p. 113; Mayer 2001, p. 577; Di Fabio 2002, p. 1289 and Craig 2004a, p. 323.
13 See in general, de Búrca 2011.
14 See in general on this issue, Senden 2004, p. 371-392; Mayer 2004, p. 29.
15 See Craig 2004b, p. 653.
16 See also, Weatherill 2003, p. 59.
17 Konstadinides 2009, p. 230. See also de Búrca & De Witte 2002, p. 201-222. See Mayer 2004.
18 Art. 4 TEU furthermore emphasises again that competences not conferred upon the Union remain with the Member States.
19 Art. 4 TEU.

respect, we can say that today EU competences have been better defined and categorised. Yet, it is also clear that the numerous powers have been conferred upon the EU in rather wide and undefined terms, particularly where the EU has been conferred upon shared competences. Whilst to some extent the Treaties have addressed the wide scope of EU powers by *inter alia* declaring that the flexibility provision of Article 352 TFEU cannot be used as a basis for widening the scope of the Union powers beyond the general framework created by the Treaties,[20] it remains difficult to define or delimit EU competences. Moreover, the Treaties fail to address the relationship between these powers and those of the Member States. This means that the issue of competence, inexorably linked with the issue of the legal basis, and the underlying question of division of powers between the EU and the Member States and the legitimate scope and limits of powers of the EU as well as the relationship between these powers and those of the Member States are likely to feature in both cases before European and national (constitutional) courts,[21] discussions in national parliaments and/or discussions on future treaty reform. To be sure, also the broader context of a European constitution and the finality of the EU are bound to return on the political agenda, albeit with the lessons of the Constitutional Treaty in mind, this will be, probably, rather later, than sooner.

3. The Legitimacy of the EU

The French *non* and the Dutch *nee* to the Constitutional Treaty made plain that the political leaders had done little to (re)gain the people's trust in the 'European project' and that much work was to be done in this respect. It was the outcome of a long process that consistently had neglected European citizens' participation in policy-and decision-making and in which national political leaders had time and again blamed 'Brussels' for unpopular decisions taken by the EU in agreement with or even at the request of the Member States.[22] Already soon after the introduction of Jacques Delors' new internal market programme of 1985,[23] new re-regulatory operations at the EU level had appeared necessary for the internal market policy.[24] This led the EU to enter into new policy areas and to gradually erode both territorial - nation-state centred - political governance and nation-state constitutionalism, that intensified questions of legitimacy of the European integration process.[25]

The legitimacy of the EU was particularly debated during the crisis surrounding charges of fraud, nepotism and mismanagement levelled against the

20 Declaration 42 to the Lisbon Treaty.

21 See for example the German constitutional court in be 2/08, *Gauwelier* v. *Treaty of Lisbon*, judgment of 30 June 2009; the Polish constitutional Court, on Polish membership of the EU, judgment K18/04 of 11 May 2005 and the Czech Constitutional Court Pl US 19/08 Treaty of Lisbon, judgment of 26 November 2008.

22 See the European Commission in COM(2001) 428 final, European Governance - A White Paper, p. 7.

23 COM(85) 310 final.

24 Majone 1996.

25 See *inter alia* Joerges 2002, p. 3-31.

Santer Commission,[26] the perceived democratic deficit, the problems relating to the 2004 enlargement[27] as well as the food crises surrounding BSE and dioxins.[28] Soon after the fall of the Santer Commission in 1999, the new President of the Commission, Romani Prodi concluded that it was necessary 'to radically rethink the way we do Europe; to reshape Europe; to devise a completely new form of governance for the world of tomorrow'. To this end, the EU needed new forms of governance, referring to the rules, processes and behaviour that affect the way in which powers were exercised at European level.[29] After elaborate intensive in-house discussions and investigations and discussions with external experts and interested parties,[30] the Commission presented in July 2001 its White Paper on European Governance.[31] Herein the Commission had sought to avoid the issues that required Treaty amendments that were to be placed on the agenda for the Convention.[32] In this Paper, the Commission recommended to improve the legitimacy of EU policies and its institutions by reforming European governance and setting as principles of good governance: openness, participation, accountability, effectiveness and coherence. This would improve the openness of and participation in EU policy-making, restore the institutional balance, improve the quality of its policies, redesign rules and promote greater use of different policy tools, in order to enhance efficiency in policy formulation and implementation, whilst these principles would also be applied to the EU's global responsibilities.[33]

The White paper thus pleaded for 'better involvement and more openness' (primarily directed to input legitimacy) and 'better policies, regulation and delivery' (primarily directed to output legitimacy[34]), whilst recognising that these two are interrelated in the need for greater involvement in, and information about, policy proposals can also enhance the quality of these proposals. Direct participation of citizens in political decision-making could so be seen as a mechanism to link political decisions with citizens' preferences. On the other hand, the involvement of stakeholders and citizens could generate better or more effective political outcomes.[35] Moreover with its 'refocused institutions' the Commission clarified its desire to optimise the efficiency and coordinative capacity of EU institutions and to increase transparency and accountability.

26 See Committee of Independent Experts, *First Report on Allegations regarding Fraud, Mismanagement and Nepotism in the European Commission of 15 March 1999*, available at: <http://www.europarl.eu.int/experts/pdf/reporten.pdf>. See Craig 2000, p. 98.

27 See e.g. Ott 2002.

28 See Vos 2000, p. 227-255.

29 Prodi 2000.

30 See for the whole archive on <http://ec.europa.eu/governance/index_en.htm>.

31 COM(2001) 428 final, European Governance - A White Paper.

32 This was very much criticized, see *inter alia* the contributions by Scharpf 2000 and Weiler 2000.

33 COM(2001) 428 final, European Governance - A White Paper, p. 10.

34 Scharpf 2003 and Scharpf 1999.

35 Therefore, the introduction of interactive governance can be seen as an attempt to improve legitimacy on the input side as well as the output side.

Although the White Paper was received with great criticism as regards *inter alia* the Commission's institutional self-interest and its opposition to Member States as well as its missed constitutional opportunity and the thin link with the IGC debates,[36] it has been the guidance in the exercise of EU powers, in particular of the Commission. In the years following the White Paper, the Commission thus set in motion various initiatives on consultation of civil society, stakeholders and citizens in EU policy-making to live up to its new commitment to better involvement and openness.[37] One important initiative was the launch of the project 'Your Voice in Europe' by means of which the Commission gives everyone interested the possibility to give an opinion of EU policies and join discussions.[38]

To live up to its promise of better policies, regulation and delivery, the Commission introduced the better regulation agenda with impact assessments,[39] whilst also improving, more on the input side, the knowledge basis of the policy-making process. That scientific expertise as a basis for EU policy- and decision-making is a very sensitive and delicate issue became painfully clear in the BSE crisis. Following the critical conclusions of the European Parliament Inquiry Committee[40] which made the then Santer Commission tremble, the European Commission hastily came up with proposals to improve the scientific basis of EU decision-making. The increasing resort to European agencies, such as the European Food Safety Authority, put at an arm's length of the European Commission, should largely be seen in this context.[41]

The Lisbon Treaty made a great effort to improve the involvement of citizens and positioned the participation of citizens and others firmly in policy- and decision-making.[42] The new provisions require the EU institutions to give citizens and representative associations the opportunity to make known and publicly exchange their views in all areas of the Union and that they will maintain an open,

36 See e.g. the contributions by Scharpf 2000 and Walker 2000.

37 See Commission Communication on general principles and minimum standards for consultation of interested parties by the Commission, COM(2002) 704.

38 See <http://ec.europa.eu/yourvoice/index_en.htm>.

39 See e.g. the Interinstitutional agreement on better law-making, *OJ* 2003, C 321/1. See the general better regulation website of the Commission, listing all relevant documents: <http://ec.europa.eu/governance/better_regulation/index_en.htm>. See for a discussion Weatherill 2007.

40 European Parliament's Inquiry Committee, Report on alleged contraventions or maladministration in the implementation of Community law in relation to BSE, without prejudice to the jurisdiction of the Community and national courts 7 February 1997 A4-0020/97/A (Medina Ortega Report).

41 See e.g. Chiti 2009; Geradin 2005.

42 Interestingly, whilst the Constitutional Treaty still formally introduced participatory democracy as a normative model for the EU, in addition to representative democracy (Art. I-47 of the Constitutional Treaty), due to the apparent sensitivity of this issue, the Lisbon Treaty makes no mention of this model. Title VI of the Constitutional Treaty, 'the democratic life of the Union' has been replaced by Title II of the Treaty of European Union, called 'provisions on democratic principles'. Yet, strikingly Art. 11 TEU includes exactly the provisions that were included in the Constitutional Treaty under the heading 'participatory democracy'. See Smismans 2004.

transparent and regular dialogue with stakeholders and civil society. The real innovation of the Lisbon Treaty is the citizens' initiative, also laid down in Article 11 TEU (3). This gives active groups of citizens the possibility to mobilise themselves in order to demand the European Commission to develop EU legislation on a certain topic.[43] The new provisions inserted by the Lisbon Treaty, especially the citizen's initiative laid down in Article 11 TEU, underline the EU's commitment to take citizens, stakeholders and civil society seriously. Yet, whether such new, participatory governance structures will be really meaningful in practice and not turn out to be a participatory myth,[44] will depend on both citizens and stakeholders but foremost on the Commission that would need to demonstrate to be truly engaged and not merely concerned with window-dressing.

4. The Global Setting of the EU

Lisbon has not only lend its name to the Treaty that amended the two existing treaties in the Post-Constitution era, it also provided the setting for a new strategy that was adopted by the European Council in Lisbon, thus called the 'Lisbon strategy', as a response to the challenge of globalisation. The European Council hereby committed the Union to become, by 2010, 'the most competitive and dynamic knowledge-based economy in the world, capable of sustainable economic growth with more and better jobs and greater social cohesion'.[45] This was to be achieved through a range of ambitious policy goals, both of an economic (becoming a dynamic, knowledge based economic) and social (modernising the European social model and building an active welfare state) nature. This strategy officially launched the open method of coordination as method to help Member States in the implementation of the 'Lisbon goals'[46] and clearly set out the EU's ambitions and role as a competitor in the global setting.[47] The strategy however gradually developed into an overly complex structure with multiple goals and actions and an unclear division of responsibilities and tasks, particularly between the EU and national levels,[48] and in 2009, it was openly declared to be a failure.[49]

In 2010 therefore, building on the lessons of the Lisbon strategy, the European Commission developed a new strategy 'Europe 2020' to recover from the crisis and prepare EU economy for the next decade, making the EU a smart, sustainable and

43 See for its implementation: Regulation (EU) No. 211/2011 of the European Parliament and of the Council on the citizens' initiative, *OJ* L 65, 2011/1.

44 Smismans 2008.

45 Conclusions of the Presidency of 23 and 24 March 2000, *EU Bulletin* 3-2000.

46 See e.g., Zeitlin, Pochet & Magnusson 2005.

47 See in general, Rodrigues 2009.

48 As the Commission itself admitted. Commission staff working document, Lisbon Strategy evaluation document, SEC(2010) 114 final.

49 See most outspokenly, Fredrik Reinfeldt, the Swedish Prime Minister on the eve of the Swedish Presidency of the European Union, <http://www.euractiv.com/en/priorities/sweden-admits-lisbon-agenda-failure/article-182797>. Surely, although some objectives had been achieved in various areas, the outbreak of the economic and financial crisis did not contribute to make it a success.

inclusive economy.[50] Importantly, two major challenges were identified: the (re-definition of the EU's role in the international order and the renewal of its development model.[51] Both challenges had featured significantly on the political agenda in the discussions on the reform of the Treaties. Pre-Lisbon, provisions on the EU's external action were scattered throughout the Treaties. The Common Foreign and Security Policy (CFSP) was laid down in the EU Treaty (second pillar), whilst trade policy, development aid and economic, financial and technical cooperation with third countries were governed by the EC Treaty (first pillar).[52] In addition, the economic and political relations with third countries and organisations were subjected to different rules and decision-making procedures. The Lisbon Treaty sought to address these complexities and to improve the coherence of external relations of the EU.[53] This was done first, by removing the pillar structure and explicitly conferring upon the EU legal personality,[54] and second, by inserting one set of common goals for EU's 'relations with the wider world', combining CFSP with economic goals.[55] These improvements however are still somewhat flawed. Notwithstanding the removal of the pillar structure, the CFSP remains clearly in the Treaty on European Union and demonstrates to possess still intergovernmental characteristics, with the European Court of Justice being largely excluded to review CFSP acts.[56] All other provisions on external relations, on the other hand, are placed in the Treaty on the Functioning of the European Union. Moreover, although the TEU presents the goals of external relations as one coherent set, and elaborates these goals,[57] it does not provide for linkages between them or a hierarchy or prioritising mechanisms. The challenge will be therefore to implement these provisions in a consistent manner, horizontally between the EU policies themselves and also vertically, between the EU and the Member States, in view of the nature of both exclusive and shared competences.[58]

To a great extent, the creation of a High Representative of the Union for Foreign Affairs and Security Policy is meant to take away these flaws and provide

50 COM(2010) 2020, Communication from the Commission, *Europe 2020 A strategy for smart, sustainable and inclusive growth.*

51 *On the EU 2020 strategy: contributions after the Lisbon agenda experience*, written by members of the so-called 'Lisbon Agenda group', <http://www.mariajoaorodrigues.eu/files/EU202020_Contributions_100112_Final.pdf>.

52 See in general Koutrakos 2011; Cremona & De Witte 2008.

53 Dony 2009, p. 149-150.

54 See Leal-Arcas 2006; de Schoutheete & Andoura 2007.

55 Namely: to uphold and promote its values and interests and contribute to the protection of its citizens; to contribute to peace, security, the sustainable development of the Earth, solidarity and mutual respect among peoples, free and fair trade, eradication of poverty and the protection of human rights, in particular the rights of the child, as well as to the strict observance and the development of international law, including respect for the principles of the United Nations Charter. See Art. 3(5) TEU.

56 Art. 24 TEU, with the exception of the competence to monitor compliance with Art. 40 TEU and the review of legality of decisions adopted on the basis of Art. 275 (2) TFEU.

57 Art. 21(2) TEU.

58 See on this C-91/05, *Commission* v. *Council* (ECOWAS) [2008] ECR I-3651. Hillion & Wessel 2009.

for more institutional consistency. The High Representative, Catherine Ashton, chairs the Foreign Affairs Council and conducts the Common Foreign and Security Policy and is supported by a European External Action Service.[59] Being at the same time also a Vice-President of the European Commission, she is to ensure the consistency and coordination of the European Union's external action. Yet, the creation of the position of a High Representative is quite problematic in itself and raises concerns as regards her workload, the impact on the collegiality of the Commission, the relationship between the High Representative and the president of the European Council and the division on labour between them on issues relating to CFSP.[60]

One of the crucial issues in relation to the EU's strive to assert its presence in the global setting remains therefore in how far the EU will be successful in ensuring effective and consistent co-ordination in view of the complex and multi-level nature of its constitutional structure.

5. Challenging the Teaching and Teaching the Challenges

This very brief account of a selected number of challenges that the EU faces in the aftermath of the Lisbon Treaty indicates that the classic methods of teaching law that rely on the mere studying of the relevant legal instruments, case law and literature do not really work. These challenges once again show that a more comprehensive, interdisciplinary approach of teaching, setting EU law in context, is necessary to provide students with a fine understanding of EU law. The challenges moreover emphasise the close intertwining of institutional and substantive issues of EU law, and the intricate linkage between national, EU and global levels. This calls for an approach that reconciles both such issues and the different levels. Together, this requires a careful selection of handbooks to be used, and teaching methods to do justice to the complexities of EU, based on problem-based learning and the Socratic method.

In addition, the ever larger Union with ever more tasks to be fulfilled, stretching far into fields of law that formerly had remained largely to the national legal setting, such as private law and very recently, criminal law, also asks for a different approach in the teaching of such fields and possibly to the development of new courses on these subject-matters. At the same time, the ever wider and intruding Union confronts those who teach EU law with the dilemma to choose and specialize in specific areas of EU law. The challenge for teaching is therefore to give general courses on EU law a flavour of the more specific settings and place courses on specific topics of EU law in the broader setting of EU law.

Surely the teaching of EU law is also affected by the general digitalisation of our society. This means that teaching EU law will need not only to ensure adequate ways to allow communication between teachers and students as well as students amongst themselves, through for example a digital environment, but also to reflect

59 Art. 27(3) TEU.

60 Dony 2009, p. 152-153.

on ways how to deal with 'digital' students and develop interactive, engaging pedagogical methods for future paper-and roomless classrooms.

Bibliography

Chiti 2009
Chiti, E., 'An Important Part of the EU's Institutional Machinery: Features, Problems and Perspectives of European Agencies', *Common Market Law Review*, 2009, p. 1395-1442.

Committee of Independent Experts 1999
Committee of Independent Experts, First Report on Allegations regarding Fraud, Mismanagement and Nepotism in the European Commission of 15 March 1999, available at: <http://www.europarl.eu.int/experts/pdf/reporten.pdf>.

Constantinesco 1974
Constantinesco, V., *Compétences et pouvoirs dans les Communautés européennes. Contribution à l'étude de la nature juridique des Communautés,* Coll. Bibliothèque de droit international, Vol. LXXIV, Paris: Librairie générale de droit et de jurisprudence, 1974.

Craig 2000
Craig, P., 'The Fall and Renewal of the Commission: Accountability, Contract and Administrative Organisation', *European Law Journal*, 2000, Vol. 6, p. 98-116.

Craig 2004a
Craig, P., 'Competence: Clarity, Conferrral, Containment and Consideration', *European Law Review*, 2004, Vol. 29, No. 3, p. 323-344.

Craig 2004b
Craig, P., 'Constitutional Process and Reform in the EU: Nice, Laeken, the Convention and the ICG', *European Public aw,* 2004, Vol. 10, p. 653-675.

Cremona & De Witte 2008
Cremona, M. & De Witte, B. (eds.), *EU Foreign Relations Law: Constitutional Fundamentals,* Oxford: Hart Publishing, 2008.

Dashwood 1996
Dashwood, A., 'The Limits of European Community Powers', *European Law Review,* 1996, Vol. 21, p. 113-128.

De Búrca 2003
De Búrca, G., ´The European Court of Justice and the Evolution of EU Law´, in Börzel, T. & Cichowski, R. (eds.), *The State of the European Union, 6: Law, Politics, and Society*, Oxford: Oxford University Press, 2003, p. 48-77.

De Búrca 2011
De Búrca, G., *Constitutional Limits of EU Action*, Oxford: Oxford University Press, 2011, forthcoming.

De Búrca & De Witte 2002
De Búrca, G. & De Witte, B., 'The Delimitation of Powers between the EU and its Member States', in Arnull. A. & Wincott, D. (eds.), *Accountability and Legitimacy in the European Union*, Oxford: Oxford University Press, 2002, p. 201-222.

De Schoutheete & Andoura 2007
De Schoutheete, Ph. & Andoura, S., 'The Legal Personality of the European Union', *Studia Diplomatica*, 2007, Vol. LX, p. 233-244.

Di Fabio 2002
Di Fabio, U., 'Some Remarks on the Allocation of Competences between the European Union and its Member States', *Common Market Law Review*, 2002, Vol. 39, p. 1289-1302.

Dony 2009
Dony, M., 'The EU's External Relations and its Evolving Framework', in Telò, M. (ed.), *The European Union and Global Governance*, London: Routledge, 2009, p. 131-155.

Estella 2002
Estella, A., *The EU Principle of Subsidiarity and its Critique*, Oxford: Hart Publishing, 2002.

Geradin, Munoz & Petit 2005
Geradin, D., Munoz, R. & Petit, N. (eds.), *Regulation through Agencies: A New Paradigm of European Governance*, Cheltenham: Edward Elgar, 2005.

Hillion & Wessel 2009
Hillion, C. & Wessel, R., 'Competence Distribution in EU External Relations after *ECOWAS*: Clarification or Continued Fuzziness?', *Common Market Law Review*, 2009, p. 551-586.

Joerges 2002
Joerges, C., 'The Law's Problems with the Governance of the European Market', in Joerges, C. & Dehousse, R. (eds.), *Good Governance in Europe's Integrated Market*, Oxford: Oxford University Press, 2002, p. 3-31.

Joerges, Mény & Weiler 2000
Joerges, C., Mény, Y & Weiler, J.H.H. (eds.), *What Kind of Constitution for What Kind of Polity? – Responses to Joschka Fischer*, Jean Monnet working paper, NYU, No. 7/00, 2000.

Konstadinides 2009
Konstadinides, T., *Division of Powers in European Union Law: The Delimitation of Internal Competences between the EU and the Member States*, The Hague: Kluwer Law International, 2009.

Koutrakos 2011
Koutrakos, P. (ed.), *European Foreign Policy: Legal and Political Perspectives*, Cheltenham: Edward Elgar, 2011.

Leal-Arcas 2006
Leal-Arcas, R., 'EU Legal Personality In Foreign Policy?', *Boston University International Law Journal,* 2006, Vol. 24, p. 165-212.

Majone 1996
Majone, G. (ed.), *Regulating Europe,* London: Routledge, 1996.

Mayer 2001
Mayer, F.C., 'Die drei Dimensionen der europäischen Kompetenzdebatte', *Zeitschrift für ausländisches öffentliches Recht und Völkerrecht,* 2001, Vol. 61, No. 2/3, p. 577-640.

Mayer 2004
Mayer, F., 'Competences - Reloaded? The Vertical Division of Powers in the EU after the New European Constitution', in Weiler J.H.H. *et al.* (eds.), *Altneuland: The EU Constitution in a Contextual Perspective,* NYU Jean Monnet Working Paper 5/04, 2004.

Ott 2002
Ott, A. (ed.), *Handbook on European Enlargement: A Commentary on the Enlargement Process,* The Hague: T.M.C. Asser Press, 2002.

Piris 2006
Piris, J.C., *The Constitution for Europe,* Cambridge: Cambridge University Press, 2006.

Pollack 2000
Pollack, M.A., 'The End of Creeping Competences? EU Policy-making since Maastricht', *Journal of Common Market Studies,* 2000, Vol. 38, No. 3, p. 519-538.

Prodi 2000
Prodi, R., President of the European Commission, *2000-2005: Shaping the New Europe,* European Parliament Strasbourg, 15 February 2000, SPEECH/00/41.

Rodrigues 2009
Rodrigues, M.J. (ed.), *Europe, Globalization and the Lisbon Agenda,* Cheltenham UK/Northampton MA USA: Edward Elgar, 2009.

Scharpf 1999
Scharpf, F.W., *Governing in Europe: Effective and Democratic?,* Oxford: Oxford, University Press. 1999.

Scharpf 2000
Scharpf, F., ´European Governance: Common Concerns vs. the Challenge of Diversity ´, in Joerges, C., Meny, Y. & Weiler, J.H.H. (eds.), *Symposium: Mountain or Molehill? A Critical Appraisal of the Commission White Paper on Governance,* Jean Monnet Working Paper NYU, No. 6/01, 2000.

Scharpf 2003
Scharpf, F.W., 'Problem-Solving Effectiveness and Democratic Accountability in the EU', MPIfG Working Paper 03/1, 2003.

Senden 2004
Senden, W., 'Is the European Union in Need of a Competence Catalogue? Insights from Comparative Federalism', *Journal of Common Market Studies,* 2004, Vol. 42, No. 2, p. 371-392.

Smismans 2004
Smismans, S., 'The Constitutional Labelling of "the democratic life of the EU": Representative and Participatory Democracy', in Follesdal, A. & Dobson, L. (eds.), *Political Theory and the European Constitution,* London: Routledge, 2004, p. 122-138.

Smismans 2008
Smismans, S., 'New Modes of Governance and the Participatory Myth', *West European Politics,* 2008, Vol. 32, No. 5, p. 874-895.

Toth 1994
Toth, A.G., 'A Legal Analysis of Subsidiarity', in O'Keeffe, D. & Twomey, P.M. (eds.), *Legal Issues of the Maastricht Treaty,* London: Chancery, 1994, p. 37-48.

Usher 1985
Usher, J., 'The Scope of Community Competence – Its Recognition and Enforcement', *Journal of Common Market Studies,* 1985, Vol. 42, No. 2, p. 121-136.

Usher 1988
Usher, J., 'The Gradual Widening of European Community Policy on the Basis of Articles 100 and 235 of the EEC Treaty', in Schwarze, J. & Schermers, H. (eds.), *Structure and Dimensions of European Community Policy,* Baden-Baden: Nomos, 1988, p. 25-36.

Vos 2000
Vos, E.I.L., 'EU Food Safety Regulation in the Aftermath of the BSE Crisis', *Journal of Consumer Policy,* 2000, p. 227-255.

Walker 2000
Walker, N., ´The White Paper in Constitutional Context´, in Joerges, C., Meny, Y. & Weiler, J.H.H. (eds.), *Symposium: Mountain or Molehill? A Critical Appraisal of the Commission White Paper on Governance,* Jean Monnet Working Paper NYU, No. 6/01, 2000.

Weatherill 2003
Weatherill, S., 'Competences', in De Witte, B. (ed), *Ten Reflections on the Constitutional Treaty for Europe,* Florence: Robert Schuman Centre at the European University Institute, 2003, p. 45-66.

Weatherill 2007
Weatherill, S. (ed.), *Better Regulation*, Oxford: Hart Publishing, 2007.

Weiler 2000
Weiler, J., 'The Commission as Euro-Skeptic: A Task Oriented Commission for a Project-Based Union', in Joerges, C., Meny, Y. & Weiler, J.H.H. (eds.), *Symposium: Mountain or Molehill? A Critical Appraisal of the Commission White Paper on Governance,* Jean Monnet Working Paper NYU, No. 6/01, 2000.

Zeitlin, Pochet & Magnusson 2005
Zeitlin, J., Pochet, P. & Magnusson, L. (eds.), *The Open Method of Coordination in Action,* Brussels: Lang, 2005.

Remco van Rhee
Tanja van der Meer

TEACHING EUROPEAN LEGAL HISTORY

1. Introduction

In the Netherlands, there are no specific admission requirements as regards the courses law students should have taken during their pre-university education. Although a sufficient knowledge of, for example, foreign languages (including Latin), economics and history is highly beneficial to such students, many of them cannot be expected to have mastered all these topics in detail. Therefore, at the Maastricht University Faculty of Law a determined effort is made to teach the various courses in such a way that a lack of the necessary background knowledge can be overcome.

This contribution deals with the way European legal history is taught in the European Law School English Track of the Maastricht Law faculty. Of course, when teaching Europe legal history, a lack of knowledge as regards European history in general, the major modern European languages (French, German and English) and Latin is especially problematic. In order to overcome this problem, we[1] have designed our compulsory first-year course in such a way that students not only acquire the necessary knowledge of European *legal* history, but also study the main events in European History in general. Additionally, we provide original texts with extensive translations, and encourage students to read both the translation and the original. During the seminars we frequently refer to the original texts in order to demonstrate their importance. This is not only beneficial from the perspective of legal history, but also from the perspective of other law courses which presuppose that students have some knowledge of the concept of Europe and European integration processes, of the major modern European languages, and of the language that for a long period helped to shape the European intellectual environment (Latin).

After the first-year introductory course on European legal history, which will be discussed below, we aim at integrating legal history into the various (modern)

1 Apart from the authors of the present contribution, 'we' refers to Prof. Dr. Louis Berkvens, Dr. Pim Oosterhuis, Mr. Emanuel van Dongen and Ms. Mariken Lenaerts.

law courses on offer in Maastricht. In our opinion, the integration of legal history helps to demonstrate the relevance of this topic in a modern European legal curriculum, especially in courses with a comparative nature, and, where necessary, also keeps the instructor aware of the fact that he/she is teaching in the law faculty and not in the history department of his/her university. Knowledge of legal history helps in avoiding anachronistic interpretations of the legal system and in building a profound knowledge of legal concepts and legal terminology.

2. General Introduction to Legal History in Year 1 of the Bachelor's Programme

In the first year of the Bachelor's programme, European legal history is taught during what may be called a 'crash course' of four weeks in January (4 ECTS). Although this is a short period of time, the benefit of concentrating the introductory course in this manner is that it is the only course the students have to focus on as in Maastricht, usually two parallel courses are taught during eight-week periods. Consequently, students are expected to devote 40 hours per week to the course, which is also stimulated by not having a written exam at the end of the course, but a series of compulsory student papers (one paper per week) that are graded and that make up the final mark.

Taking into consideration what has been stated above, it may not come as a surprise that the introductory course not only puts an emphasis on European *legal* history and its chronology, but also provides – as far as relevant from a legal point of view – the necessary information on European history in general. The chosen didactical approach ties in with the comparative method employed by most European Law School courses, as well as with the methods of case and rule analysis developed in the first year Skills trajectory, elements of which are incorporated in most subsequent courses.

The subject matter is divided into three periods: (1) Roman Law in Antiquity, (2) the *Ius Commune* period (Middle Ages and early modern period),[2] and (3) the Codification Period. The course consists of two weekly lectures and two weekly seminars.

2.1. *Lectures*

In the two lectures, which are scheduled at the start of each week, external European legal history and European history in general are focused on. The students are required to prepare for the lectures. This is facilitated by the fact that the various power-point presentations used during the lectures are made available in advance. The presentations assist the students in focusing on the major issues while reading the relevant parts of Peter Stein's book 'Roman Law in European Legal History'.[3]

2 We refer to this period as the 'Ius Commune period' only for reasons of convenience.
3 Cambridge University Press, 1999.

Students bring print outs of the power-point presentations to the lectures in order to make notes. The lectures are inter-active in the sense that the lecturer submits questions to the audience (individual students are selected at random) and gives the students frequent opportunities to ask questions. Students who have not been able to prepare for the lecture will need to mention this at the start of the lecture and will as a result not be asked questions. The lectures are recorded on video and made available on the Intranet site.

After the lecture, students are required to reread the relevant parts of 'Roman Law in European Legal History'. Although this book might be considered condensed for a beginning law student, the lectures provide the relevant framework needed for a proper understanding of the book. A more extensive book cannot be used during a four-week course. We are, however, currently in the process of writing a book specifically designed for teaching European legal history in Maastricht.

2.2. *CALI Modules*

A further aid to the students in studying 'Roman Law in European Legal History', in addition to the lectures, is offered in the electronic learning modules that have been developed at the Maastricht faculty for the specific purpose of this course.[4] Students need to complete the electronic learning modules covering the subject matter of the particular week. The modules consist, first of all, of an outline of the subject matter. In addition, and most importantly, the modules contain questions which allow the students to check whether they have studied the materials attentively and suggested further reading and Internet links. The modules provide the students with feedback when they submit the wrong answer, by indicating which parts of the materials should be studied again in order to be able to answer the question in a satisfactory manner.

4 The modules were developed by Prof. Dr. A.M.J.A. Berkvens and Prof. Dr. C.H. van Rhee, with contributions of Dr. J.A.J.M. van der Meer. Some of these modules are available on <www.cali.nl>.

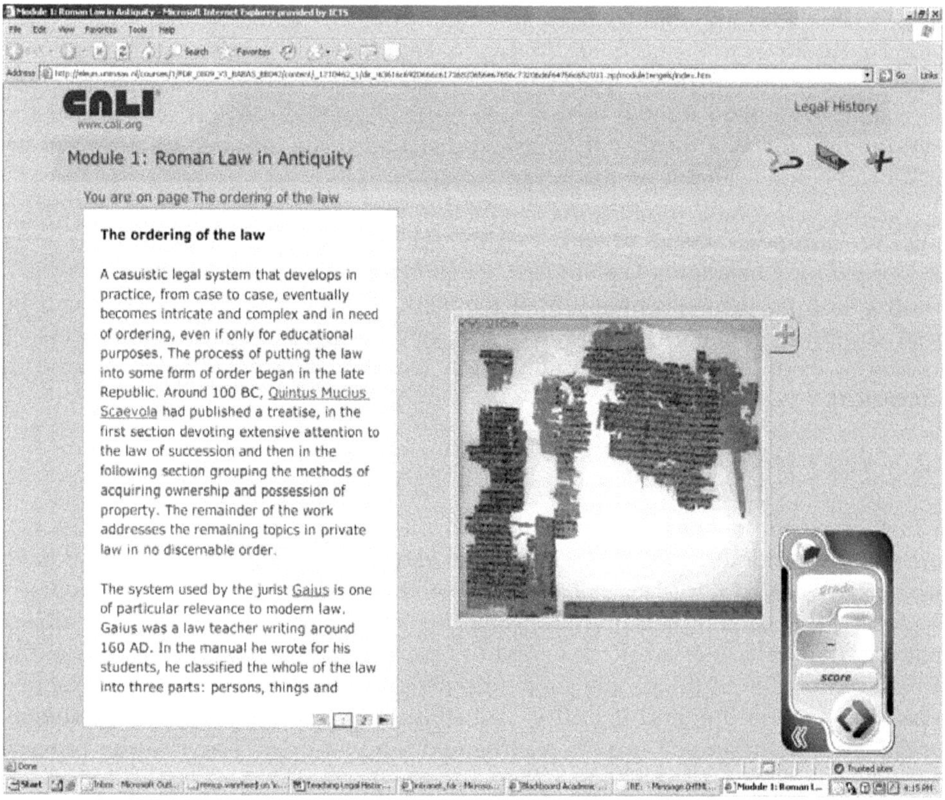

Example of a page from an electronic module with an outline of the subject matter, with hyperlinks and an illustration.

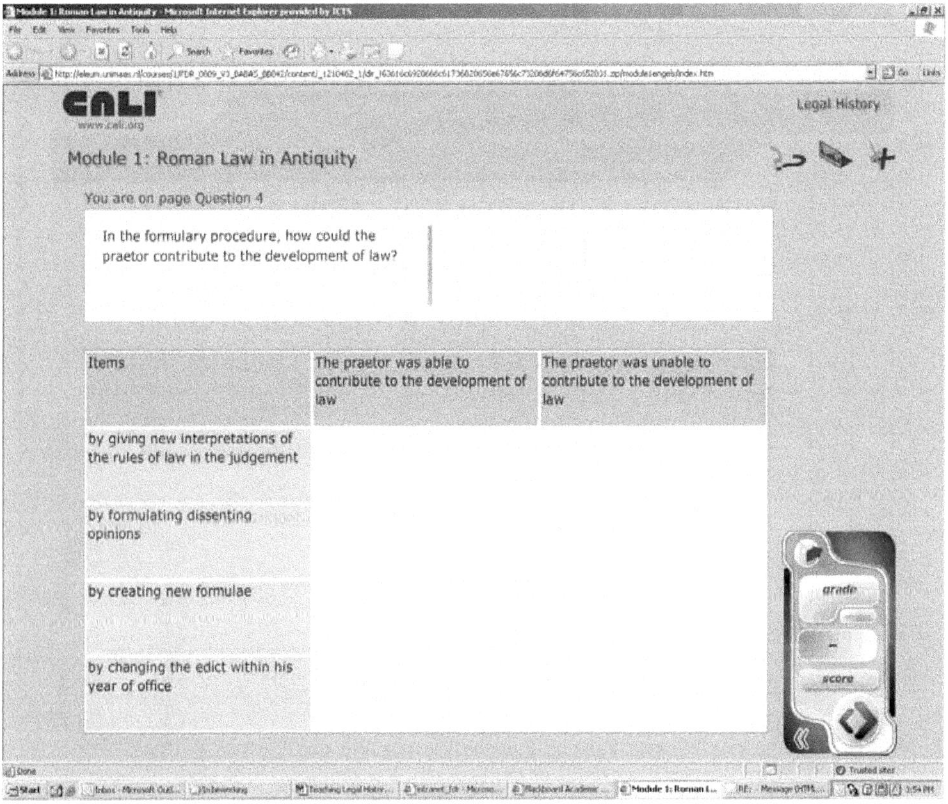

Example of a page from an electronic learning module containing a question. Students have to categorize the four statements on the left ('items') under the correct heading by dragging them into one of the two columns on the right hand-side. It should be noted that each question in the module follows a different format.

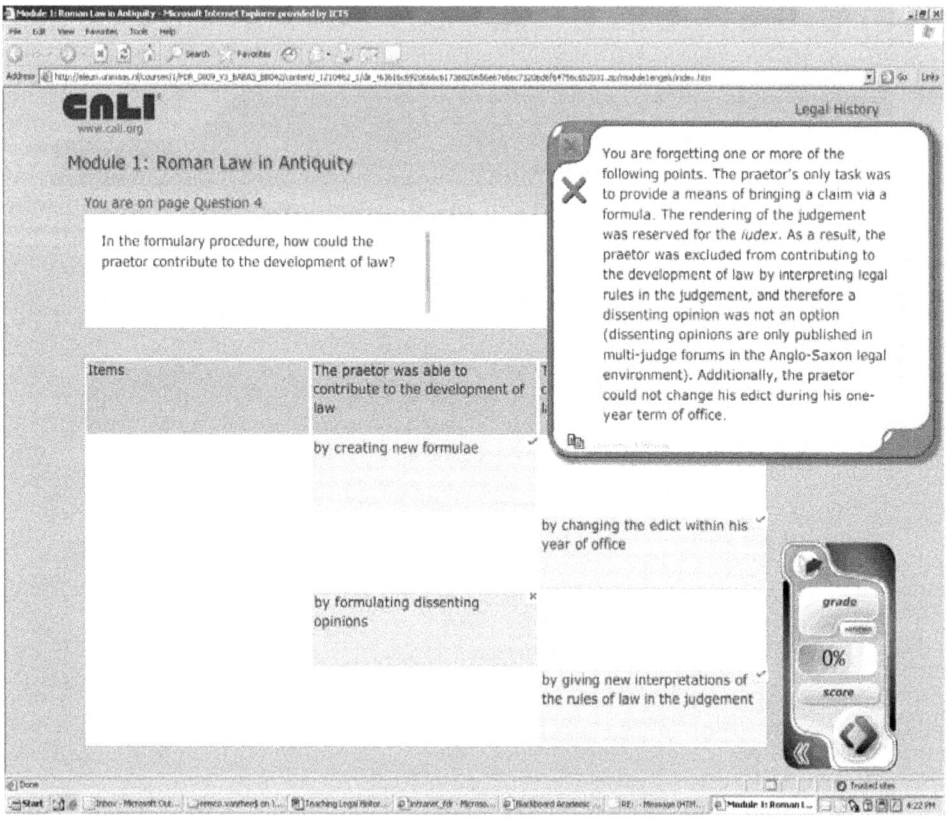

Example of the same page where the student has provided the wrong answer to the question.

2.3. *Seminars*

In the second half of the week the students attend two seminars. Each of these two seminars is offered with a particular didactic objective in mind and is geared to a specific element in the individual student papers on the subject matter of the particular week (see below). This is very important, since the papers constitute the course exam and together provide the final grade for the course.

The first seminar is concerned with external legal history, focusing on the legal history of a series of selected time periods and places within the general historical period of the particular week. The aim is to allow students to analyse primary historical sources in their specific historical context.

Students have to prepare for this first seminar on the basis of a series of rather broadly formulated assignments. These assignments serve several aims. One of these aims is making the students more familiar with the most important developments in the period under scrutiny. A further aim is familiarizing the students with the components that constitute a legal system, and to help them gain the necessary insights and skills for this element in their student papers. An example of an assignment from the week devoted to Roman law in Antiquity is:

> Suppose, you have to write an essay on Marcus Tullius Cicero as lawyer and statesman. To that end, it is important for you to know exactly how things stood in Rome in the years 64-62 BC. Find out what form of government Rome had in those days and who stood at the helm of the Roman state. What territory was encompassed by the Roman state in those days? Discuss the structure of Roman society, the economical state of affairs, the demographic structure of the populace and possible social unrest.

Of course, some of these questions may be hard to answer for a first-year law student, and therefore the teaching staff devotes a sufficient amount of time to discussing how the relevant information could have been uncovered by using the appropriate research methods

The second seminar of the week is different in character. During this second seminar, students study aspects of the history of contract law. In each week, developments of the particular period that is focused on in this week are discussed. The book we use for this part of the course is that of Robert Feenstra & Margreet Ahsmann on the Law of Contract (translated into English).[5] We use this book since it is sufficiently short for our four week period and, most importantly, because it contains a large selection of relevant historical texts, both in the original language and in translation, from the various periods studied by the students.

In Week One of their course, students focus on the system of contracts and *pacta* in Roman law. The aim is to contrast the modern continental situation, with its general law of contract, with a situation where a general law of contract is virtually absent. The absence of a general law of contract caused difficulties for those subject to the law in the past. These difficulties are highlighted in the course material, and students are offered the necessary tools to appreciate the advantages and disadvantages of the modern approach. Additionally, students study early developments pointing in the direction of a more general approach to contract. Students study the *numerus clausus* of contracts recognized in Roman law, the transformation of *consensus* into a general requirement for contracts, as well as the late post-classical growth of the number of binding agreements due to the introduction of the *actio praescriptis verbis* (available to parties having performed on the basis of a non-binding agreement (*pactum*), enabling them to obtain restitution or performance of the opposing party; consequently, the non-binding agreement becomes binding, at least to a certain extent).

Developments in these particular fields from the 'rediscovery' of the Roman Law in the High Middle Ages until (and including) the codification period are the subject of the seminars in the subsequent weeks. This means that students concentrate on the contributions of Canon Law, Natural Law and the Law Merchant

5 Feenstra & Ahsmann, available on the Intranet site. This is a translation with modifications and additions of Feenstra & Ahsmann 1988.

to the development of a general law of contract in which both formal and substantive freedom of contract are central issues.

As stated above, students have to use original texts with a translation to answer a set of questions and to solve cases. The relevant texts are to be selected by them from a larger group of texts prescribed in a particular week which can be found in the book of Feenstra & Ahsmann mentioned above. In the area of contract law, an obvious text to be studied is printed below.

> Decretals of Gregorius IX (Liber Extra) 1,35,1 (c. Antigonus, title De pactis = 'On *pacta*'; text based on manuscripts and 16th century editions)
> *Ex concilio Africano*
> *Pacta quantumcumque nuda servanda sunt.*
> *Antigonus episcopus dixit et infra. Aut inita pacta suam obtineant firmitatem aut conventus (si se non cohibuerit) ecclesiasticam sentiat disciplinam. Dixerunt universi: pax servetur et pacta custodiantur.*
>
> From the text of the African Council [Council at Carthago 348 AD]
> Agreements, however naked, must be honoured.
> Bishop Antigonus etc. etc. [the *Liber Extra* omits the charge pronounced by bishop Antigonus against his opponent as well as the beginning of an opinion put forward by one of the bishops present at the Council; after 'etc. etc.' follow immediately his conclusion and the verdict of the assembly:] 'either agreements must be in force or the defendant, if he does not contain himself, must undergo ecclesiastical discipline.' All said: 'peace must be maintained and agreements must be honoured.'

Students are first of all required to put the texts in their historical context. To this end and in this particular case, they need to make use of their knowledge about the role of the Church and Canon Law in the medieval context. They need to be precise and, for example, discuss the role and significance of the *Liber Extra*. They also need to discuss the link between Roman Law and Canon Law. Subsequently, after having studied all the relevant texts in their context, they will have to reflect on a series of cases. An example of such cases is provided below. As regards this case, students need to mention that it took place before the *Liber Extra* came into being and must reflect on the possible relevance of the text cited above.

> Falco is a young man who lives in Padua. He was born in 1125, and is now 23 years old. Five years ago, he started working for Ricardo, who is a master tapestry weaver. They agreed that Ricardo would teach Falco how to design and weave tapestries. If Falco worked hard in Ricardo's atelier for five years and did well, Ricardo would help Falco being admitted to the guild of tapestry weavers. In addition, he would help him to found his own atelier and eventually to attain the master status.
> Falco worked hard and is now the designer and supervisor of half the tapestries that come out of Ricardo's atelier. Ricardo does not want to lose such a good employee only to create a formidable competitor. Consequently, he changes his mind: he forgets about his promise made to Falco: he will not make him a guild member, let alone help him found his own atelier. Falco decides to take Ricardo to court, but as he asks the advice of a lawyer he hears that his agreement with Ricardo, though valid as such, is not actionable according to Roman law since that law only recognizes a set series of contracts. Falco cannot, therefore, force Ricardo to comply with his earlier promises by going to a secular court that applies Roman law. In confusion, he wanders into his

parish church, where the local priest is reading his breviary. The kind old man asks Falco what is the matter, and Falco tells him about his problems. The priest advises him not to go to the secular court, but to the ecclesiastical court. There Falco might win his case ...

By having the students study the relevant texts, they simultaneously reflect on the context in which these texts functioned as well as on their possible legal significance in a particular historical period. In this way, students are made aware once more that knowledge of external legal history, i.e. the historical context, is a necessary prerequisite for understanding the law in action.

After having attended the last seminar in a particular week, the students are well prepared to write their paper for that week.

2.4. *Individual Student Paper*

We aim for students to start preparing their paper early in the week during which the lectures and seminars for the particular period at hand take place. Therefore, we post the case description that is the basis for the paper at the beginning of the week in the Intranet environment rather than at the end.

The paper consists of three parts. The first part is devoted to situating the case in its general historical context. The aim of this first part is to highlight the importance of the general historical and societal context for a proper understanding of the law.

The second part focuses on the legal system of the territory where the case is situated. This part studies the effect of a legal rule or a legal institution within the parameters of the existing legal system. In order to help students they are offered a *questionnaire* which contains the questions which need to be answered in this second part of their paper. Addressing these questions is rehearsed during the first seminar of the week, although for a different place and a different time period. Examples of such questions are:

- Where does the case take place?
- In the period in question, what was the political, administrative and social situation in the area in which the case took place?
- What important legal developments can be identified in this period?
- What sources of law were known in the period in question?
- What was the relationship between these sources of law?
- Name at least two important jurists who practiced in the period in question. Discuss their influence on the development of law.

The third part of the paper is devoted to solving the case. In doing this, students have to make sure that they use the information from the first and the second part of their paper, which provides e.g. an answer to the possible procedural avenues open to the proponents in the case. Students must use all relevant texts (source materials) that have been provided. Just as in the first two parts of their paper, students should use footnotes referring to their sources. In the third part, this also means that explicit references to the relevant historical legal texts from the book by Feenstra & Ahsmann should be included.

An example of a possible case may be found below.

> Mario Benedetto is a carpenter in Perugia. His business is booming, especially after he decided to specialize in making coffins. Unfortunately, many of his customers do not have the money to pay him immediately. Consequently, he lacks the money to buy enough wood for his business and proposes his supplier, Claudio Fregoli, to exchange a series of expensive gems for a large amount of wood to be delivered in June 1352. Claudio agrees, especially when Mario states that he intends to deliver the gems to Claudio in April 1352, i.e. before the delivery of the wood.
> Early 1352, the number of customers interested in coffins declines dramatically. Mario despairs, especially because it seems that the amount of wood promised in exchange for his gems is much more than he will need in the coming few years. Additionally, he would rather keep the gems to support his family in the months to come, given the fact that he has realized that many of the unpaid coffins will most likely never be paid for given the fact that in the meantime most of the people who bought these coffins for their family members have also died. Claudio, however, is of the opinion that 'pacta sunt servanda.'
> In despair, Mario consults you. He asks you whether he is bound by the agreement reached with Claudio. Since you are *doctor utriusque iure*, you have a tendency to base your answer on the so-called 'learned laws' and to advise your clients to litigate before courts where these laws are taken into consideration. What would your advice be?

Students have to recognize that this case is situated at the height of the Black Death period, a time when impossibility to perform a contract was not just a legal concept but very much a fact of daily life (and death). Another example of a case is situated in the seventeenth century.

> 's-Hertogenbosch, 15 April 1629. Laurent de Crèvecoeur is very much afraid. He has just received a visit from Marten van Cromvoirt, distant relative to the city's garrison commander Antonie Schetz, baron Grobbedonk. Marten threatened to tell his son, Adrian van Cromvoirt, secretary to bishop Michael Ophovius, that he has found Laurent out to be a secret Protestant. Laurent did not go to Mass when it was Easter, a week earlier, and Marten had him followed to a secret meeting in a warehouse on the outskirts of the city. Should Marten denounce Laurent? The circumstances being what they are, it is quite probable that Laurent would be seen as a traitor to the city and dealt with accordingly!
> Laurent is, however, also very angry. Marten told him that he would not denounce Laurent if he only would sell him the valuable painting 'Adoration of the Christ Child' by the famous painter Jeroen van Aken – also known as Hieronymus Bosch – for about 10% of its value. Laurents father bought this painting to celebrate Laurents birth, 38 years earlier from the heirs of the painter. Laurent saw no way out, so Marten left with the painting, leaving behind an official document of sale saying that Laurent sold him the painting very much of his own free will. On 24 September 1629 Laurent de Crèvecoeur visits you, a *magister utriusque iuris* with a law practice in 's Hertogenbosch, and tells you the story about the sale of the Bosch painting. He asks advice as to what he can do to get it back.

In solving this case, students should discuss the procedural avenues open to Laurent to reclaim his painting. These have changed completely between 15 April and 24 September due to the conquest of 's-Hertogenbosch by Stadholder Frederic Henry and the Dutch Republic and the ousting of the Spaniards on 14 September. Discussing these historical circumstances make the students aware of the necessity to check not only the facts of the case itself, but also its broader historical context.

The paper needs to be submitted electronically in order to allow for a plagiarism test (papers are checked both against the Internet, and against the papers that have been handed in by other course participants, both current ones and those who participated in previous years) and in order to be able to check whether the papers have been submitted at or before the deadline indicated in the course materials (papers submitted after the deadline will not be taken into consideration). After the papers have been submitted, students are provided with an example of what their paper ideally should have looked like and they are allowed to ask questions during the seminars and lectures. They can apply the additional knowledge obtained in this way in more adequately researching and structuring subsequent papers.

As stated, the final mark for the course is based on the various papers submitted by the students. We have opted for taking into consideration only a specific part of each paper due to constraints as regards the number of staff available for grading the papers. It may, for example, happen that in a certain academic year, we decide to grade the section on the general historical context of the case in the paper submitted for Roman Law, the section on the legal context from the paper submitted for the codification period and the part devoted to solving the case from the paper submitted for the *Ius Commune* period. Each year a different combination is chosen.

In the introductory course, the emphasis is on the learned laws (Roman and Canon Law). Nevertheless, some attention is given to customary law/the *ius proprium* whenever this is necessary. Additionally, some attention is given to English legal history, although time constraints do not allow us to pay sufficient attention to this important subject, which is unfortunate, especially in the European Law School programme.

3. Legal History in other Courses of the Bachelor's Programme

As stated, after the introductory first year course, solely devoted to European legal history, legal history is taught within the context of other courses devoted to modern topics. In the course on Comparative Contract Law, for example, the focus is on good faith (*bona fides*), fraud (*fraus*), duress (*metus*) and *causa/consideration*. In the course on Property Law, the historical origins of the consensual and traditional systems of transfer of ownership are discussed, as well as the origins of abstract and causal systems of transfer. Additionally, specific attention is given to the influence of the feudal system and the French Revolution on the development of continental land law. In the course on International & European Law, the history of public international law, especially in the eighteenth and nineteenth centuries, is focused on, while European integration before the establishment of the European Coal and Steel Community also gets some attention.

In addition, there is an elective course solely devoted to legal history at the end of the third year of the Bachelors programme. Its content varies each year and depends largely on the interests of the participants. Students have to choose topics from a series indicated in the course book and, on the basis of these materials and additional sources, they have to prepare presentations and discussion sessions. The seminars are supervised by a legal historian, but the emphasis is on student input. This course is graded on the basis of a final paper, class participation and the slides of the various power point presentations prepared by the individual students.

4. Legal History in the Master's Programmes

In the Master's programme, legal history is again taught in an integrated manner. An example is the course Civil Litigation in Europe, also discussed in this volume. This course, which is comparative in nature, discusses the differences between, and the similarities of, the various systems of civil procedure in Europe. A central question is to what extent harmonisation of procedural law is necessary from the perspective of the proper functioning of the internal market, to what extent harmonisation has already been achieved, as well as the chances of further harmonisation. In this course the starting point is always historical. For example, students are familiarized with the distinction between pre-trial and trial in the Anglo-American system of civil procedure by looking at the history of the jury in civil matters. Additionally, they study the continuing existence of these two procedural phases despite of the fact that the civil jury has nearly disappeared in England and many other Common Law countries. The advantages of this division from the perspective of expediency and efficiency are discussed and subsequently parallel developments on the European Continent are taken into consideration. The ideas of the nineteenth century Austrian jurist Franz Klein are especially interesting from this perspective.[6]

As regards the feasibility of a further harmonisation of civil procedural law, we take into consideration various nineteenth and twentieth century authors who have claimed that civil procedure is a topic that is purely national in character and is not fit for harmonisation. We contrast these views with the history of the Romano-canonical procedure, taking into consideration that this procedure served as an international framework while allowing national particularities.

5. Final Remarks

Obviously, the approach to the teaching of legal history in Maastricht described above has many virtues. In our opinion, the most important virtue is that it necessarily establishes a strong link with modern law and is especially of interest to comparative lawyers such as the students of the European Law School. There is no

6 See Van Rhee 2005.

possibility of adopting an antiquarian approach, since the professor of legal history continually needs to link his teaching to the contemporary issues taught in the various law courses. This forces him or her to follow developments in contemporary law thoroughly. Without such knowledge, it is obviously hard to explain these developments from an historical perspective. At the same time, the Maastricht approach allows him or her to demonstrate the relevance of legal history for the future studies and legal career of the students and, most importantly, to make the largest number of students enthusiastic about the topic. When this approach is combined with a willingness to teach students with an interest in legal history, one that goes beyond the interest of ordinary law students, in small seminars - or even individually when they have opted for writing a thesis on legal history - we find it very satisfactory, which may, however, not come as a surprise for the reader.

Bibliography

Feenstra & Ahsmann
Feenstra, R. & Ahsmann, M., *Contract: 'Contract' and 'Freedom of Contract' in Historical Perspective*, available on the Intranet site of the course.

Feenstra & Ahsmann 1988
Feenstra, R. & Ahsmann, M., *Contract. Aspecten van de begrippen contract en contractsvrijheid in historisch perspectief*, Deventer: Kluwer, 1988.

Van Rhee 2005
Van Rhee, C.H. (ed.), *European Traditions in Civil Procedure*, Antwerp: Intersentia, 2005.

Bram Akkermans
Aalt Willem
Heringa

CONCLUSION: TOWARDS A COALITION FOR EUROPEAN LEGAL EDUCATION (CELE)

Taking into account our motivation to edit this book and invite authors who have researched various aspects of European law and integration, who have taught in the Maastricht European Law School project, who have one time or another reflected upon the future of legal education in Europe or European legal education, it is difficult to draw definite, unchallengeable conclusions, because we believe there are many variations. However we would like to draw attention to some inescapable trends; focus upon our approaches as an example of how the future of European legal education might be approached; and point at the (many) obstacles which lie ahead and the many challenges connected to it.

Our first firm conclusion, however, is that there can be no doubt that a curriculum can be built upon European law, comparative law and globalization trends, whilst training good lawyers and critical academics. The growth of the body of law, in domains such as European law *strictu sensu*, European private law, -criminal law, -administrative law, *etcetera* is such that a good legal education can be build around it. Teaching materials have been developed: not nearly enough, but it is unquestionable that many academics now work on these domains of European law, Europeanization/globalization of the law and comparative law, such that we witness an increase of textbooks and casebooks and legal materials. Increasingly comparative law is even incorporated in domestic textbooks enabling students in non-comparative programmes to gain comparative knowledge and develop more critical attitude towards their own domestic legal system.

In the European context, in our opinion, THE main obstacle and issue to be overcome is related to how ensure that law graduates of a new European Law programme, assuming that they possess all necessary lawyering skills (which we will discuss later) can freely enter the labour market of lawyers and can find employment as what they are: European lawyers! Currently this is impossible due to the fact that professional qualifications for lawyers are regulated at a domestic level. Solving this requires a strategic mission and discussion with all stakeholders: bar associations, national legislatures and the European Commission. It does also fit in the strategy for 'European universities', or a European Charter for some specific academic/professional programs, in order to promote that they will have a sound legal basis to perform the tasks of a European education in a specific field. Law would be in our opinion a prime example.

In constructing a truly European curriculum many variations and options do exist. We will name a few. The first is that adequate reflection must be given to the positioning of the program: a focus on Europe and Europeanization, or also including globalization aspects and the role of international law and international organizations.

Secondly, the question can be asked (and Jan Smits very pertinently dealt with this issue in his contribution to this book) whether a legal curriculum ought not to a much lesser extent be constructed on a given legal system (domestic or European) and more on a comparative academic training in legal thinking. In which model in a post-graduate (master) program of one or two years a student can subsequently opt for a training in one specific model and system.

And thirdly, what has to be taken into account is the position of a legal education programme in a domestic legal setting. In many if not most European countries, studying law is primarily an academic endeavour in the setting of a university. That model pleads in favour of the Smits' approach. It also supports the Maastricht model: the European Law School as an academic training after which students can delve into one specific legal system.

Evidently, this project is strongly related to perceptions about the role and substance of legal education and lawyering skills. And it is also linked to didactical visions as to the best ways to teach law and to learn those skills and to learn in general.

In that respect it is submitted that learning is an interactive exercise: the best way to learn is to be actively engaged and to be challenged to participate. Linked to interactive modes of teaching is the notion that students must also be trained in 'evaluating' laws, statutes, text books, cases, in short the positive law. Since studying law in academia is an academic endeavour it is crucial that students grasp and train critical minds and will be able to reflect on the quality of a legal system, laws, decisions, *etcetera*. And one way of doing just that is by resorting to comparative methods. But, and, also to other disciplines: philosophy of law, law and economics, behavioural sciences. Furthermore, we have to train students to be able to engage with lawyers from other jurisdictions, countries and legal cultures, and to be able to do so in a multi-level setting. Law-making and decision-making on the domestic level is strongly and increasingly influenced by European aspects and globalization items; and rule- and decision-making at the European level is to a great extent a process in which communication skills are relevant, through networking, cooperation procedures, negotiations and the ability to interact among legal cultures and backgrounds. When these characteristics are shared it seems imperative to include those elements in all legal education and curricula, but also, in our opinion, to construct specific law schools, with a European mandate so to speak, where the focus lies on a generation of lawyers specialized and trained to cope with these new challenges.

In this book we have tried to open up our experiences with trying to do so and to show how we did it. How we think it is possible and indeed necessary to teach in the European legal lingua franca: the English language. How we have set up courses that teach company law and property law, and constitutional law and private law and civil procedure, and made these courses fit in our philosophy of a European legal curriculum, which builds upon common principles, comparative law and European law, and does not necessarily focus upon one domestic system.

It is a project which led to a curriculum of undergraduate studies in three years and a postgraduate program of one year; but also allows students to initially start with the European Law School and afterwards specialize in a legal system.

The European Law School project is a work in progress. We have developed many course materials over the recent decade also because this teaching project has been very much linked with the research focus of the Faculty of Law. However, many more materials have to be developed if we would work towards a truly European legal education.

We have to work out and lobby for a more perfect link with the labour market and the stakeholders. It is helpful that in many European countries university legal education also trains students for many other occupations but the bar: NGOs, civil service, companies, international organizations. The European Law School bachelor therefore also serves as a truly academic undergraduate program, such as university colleges offer as well.

How do we intend to further go about our project, trying to achieve our ambitions that more thought must be given to the future of European legal education? We submit that there are a variety of avenues and strategies. What they have in common is the necessity for law schools in Europe to discuss the issue of the future of European legal education, also in the light of the implementation of the Bologna-process and the growing need for more and better trained European lawyers. In that vein we hope that a group of law schools, who share a same vision as we do, might be willing to meet in order to come up with a shared perspective and possibly a list of principles, as to how European legal education in a number of law schools might take place. A Coalition for European Legal Education (CELE) if you will. Whilst at the same time taking political action campaigning for a European charter for those schools which participate in the project. We would propose to involve bar associations and other stake holders in this discussion to undertake action in the direction of a dichotomy of legal education in Europe: schools training domestic lawyers, with evidently an input from European law in the curriculum; and some schools (European charter law schools) focusing on the European labour market for transnational and truly European lawyers.

The least such a discussion hopefully might entail is an intense reflection on the quality, harmonization, Bologna-isation and Europeanization of legal education, with an aim to reflect the Europeanization of the job market, of law firms, of decision-making and of rule making in Europe. And by doing so, increase the quality of lawyers, lawmakers and litigators and acknowledge that legal education is more than a professional training programme, but a truly high level academic education, which truly benefits from a European, comparative and globalization perspective.

A peer-reviewed book series in which the common foundations of the legal systems of the Member States of the European Community are the central focus.

The *Ius Commune Europaeum* series includes horizontal comparative legal studies as well as studies on the effect of treaties within the national legal systems. All the classic fields of law are covered. The books are published in various European languages under the auspices of METRO, the Institute for Transnational Legal Research at the Maastricht University.

Recently published:

Volume 80: *Rechtsbescherming en overheidsovereenkomsten*, K. Wauters
Volume 81: *Derden in het contractenrecht*, I. Samoy (red.)
Volume 82: *The Right to Specific Performance. The Historical Development*, J.H. Dondorp and J.J. Hallebeek (eds.)
Volume 83: *Financial Supervision in a Comparative Perspective*, M. Poto
Volume 84: *Enforcement and Enforceability – Tradition and Reform*, C.H. van Rhee and A. Uzelac (eds.)
Volume 85: *Fact-Finding in Civil Litigation. A Comparative Perspective*, R. Verkerk
Volume 86: *The Making of Chinese Condominium Law. A Comparative Perspective with American and South African Condominium Laws*, L. Chen
Volume 87: *Effective Criminal Defence in Europe*, Z. Namoradze, R. Smith, T. Spronken and E. Cape (eds.)
Volume 88: *Conflict of Laws and Laws of Conflict in Europe and Beyond. Patterns of Supranational and Transnational Juridification*, R. Nickel (ed.)
Volume 89: *The Regulation of Architects in Belgium and the Netherlands. A Comparative Analysis*, S. Schoenmaekers
Volume 90: *Evolutie van de basisbeginselen van het contractenrecht*, I. Samoy (red.)
Volume 91: *Recidive in België en Nederland. Een analyse van 200 jaar rechtspraak en rechtsleer*, M. Dams
Volume 92: *An EU-wide Letter of Rights. Towards Best Practice*, T. Spronken (ed.)
Volume 93: *The Costanzo Obligation. The Obligations of National Administrative Authorities in the Case of Incompatibility between National Law and European Law*, M. Verhoeven
Volume 94: *The Effect of a Change of Circumstances on the Binding Force of Contracts. Comparative Perspectives*, R. Momberg Uribe
Volume 95: *The Landscape of the Legal Professions in Europe and the USA: Continuity and Change*, A. Uzelac and C.H. van Rhee (eds.)
Volume 96: *Constitutional Constraints on Ad Hoc Legislation. A Comparative Study of the United States, Germany and the Netherlands*, A. Jasiak
Volume 97: *The Social Security Position of Irregular Migrant Workers. New Insights from National Security Law and International Law*, K. Kapuy

www.ingramcontent.com/pod-product-compliance
Ingram Content Group UK Ltd.
Pitfield, Milton Keynes, MK11 3LW, UK
UKHW051926100926
8556IPUK00022B/1402

9 781780 680187